Making Working Relationships Work

The TRIPS Toolkit for Handling Relationship Challenges and Promoting Rapport

Making Working Relationships Work is for all those wanting to develop collaborative and inclusive workplaces and to improve relationship building capabilities – their own or that of others. It provides a powerful set of tools and concepts for leaders, managers, and employees of all levels to deal with relationship challenges at work with greater success. Full of authentic case studies and engaging activities, it enables readers to reflect meaningfully on working relationships in their own context and to select the most suitable strategies for promoting rapport and wellbeing.

Helen Spencer-Oatey is Managing Director of GlobalPeople Consulting Ltd. (GPC) and Emeritus Professor of Intercultural Communication at the University of Warwick, UK. She is internationally renowned for her work on communication and rapport management, especially in contexts of cultural diversity. She has published extensively in these areas, including the books Global Fitness for Global People, Intercultural Politeness, Developing Global Leaders, Intercultural Interaction, and Culturally Speaking.

Domna Lazidou has a PhD in Culture and Communication and a background in Internal Communication Management in complex, intercultural workplaces. As well as teaching on the subject, she works with organisations, global leaders and teams to help develop diverse relationship building capabilities, supporting them in creating more effective, inclusive working environments, including in hybrid and remote contexts. She is co-author of Global Fitness for Global People.

Praise for Making Working Relationships Work

A truly impressive book! Its accessible and easy manner belies its sophistication, resting as it does on a rich foundation of serious scholarship skilfully distilled from linguistics, psychology, sociology and more. I was expecting to read the book from an academic perspective, but I kept finding myself making mental notes on how to deal with my own workplace problems, both as an employee and as a manager – where was this book when I first had to run a department!

> *Professor Jonathan Culpeper, Head of Department of Linguistics and English Language, Lancaster University*

Making Working Relationships Work is a practical and insightful read. From the clear and informative study of rapport, to the perceptive examination of workplace roles and relationships, the authors have organised multiple concepts and theories into a useful guide with real-world examples and useful tools.

The TRIPS rapport management framework simplifies the many variables that affect rapport, and this provides the basis for a fascinating look at how humans relate to each other. Most importantly, the book's exploration of the complexities and entanglements of workplace relationships encourages the reader to reflect on their own approach to building connections and rapport with their colleagues.

There is no doubt that *Making Working Relationships Work* will become a vital guide for leaders, managers, and professionals leading people through change in the workplace.

> *Roisin Reilly, Internal Communication and Management of Change, Hewlett Packard Enterprise*

This book provides a robust framework (the TRIPS Toolkit) for building excellent working relationships within the workplace and acts as a valuable guide for solving team-relationship problems within any organization striving for growth. It illustrates effectively the complex and nuanced challenges people often face in different workplace settings and that may affect their motivation. It reveals how these factors may be perceived differently by different people, and what can be done to enhance productivity and team harmony. I highly recommend this book as a working manual for all business leaders, managers and individual employees seeking to foster an environment that promotes wellbeing and productivity for all.

> *Boboye Adeniji Oluwafemi, Managing Partner, PELSE Consulting*

Helen Spencer-Oatey and Domna Lazidou have achieved the impossible in writing an engaging and genuinely insightful book about the challenges of workplace relationships that is relevant for professionals, scholars, and students alike. *Making Working Relationships Work* introduces an accessible and practical framework for navigating relationships in the workplace that is carefully grounded in decades of painstaking empirical research. It's a truly remarkable volume and a must-read for anyone who wants to know how to better manage working life.

Professor Michael Haugh, School of Languages and Cultures, The University of Queensland

We all have questions about human dynamics in the workplace, from "why is it so hard?" to "why are some people so awkward?!" This book is a comprehensive and insightful guide to the complexities & intricacies of how we relate to each other, get annoyed & fall out – and what to do about it. Read this & follow the step-by-step reflections and actions, to improve your communication & relationships.

Helen Frewin, Business Psychologist, CEO Totem Consulting & author of Better Than Confidence

Effective workplace relationships are central to a thriving work environment, yet the skills of navigating challenges and fostering connections are so often overlooked. Making Working Relationships Work provides clear frameworks and practical strategies that would be useful in any workplace context. You will recognise yourself, your colleagues, and managers throughout the many case studies – for better or worse!

Dr Matthew Iasiello, Mental Health & Wellbeing Program, South Australian Health & Medical Research Institute

Helen Spencer-Oatey and Domna Lazidou's new book "Making Working Relationships Work" is a perfect guide to creating better relationships with colleagues. It offers meaningful and concrete suggestions for solving some of our most pressing challenges. I loved the guided reflection, case studies, and suggestions for leading more productive conversations with others and becoming the best communicator I can be. For any professional, this book is a must-have.

Julien C. Mirivel, PhD - Professor of Applied Communication, University of Arkansas at Little Rock, and Founder of the Positive Communication Network

As a consultant focused on working with organisations interested in creating inclusive workplace cultures, Making Working Relationships Work is an excellent addition to my toolkit. It offers a comprehensive yet practical and accessible guide to gaining a deep understanding of workplace relationships and their dynamics. The TRIPS rapport management framework is super helpful in that it asks us to pause and reflect on the complexity of what influences our relationships. With an emphasis on self-awareness and mutual understanding, a strong theoretical underpinning, and plenty of relatable case studies that demonstrate the applicability of the tools to a variety of workplace scenarios, this book supports us in making our relationships work. If you're looking for a quick fix to building healthy communication cultures at work, this is not the book for you. If you're looking to make lasting and meaningful change to professional interactions in your workplace, I recommend getting a copy.

Tanya McCalmon, Director, Inclusion Consultant, Lennox Learning & Development

Making Working Relationships Work inspires us to reflect on the challenges of our own contexts at work with authentic case studies. It is superbly researched and grounded in a deep understanding of both psychology and pragmatics. The TRIPS rapport management framework introduced in the book contains tools and strategies to resolve the toughest issues arising at the intersection of the interpersonal and the organizational. As a practitioner in the complex organizational landscape of higher education, the book has supplied me with a harvest of new insights that will enhance the variety of working relationships I must engage in daily.

Dr Brandon Conlon, Assistant Director of Faculty and Postdoctoral Professional Development, Okinawa Institute of Science and Technology

Making Working Relationships Work

The TRIPS Toolkit for handling relationship challenges and promoting rapport

Helen Spencer-Oatey
Domna Lazidou

Ground Level, 470 St Kilda Road, Melbourne Victoria 3004, Australia

4th Floor, Silverstream House, 45 Fitzroy Street Fitzrovia, London WIT 6EB United Kingdom

2nd Floor Daiya Building, 2-2-15 Hamamatsu-cho, Minato-ku, Tokyo 105-0013, Japan

447 Broadway, 2nd Floor #393, New York NY, 10013 United States

First published 2024 by Castledown, Melbourne

Information on this title:
https://castledown.online/reference/9780648184461/
DOI: 10.20140/9780648184461

Making Working Relationships Work: The TRIPS Toolkit for Handling Relationship Challenges and Promoting Rapport

© Helen Spencer-Oatey & Domna Lazidou, 2024

All rights reserved. This publication is copyright. Subject to statutory exception and to the provisions of relevant collective licencing agreements, no reproduction, transmission, or storage of any part of this publication by any means, electronic, mechanical, photocopying, recording or otherwise may take place without prior written permission from the author.

Typeset by Castledown Design

ISBN: 978-0-648184-46-1 (Paperback)
ISBN: 978-0-6481844-7-8 (eBook)

Castledown takes no responsibility for the accuracy of URLs for external or third-party internet websites referred to in this publication. No responsibility is taken for the accuracy or appropriateness of information found in any of these websites.

Contents

Acknowledgements xi
Part 1 Foundations 1
   Chapter 1: Introduction: The why's and what's of working relationships and rapport 2
      1.1 Introduction 2
      1.2 The current workplace 5
      1.3 What are 'working relationships'? 6
      1.4 What is rapport? 9
      1.5 The TRIPS Rapport Management Framework 11
      1.6 Organisation of the book 12
      1.7 Making the most of the book 15
   Chapter 2: The TRIPS Rapport Management Framework: A Case-based Overview 17
      2.1 Introduction 17
      2.2 T – Triggers 19
      2.3 R – Reactions 22
      2.4 I – Interactions 24
      2.5 P – People 27
      2.6 S – Settings 29
      2.7 Summary of the TRIPS Rapport Management Framework 34

Part 2 Relationship challenges at work: Tools and strategies for promoting rapport 35
      Introduction to Part 2 36
   Chapter 3: Upset or annoyed? How to manage and learn from adverse experiences 38
      3.1 Introduction 38
      3.2 Identifying emotions 40
      3.3 The Reaction Management Tool 42
      3.4 The Reaction Management Tool and a diversity/intercultural perspective 51
      3.5 Using the Reaction Management Tool 52
      3.6 Key takeaways 53

Contents

Chapter 4: Divided by conflict? How to handle disagreement constructively 54
    4.1 Introduction 54
    4.2 Disagreement: key features 55
    4.3 The Discord Management Tool 60
    4.4 Key takeaways 74

Chapter 5: Silence(d) in meetings? How to overcome sidelining and promote inclusion 75
    5.1 Introduction 75
    5.2 Background information on participation and 'speaking up' issues 77
    5.3 The Participation Management Tool 82
    5.4 Key takeaways 95

Chapter 6: Troubled by colleagues? How to reduce divisions and foster cooperation 96
    6.1 Introduction 96
    6.2 Challenges from colleagues 96
    6.3 The Cooperative Colleague Tool 100
    6.4 Key takeaways 116

Chapter 7: Problems with bosses? How to 'manage up' and enhance alignment 117
    7.1 Introduction 117
    7.2 'Boss behaviour' challenges 118
    7.3 Power and psychological safety 124
    7.4 The Upward Management Tool 125
    7.5 Key takeaways 136

Chapter 8: Exercised by leadership? How to manage supportively and bravely 137
    8.1 Introduction 137
    8.2 Challenges to providing supportive and brave leadership 137
    8.3 The Supportive Leadership Tool 140
    8.4 Key takeaways 161

Contents

Part 3 The TRIPS Rapport Management Framework 162
   Introduction to Part 3 163
   Chapter 9: Triggers: Understanding what undermines or enhances rapport 164
   9.1 Introduction 164
   9.2 G – Goals 165
   9.3 A – Autonomy 167
   9.4 A – Attention 170
   9.5 F – Face 172
   9.6 F – Fairness 175
   9.7 E – Ethicality 177
   9.8 GAAFFE Priority clashes 179
   9.9 Summary and follow-up reading 180
   Chapter 10: Reactions: Understanding emotional reactions, thinking and evaluative judgements 181
   10.1 Introduction 181
   10.2 Understanding emotions 181
   10.3 Displaying emotional reactions 183
   10.4 Regulating emotional reactions 185
   10.5 Perceiving emotions in others 190
   10.6 Cognitive reactions – sensemaking & evaluating 191
   10.7 Summary and follow-up reading 195
   Chapter 11: Interactions: Understanding how communication can trigger rapport reactions 196
   11.1 Introduction 196
   11.2 How communication works 196
   11.3 Disclosure – non-disclosure of information 197
   11.4 Communication style: deciding how to frame the message 199
   11.5 Communication dynamics: handling the dynamics of interactions 205
   11.6 Microinsults 208
   11.7 Summary and follow-up reading 210
   Chapter 12: People: Understanding the impact of the people involved 212
   12.1 Introduction 212
   12.2 Number of participants 212
   12.3 People's identity characteristics 214
   12.4 People's links with each other 220
   12.5 Summary and follow-up reading 226

Contents

Chapter 13: Settings: Understanding the impact of contexts.....227
13.1 Introduction.....227
13.2 An overview of settings.....227
13.3 Settings and norms: the 'way we do things round here'.....229
13.4 Settings, rules and regulations.....233
13.5 Settings and Values/Beliefs.....235
13.6 The dynamic interplay between Settings, norms and values.....238
13.7 Settings and psychological atmosphere.....240
13.8 Summary and follow-up reading.....244

Part 4 Your TRIPS Toolkit: Templates for applying the tools.....245
Introduction to Part 4.....246
Chapter 14: The TRIPS Challenge Tool Templates.....247
Reaction Management Tool: Steps and Prompts....247
The Discord Management Tool: Steps and Prompts.....249
The Participation Management Tool: Steps and Prompts.....250
The Cooperative Colleague Tool: Steps and Prompts.....252
The Upward Management Tool: Steps and Prompts.....253
The Supportive Leadership Tool: Steps and Prompts.....255
Chapter 15: The TRIPS Concept Tool Templates.....258
Triggers: Reflection questions.....258
Reactions: Reflection questions.....258
Interactions: Reflection questions.....259
People: Reflection questions.....260
Settings: Reflection questions.....261
Chapter 16: The RelATE family of strategies and concluding comments.....263

Activity and Case Study Answers.....265

References.....270

Index.....278

Acknowledgements

Many people have helped to make this book possible and we are sincerely grateful to them all for their various contributions.

First, we would like to express our thanks to all those who generously gave up their time to be interviewed by us. Their insights and experiences helped shape our thinking around several of the chapters. We are also extremely grateful to the numerous colleagues, clients, friends, family members, writers, researchers, and students – known to us personally or through their published work – who have also contributed to our thinking through sharing their experiences and ideas. Some of them feature in the book – referenced if their work is published, or otherwise with pseudonyms. All have made a very valuable contribution to the book, stimulating our thinking and helping us develop new insights.

We are very grateful to the team at Castledown Publishers, who have taken a very personalised and supportive approach to the creation of this book; in particular, Blake Tanner and Chika Fujimoto, our editors, for their encouragement and flexibility as we discussed the whole project and developed the manuscript. We would also like to thank Lauren Harcombe for dealing with numerous administrative issues, Alicia Moodley for her creativity in designing the book cover and extensive formatting work, and Dan Spencer and Emily Hutchinson for their design feedback, suggestions and advice.

We are very grateful to each other for the numerous stimulating discussions that we have enjoyed and for each person's detailed feedback on the developing drafts. We experienced in real-time some of the issues we were writing about – particularly the challenge of managing competing demands on our time. This helped to keep us grounded in the realities of collaborative working!

Finally, we are thankful to our families and friends for their patience as we sat in front of our computers for hours on end, drafting the chapters or participating in numerous discussions with each other, online or face-to-face. Without their support, the book would never have been possible.

Part 1

FOUNDATIONS

Part 1 – Foundations

Chapter 1: Introduction

The why's and what's of working relationships and rapport

1.1   Introduction

In the second year of the Covid-19 Pandemic a senior manager working for a global company in Europe complained about one of her direct reports, a new hire who, because of the travel restrictions, was still working from his base in the USA.

> I must admit I am deeply disappointed; on paper Caleb has so much experience and I thought he was going to make a lot of difference to our ability to professionalise our marketing function, but in practice this has not happened. He seems unwilling to take the initiative and drive projects, he has little understanding of the team's work and priorities and seems to prefer to work on his own which does not really endear him to the team. I have tried to suggest that he spends more time getting to know his colleagues and collaborating online, but this has not gone down very well, and I am at a loss how to direct him or motivate him.

Caleb, when interviewed had a completely different take:

> I find it exasperating that no one is willing to listen to my professional advice and that includes my boss. Whenever there is a new project we all have to come together to discuss it for ever and ever … sometimes we seem to do nothing but talk … to do any work we have to have a meeting. Rather than just agree what needs to be done and then do it. And, you would think that given how many meetings we have it would be easy to get the information I need – not so. It is one thing to say 'your task is to professionalise the function'. Well, I need to know certain things to be able to put a strategy and plan together. I don't even know who I can talk to get the information I need … My manager has no understanding of what I am trying to achieve or indeed what I can achieve if I have the right support. I need trust and access to other senior leaders, not constant unhelpful interventions!

Caleb did not stay long after that.

Part 1 - Foundations

This book is about working relationships at work: relationships that go awry like that between Caleb and his boss, the reasons this happens, and how you can work to fix them. Most of us spend a huge proportion of our lives at work and our relationships with managers and colleagues can have a major impact on us: on our ability to do our job, our professional growth and development, and our physical and emotional wellbeing. Most of us know this, yet we frequently have difficulty handling relationships well. Sometimes we may seem to have little control over events, as illustrated by Erica's story. Erica is a public sector manager who loved her job and was loved by her customers yet has had health issues because of work stress. She says:

> *I used to like to spend time in the front office to engage with the public and be helpful; even if it was not part of my job description, I did not mind putting in the extra time. I enjoyed it a lot and also felt I was helping the younger members of the team to learn about their customer facing role. I was told by my superiors to stop doing it as I was 'showing up the rest of the team'! Eventually I was disciplined (for this and other things). It turned out that a member of the team had put in a complaint about me – in fact several complaints. They had compiled a whole list! Yet she never once came up to me to say that anything bothered her or to ask me to do anything differently. I would like to understand and try to sort it out and yet I'm not even allowed to speak to her. We now have this charade where we are working next to each other and I am not supposed to know she complained and I am pretending to be nice and she is perfectly pleasant, but I know this is rubbish really – it doesn't make for an engaging workplace.*

All these real-life experiences reflect some common features of workplace life that can easily undermine good working relationships:

- Differences in ways of working;
- Difficulties in creating trust and inclusion while working remotely;
- Divisions and mistrust among colleagues;
- Pretending that such division and disagreements do not exist.

Other examples include:

- Unclear or unrealistic objectives and targets;
- Mismatched expectations;
- Micromanagement or too little management;
- Favouritism and discrimination.

How do these issues compare with those you are experiencing? Maybe you aren't facing any particular challenges yourself at all – you are just interested in working relationships, factors that affect them, and how to maximise the positives. Or perhaps you are facing similar or different challenges to those reported above. If so, consider your own situation by looking at Activity 1.1.

Part 1 – Foundations

Activity 1.1: Challenges in working relationships at work
What working relationship challenges (if any) are you or your colleagues experiencing at work?

Who is the relationship with?	What is the issue/issues?
Your boss?	
Direct report(s)?	
Colleague(s)?	
Other (e.g., customer, client, supplier etc)?	
Overall workplace culture?	

This book does not offer simplistic tips or easy fixes to any of the above difficulties, because there are never easy solutions to managing working relationships (if they were you would not be reading this book, and we would not have bothered to write it!). Rather it provides a powerful set of tools for everyone – leaders, managers, and employees of all levels – that will enable all concerned, whatever their role and situation, to deal with relationship challenges at work with greater success.

We do this by helping you uncover the hidden mechanisms behind what we so often take for granted in the way we relate to each other. This will enable you to 'read the context' more accurately, identify the factors that affect people's working relationships at work, and learn how to select the most suitable strategies for overcoming any challenges. Later in this chapter we introduce you to the TRIPS rapport management framework that will help you achieve this. Subsequent chapters will help you understand it and apply it increasingly widely and thoroughly.

Here, we first consider the current workplace – how it has changed in recent years. We then explore what we mean by 'working relationships' and 'rapport at work'. Finally, we explain the design of the book and how to make the most of it – what we cover in each part and how to benefit from the activities.

1.2 The current workplace

Business experts agree that positive working relationships can drive high performance cultures through delivering a number of benefits, including:

- Productive collaborations among diverse and remote teams;
- Sharing of skills and knowledge and enabling continuous organisational learning;
- Open conversations, discussions and exploration including positive management of conflict;
- High levels of creativity and innovation;
- Management of uncertainty and maintenance of motivation during change and transition;
- Sense of wellbeing;
- High retention of employees.

The converse of all these benefits typically apply, of course, if working relationships are problematic or even toxic.

So, this is the challenge for modern workplaces: On the one hand, instability, constant change and the need to solve increasingly complex problems with fewer and fewer resources, necessitate the presence of more of the benefits that positive relationships engender.

On the other, the continuing economic and health impact of the pandemic on individuals and groups, more and more popular remote and hybrid work patterns, as well as increased diversity and identity related tensions, make working relationships more difficult to navigate than ever before. As a result, such benefits are more challenging to attain.

In other words, even though there has never been a greater need for the building of positive relationships and stronger connections in today's workplaces, there are nevertheless, as Caleb and Erica experienced, extraordinary forces that ironically work against the effective building of such relationships.

One manifestation of problematic working relationships can be loneliness. The British Red Cross recently carried out a study of loneliness at work[1] and found that:

- around one in ten workers (10-11 per cent) often feel lonely at work;
- around 32 per cent of senior managers are often or always lonely.

They linked loneliness at work with relationships, defining it as:

"a subjective, negative experience that happens when we have a mismatch between the relationships that we have and those that we want and need."

---

[1] Jopling et al., 2023, p. 7, p. 11

Part 1 – Foundations

They argued that loneliness is bad for several reasons:
- It reduces employee engagement, which has a direct impact on productivity;
- Makes workers more likely to leave, increasing turnover costs;
- Affects workers' health and wellbeing.

Clearly, relationships at work have a major impact on people's sense of wellbeing, as well as their workplace productivity. Interestingly, though, they found that contact with colleagues is not enough on its own to prevent loneliness. As Caleb found, for example, contact with his colleagues in endless online meetings was not enough to enable him either to feel part of the team or to work effectively them with. This implies that some kind of sense of meaningful connection is also required. In this book we explore what it means to have 'meaningful connections' and suggest ways of achieving it.

1.3   What are 'working relationships'?

The term 'relationship' can have multiple meanings. Here are some dictionary definitions:

1. The way in which two or more people or things are connected. (Britannica Dictionary)
2. The way in which two or more people or groups feel and behave towards each other. (Collins)
3. A close connection between two people, especially one involving romantic or sexual feelings. (Collins)

In this book we do not deal with the third definition, except possibly insofar as the connection might be unwanted by one party and hence cause a problem. Rather, we focus on the first and second definitions.

In the workplace, the first definition can be interpreted in terms of role relationships. How are we connected to the other employees?

- Are we colleagues in the same section/department?
- Are we colleagues in different sections/departments?
- Are we boss/line manager – supervisee/direct report?
- Are we members of the same project team?
- Are we internal supplier/internal customer?
- Are we mentor/mentee?
- Other type of role relationship?

These role relationships differ in types of connection in three main ways:
- How equal or unequal/hierarchical they are;
- How familiar, close or distant they are;
- What mutual responsibilities the parties have towards each other.

Needless to say, individuals vary in how they implement their roles and connections, which brings us to the second definition of relationships: the way people feel and behave towards each other. In other words, people's connections (equal–unequal, familiar–unfamiliar, mutual responsibilities) can be reflected very differently in the way they interact with each other. So, some people – whatever their hierarchical position – are more controlling and directive than others; some are friendly and team-oriented while others are more distant and prefer working alone; some tend to be highly responsible and pro-actively involved, while others often seem unmotivated and disengaged.

These differences map closely onto two fundamental dimensions of interaction between people that psychologists have identified: people's general disposition to relate to each other (a) in terms of relative power and control, and (b) in terms of relative distance and affiliation. The framework is often known in psychology as the Interpersonal Circle. In our work, we call it the Interaction Compass, and label the two intersecting axes as Control (high–low) and Connection (high–low). Figure 1.1 illustrates it. (For more details, see Chapter 9, Triggers.)

These two dimensions are of major importance in managing relationships. People are very sensitive to issues of control – whether, from their perspective, they are being controlled too much or not enough, whether they are being given helpful guidance or micromanaged. People are also very sensitive to issues of connection – whether, from their perspective, they are being included or excluded, whether they are being given enough 'space' to work individually or whether they can collaborate fruitfully with colleagues. Both these issues are reflected in the negative experiences of Caleb and Erica.

In subsequent chapters, we regularly refer to these two dimensions – issues of control and connection.

Part 1 – Foundations

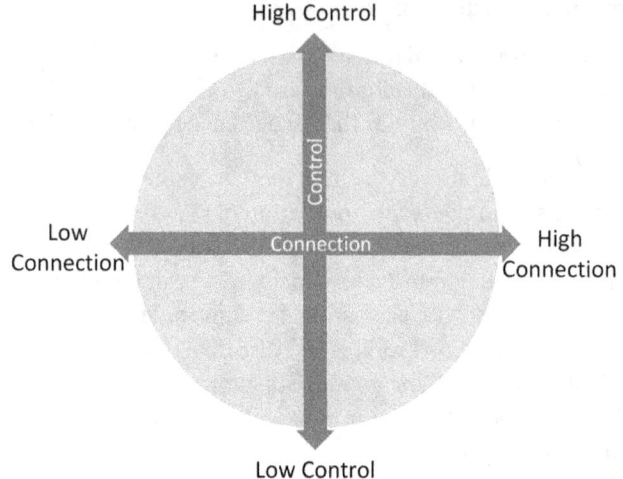

Figure 1.1: The Interaction Compass and its two key axes

How do these issues of control and connection play out in your workplace? Activity 1.2 will help you think this through.

> **Activity 1.2: Reflecting on Control and Connection at work**
> **1. Think of your line manager at work:**
> a. How much do you feel controlled by them?
> b. Think of an interaction where you felt your line manager was being too controlling. What happened/what was said?
> c. How did this make you feel?
>
> **2. Think of a particular colleague at work:**
> a. How closely connected do you feel to them?
> b. Think of an interaction where you felt your colleague did not include you as much as you would have liked or kept talking with you more than you wanted. What exactly happened/what was said?
> c. How did this make you feel?

1.4 What is rapport?

In this book, we often refer to 'rapport' as well as 'working relationships' and 'relationship management'. Professionals in many different spheres of work often refer to the importance of rapport in managing relationships. For instance, in healthcare, doctors and nurses are encouraged to develop it with patients; in the police and security services, officers seek to use it in questioning suspects; in sales settings, salespeople try to build rapport to seal a deal.

So, what is rapport and how does it complement the notion of relationships?

The aim of rapport is to make the interaction more effective in some way; for instance, in the sectors just mentioned, to make a patient feel more comfortable, to elicit more information from a suspect, and to increase the likelihood of a sale.

Rapport itself is often linked with concepts such as mutual trust, empathy, and responsiveness to each other's needs; some think it involves 'liking', others disagree. Most would agree that it's a subjective phenomenon. One helpful definition is as follows:

> We use the term 'rapport' to refer to people's subjective perceptions of (dis) harmony, smoothness–turbulence and warmth–antagonism in interpersonal relations.[2]

If we are to manage rapport, it's important not only to know what it is and why it is useful; we also need to understand the factors that affect it – the factors that can affect smoothness–turbulence and warmth–antagonism in workplace relationships. The factors are issues that we are each personally concerned about and that can influence how we feel about others. We call these factors Triggers, because if they are not handled well, they will cause or trigger some kind of reaction – in us, or in others.

The two axes of the Interaction Compass are two of these factors. Let us take control as an example. Suppose as a manager, I want my team members to use their own initiative in planning their work and I give them a lot of freedom and autonomy to do this. But also suppose those members want me to give them more direction, and I fail to do this. When this happens there will be a mismatch or imbalance in the desired level of control/direction that they want and that I am giving them. This mismatch or imbalance will undermine rapport.

There are six such Trigger factors: Goals, Autonomy, Attention, Face, Fairness, and Ethicality; in other words, personal sensitivities and desires that will trigger a reaction if they are not handled as each party wants them (see Figures 1.2 and 1.3, the first illustrated with two fictitious individuals, Ed and Di). We will explain these six Triggers in more detail in subsequent chapters.

---

[2] Spencer-Oatey & Franklin, 2009, p. 102

Part 1 - Foundations

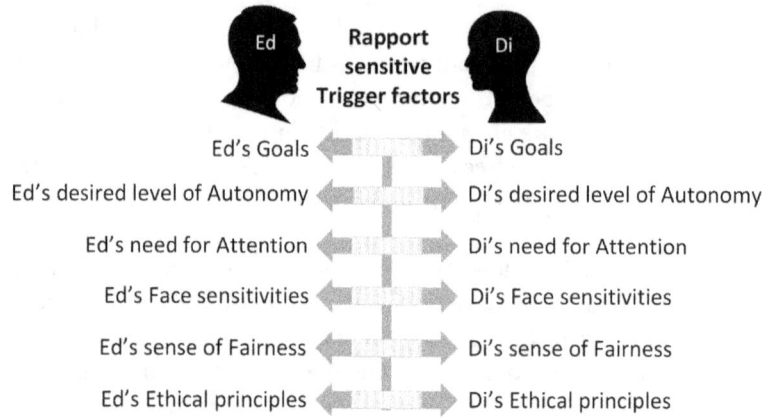

Figure 1.2: The six Trigger factors that form the bases of rapport and rapport management

Figure 1.3: The dilemmas associated with the Trigger factors that affect perceptions of rapport

Here the key thing to note is this: each person's Trigger concerns and sensitivities need to be respected as far as possible, if rapport is to be built and maintained. When this occurs, rapport is positive. When one person's Trigger concerns and sensitivities are ignored, undermined, or challenged in some way, rapport diminishes. This happens dynamically, so rapport needs to be constantly attended to by managing the Triggers. Failure to do this leads to a breakdown in rapport because there is no longer equilibrium in the handling of each person's rapport sensitive concerns.

This raises the next set of questions: how are the Trigger factors handled and what variables influence them? The TRIPS rapport management framework explains this bigger picture.

1.5 The TRIPS Rapport Management Framework

TRIPS is an acronym standing for Triggers, Reactions, Interaction, People, and Settings (see Figure 1.4). They represent the key variables that play a role in rapport and rapport management.

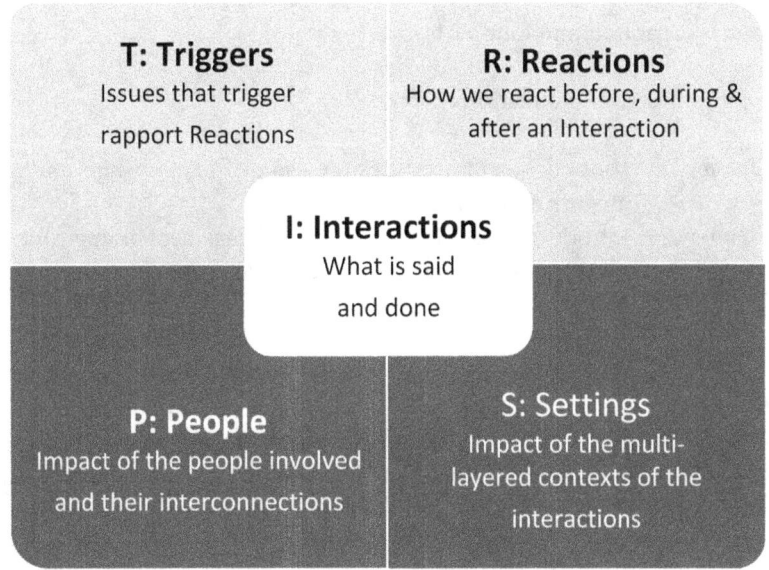

Figure 1.4: The TRIPS rapport management framework

As explained above, when Triggers are activated, they lead to Reactions of some kind, such as positive or negative emotions and evaluative judgements. It is usually people's Interactions with others – what they say and/or do to each other or fail to say and do – that activate one or more of the Triggers.

The features of these Interactions in turn are influenced by the People involved – their personal characteristics (e.g., personalities, social identities) and the links between them (e.g., their hierarchical relationship and distance–closeness). Similarly, Interactions are influenced by the Settings in which they take place (e.g., the physical setting of the Interaction and the organisational cultural setting).

Furthermore, these contextual factors – People and Settings – also influence the sensitivity of the participants to the Triggers and their Reactions to them. In fact, all five elements of the TRIPS rapport management framework (Triggers, Reactions, Interactions, People, Settings) are closely interconnected, each influencing the other.

This may sound complex, but as you work through the book, you'll gradually understand them more clearly and learn how to manage them.

1.6   Organisation of the book

The book is organised into four parts.

Part 1 comprises two Foundation chapters.

> Chapter 1:   (this chapter) introduces the topic of relationships and rapport at work and some key concepts.
> Chapter 2:   introduces the TRIPS rapport management framework and is foundational to the whole book. We strongly recommend that you read Chapter 2 before moving to subsequent chapters.

Part 2 deals with a range of challenges in working relationships and provides you with the insights and tools needed for handling them well and for promoting rapport. It begins with a brief introduction to the suite of strategies used in the tools – the RelATE family of strategies associated with managing Relationships: Attending, Thinking and Engaging. Then there are six chapters, each dealing with a different kind of challenge to working relationships. Each chapter starts with some introductory background information to the issue or situation, and then explains and illustrates a specific tool for addressing it, drawing from the RelATE family of strategies. Each chapter also explains how the TRIPS rapport management framework applies to the issues at stake. All of the chapters are illustrated with authentic case studies (some brief and some extended) and include activities for reflection and application.

Part 1 - Foundations

Chapter 3: From time to time, each of us experience incidents that upset or annoy us. This chapter explains ways of managing our Reactions in these circumstances, including learning to identify our emotions more precisely. With the help of an extended case study, it introduces the Reaction Management Tool to help us handle our Reactions more effectively.

Chapter 4: This chapter explores a specific interactional challenge – handling disagreement and conflict. After considering key background information on disagreement, it explains how the Discord Management Tool can be used to address this issue.

Chapter 5: This chapter focuses on a specific issue in a specific setting: the difficulty of participating in meetings. Using an extended case study, it considers why this happens and presents the Participation Management Tool to help overcome the exclusion that can happen in this context.

Chapter 6: This chapter considers relationships between colleagues and the challenges that can occur. Starting with some case study examples of relationship problems with colleagues, it then introduces the Cooperative Colleague Tool to help address these challenges and promote rapport among colleagues.

Chapter 7: This chapter focuses on the relationship challenges that employees may experience with their bosses. First some research data is presented on challenges that staff may experience with their boss. Then it introduces the Upward Management Tool that is valuable for handling these challenges and for building rapport whenever possible with managers.

Chapter 8: This chapter looks at the same role relationship as Chapter 7 but considers it from the manager's or leader's perspective. After considering some of the challenges that leaders and managers often experience, it introduces the Supportive Leadership Tool to help deal with the challenges associated with managing employees and promoting rapport.

Part 3 presents the five elements of the TRIPS rapport management framework in detail. Each chapter includes research and conceptual background to the component concerned, drawing especially on work in psychology and pragmatics (politeness theory and rapport management theory). Each chapter also ends with a tool that summarises the key issues to pay attention to and to ask yourself when reflecting on the impact of that element.

Part 1 – Foundations

Chapter 9: This chapter presents a detailed explanation of the notion of Triggers. It explains each of the six Triggers in turn – Goals, Autonomy, Attention, Face, Fairness, Ethicality (GAAFFE Triggers) – and their importance for managing rapport.

Chapter 10: This chapter presents a detailed explanation of Reactions. It focuses particularly on emotions – what they are, how much to display them, and how to manage them. It also considers cognitive reactions.

Chapter 11: This chapter presents a detailed explanation of Interactions. It takes communication as its core focus – how communication 'works', how to promote mutual understanding, differences in communication style, the dynamics of interaction, and the risk of microinsults.

Chapter 12: This chapter presents a detailed explanation of People. It covers the potential impact on rapport management of three main aspects: (a) the number of people present, (b) the characteristics of the people involved, both as individuals (e.g., individual working style) and as members of a social group (e.g., an ethnic minority group), and (c) the links between the people involved, such as hierarchy, familiarity, and role responsibilities.

Chapter 13: This chapter presents a detailed explanation of Settings. It explores this element from different perspectives. First, it considers settings from a multi-level perspective – the interactional setting, the organisational setting, and the societal/world setting. Next, it considers the impact of settings on ways of doing things (i.e., norms, regulations, and values). Thirdly, it examines the potential impact of settings on psychological atmosphere (i.e., healthy versus unhealthy cultural climates).

Part 4 Your TRIPS Toolkit, provides templates of each of the tools making up the full TRIPS Toolkit.

Chapter 14 contains the TRIPS Challenge Tool Templates – templates providing steps and prompts for dealing with the challenges explored in the Part 2 chapters.

Chapter 15 contains the TRIPS Concept Tool Templates – templates providing reflection questions to help you gain insights into the potential influence of the key facets of each of the TRIPS elements.

Chapter 16 summarises the RelATE family of strategies and suggests some follow-up opportunities.

1.7 Making the most of the book

We have divided the book into Parts 1, 2, 3 and 4 to try to cater to different needs.

Part 1 provides foundational information and is important for all readers. This is because rapport is not easy to manage and build. It requires time and effort, and understanding the core principles, as covered by the TRIPS rapport management framework, is fundamental to this.

Part 2 focuses on specific challenges to managing working relationships. These chapters are particularly relevant to those who are personally facing such challenges or to those who provide support to others in dealing with these difficulties. These chapters are fairly (although not totally) self-standing, and if preferred, could be read in different sequences, depending on need.

Part 3 is for readers who wish to dig deeper. Often this additional information can significantly enhance understanding and application of the Part 2 tools, and where this is the case, the Part 2 chapters include cross-references to material in the Part 3 chapters. In such situations, Part 3 material will be relevant to everyone. However, this section of the book will also be particularly relevant to readers wishing to gain a deeper, more conceptual understanding of the field of rapport management. It builds on Spencer-Oatey's previous work on rapport management and provides a professionally-oriented current version of her thinking.

Part 4 provides handy access to all the tools presented in Parts 2 and 3 of the book, so that they can be consulted easily and used as reference points.

References in the book have been handled in two ways. In Parts 1 and 2, they have been kept to a minimum, with authors referenced by surname and year of publication in footnotes. Full publication details are given in a bibliography at the end of the book.

Throughout the book we have included numerous authentic case studies with associated questions for reflection (pseudonyms are used for all individuals). We strongly believe in the value of case studies for bringing the issues at hand to life. As you read them, we encourage you to think of your own experiences and situations – whether you've experienced something similar or different. We also include activities to help you apply the ideas and concepts introduced, again with questions for you to consider and reflect on.

The reflection questions serve two purposes:
a. to help you understand more fully the concepts you've been reading about and how they apply to real life situations;
b. to help you reflect on your own experiences, attitudes, and situations.

Part 1 – Foundations

Where appropriate, we've given our own thoughts on the questions at the end of the book.

Self-reflection is never easy. We include a lot of prompts to help you with this, but there are always limitations to working on your own. We strongly encourage you, therefore, to find a suitable friend or colleague who could be a helpful sounding board for you as you grapple with the issues. Seeking consultancy or coaching support is an alternative or additional possibility.

There is one more important thing to bear in mind. The quality of a relationship is always dependent on both parties. Ideally, if there is a problem in a working relationship, both would want to work at their attitudes and interactions, and to improve and change, using the tools and TRIPS framework in this book to enhance their mutual understanding and mutual rapport. Unfortunately, however, this is not necessarily the case in all (or even many) circumstances.

Nevertheless, working on the challenges on your own can still be very useful, especially when you are patient and persevering. We wish you the very best as you grapple with the challenge of improving your working relationships and building rapport by working through this book.

Chapter 2: The TRIPS Rapport Management Framework

A case-based overview

2.1 Introduction

This chapter introduces the TRIPS rapport management framework – the framework that underpins the whole book. As explained in Chapter 1, we are using TRIPS as an acronym, with the sense that if we don't take adequate account of the five components of the framework, we can easily be 'tripped up' in our handling of workplace relationships.

These five interconnected and mutually influencing elements (see Figure 1.3 in the previous chapter for a diagrammatic representation) can be briefly explained as follows:

- T: **the Triggers:** factors (e.g., injustice) that can trigger a reaction and thereby affect our sense of rapport with other people;
- R: **the Reactions:** how we react to a Trigger (e.g., embarrassment, anger, pleasure);
- I: **the Interactions:** the behavioural exchanges (e.g., workplace discussion) in which the Trigger(s) occur;
- P: **the People:** the people (e.g., line manager, colleagues) involved in the interaction and their identities, backgrounds and interconnections;
- S: **the Settings:** the situational background (e.g., location, type of organisation) that form the context to the Interaction.

All of these have an influence on rapport and how effectively we manage it on an ongoing basis. Understanding and being mindful of the five elements can help us avoid 'tripping up' over the relational challenges that we all regularly experience and lay the foundations for better rapport. Together they form the TRIPS Rapport Management Framework that helps us understand, interpret and manage rapport in the workplace.

Case Study: A procedural failure with impact on rapport
We start with a case study that we'll draw on through much of the chapter. It concerns the experiences of Louise, a university academic.

> **Case Study 2.1: A procedural failure**
> An academic colleague of Louise's at another university in the UK asked her to be the external examiner of one of his PhD candidates. She agreed, submitted the required paperwork, and her appointment was

Part 1 – Foundations

formally approved by the university's Graduate School. The candidate submitted her thesis a few months later and in early May the date for the viva (i.e., oral examination) was set for 24 July.

At the beginning of July, Louise had not yet received a copy of the thesis, nor any of the relevant forms that she needed – a report form, the university's regulations for PhD examination, and an expense claim form. She emailed the Graduate School and received an automated reply saying "we are currently focusing on thesis submissions and vivas which are scheduled within the next 4 weeks". Since it was only 3 weeks to the viva, Louise assumed she would receive a response very soon.

Another week went by and there was still nothing – no thesis and no forms. By this time Louise was getting annoyed and felt that the Graduate School must be completely incompetent and inefficient. So, on 11 July she sent an email to the Graduate School and the candidate's supervisor, reiterating her need to receive the thesis and the forms, and then saying "Given all these uncertainties, if I have still not received proper communication from the Graduate School, with all relevant forms, by Monday 17 July, I'm afraid I'll have to withdraw from being the external examiner. I'm really sorry about this, but this is truly extraordinarily unprofessional behaviour on the part of the [name of university] Graduate School."

She was annoyed that she needed to keep chasing for essential documents. She felt she shouldn't have to waste so much time on this, that this was unfair on her – especially since examining a PhD thesis is already a time-consuming process for which the pay is minimal. But she didn't want to upset the supervisor so added a personal note to him saying "sorry for the worry and hassle that the Graduate School behaviour is causing you."

Two days later (13 July) Louise received an email confirming the date and time of the viva and was sent a link to download the thesis and forms needed. When she clicked on the link, there was a red alert symbol, saying the completed report form was overdue – that it should have been submitted by 3 July. This was followed by a reminder email on 15 July, asking her to complete the report form as a matter of urgency. Normally Louise would have been very embarrassed to receive such communications, but given the failure on the Graduate School's part, it just further annoyed her and underlined in her mind the Graduate School's incompetence.

Meanwhile, the candidate's supervisor emailed Louise saying "I am so very sorry about this. If there's any consolation it has sparked a review of processes. Thanks once again for bearing with us. I do personally and professionally appreciate it."

From this account, we can see that Louise was annoyed (a Reaction) because she could not start reading and evaluating the thesis (a Trigger) because the documentation had not been sent to her (an Interaction failure). Later, when the documentation was sent (an Interaction), they included a criticism (a Trigger) – that Louise had not completed her work by the required deadline. This further annoyed Louise and confirmed her negative evaluation of the Graduate School (a Reaction).

It may be that you have found this case study a little difficult to follow in detail. This is because we always draw on background knowledge when interpreting interactions. This background knowledge gives rise to expectations, and any noticeable breach of these expectations can trigger a reaction. The other two elements of the TRIPS rapport management framework – P: People and S: Settings – are the sources of that background knowledge. They feed into participants' expectations and when those expectations are not met, problems can arise. For that reason, they always need to be considered, especially when there is a risk of people holding different background knowledge (e.g., when they are from different cultural groups) and hence of holding different expectations.

Below we explain each of the TRIPS elements in a little more detail. This will help you to understand and apply the framework effectively in different contexts.

2.2 T – Triggers

'T' stands for 'Triggers' and refers to issues that people are particularly sensitive to from a relational perspective. If someone's expectations are not met, this often triggers a reaction of some kind. Triggers therefore need to be handled carefully in order to avoid undermining or threatening rapport. However, they can also be used to promote rapport. Triggers thus function as risks and opportunities – risks to rapport if mishandled but opportunities for enhancing rapport if handled well.

We use the acronym GAAFFE to refer to these potential triggers. They are summarised in Figure 2.1 and in Table 2.1. We explain them step by step through the book and in detail in Chapter 9. It is important to remember, though, that although they are identified as six separate rapport triggers, in reality they are quite closely interconnected. In fact, it is common for concerns about rapport to be triggered by more than one type of sensitivity at the same time.

Part 1 - Foundations

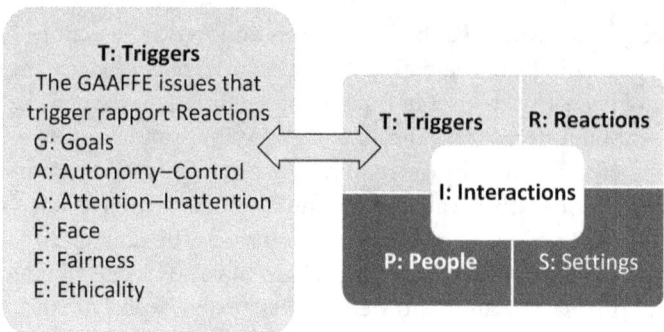

Fig. 2.1: The GAAFFE rapport Triggers

Rapport Triggers	Potential impact on rapport - risks and opportunities
G: Goals	If someone prevents us achieving a goal, whether big or small, this typically undermines rapport. If someone helps us achieve a goal, this can enhance rapport.
A: Autonomy–control	We like to be given an appropriate amount of autonomy for the type of role relationship we have with the other party – not too little and not too much, according to the circumstances. Rapport will typically be undermined if the balance is mismanaged and enhanced, if it is managed well.
A: Attention–inattention	We like to be given an appropriate amount of attention for the type of role relationship we have with the other party. We usually don't like to be ignored, but we also don't like unwanted attention. Rapport will typically be undermined if the balance is mismanaged and enhanced, if it is managed well.
F: Face	We like to feel respected and appreciated for our skills and qualities, and just for who we are – this enhances our face and promotes rapport. If we feel disrespected or unappreciated, our face will be threatened and rapport will be undermined.
F: Fairness	We like to be treated fairly – this can enhance rapport. If we feel we have been treated unfairly, especially in comparison with others, this can undermine rapport.
E: Ethicality	If we are asked to do something that we regard as illegal or unethical, we will feel concerned and uncomfortable and rapport will be undermined.

Table 2.1: The GAAFFE Rapport Triggers

Part 1 – Foundations

There can be both individual and cultural differences in people's sensitivities to each of these trigger elements, as well as the relative importance they attach to each of them.

Thinking back to the Case Study, it was Goals that primarily triggered Louise's reaction – she wanted to fulfil her goal of completing her external examining work in good time, and not receiving a copy of the thesis, nor the relevant forms, prevented her from doing so. This caused her to React. The Graduate School's lack of Attention to her communication was another Trigger – she expected her emails to be attended to and when they failed to do so, it also caused her to React. There was also an element of unfairness – she felt they were unfairly wasting too much of her time, and so lack of Fairness was a third, more minor Trigger.

When the Graduate School later signalled with a red warning that she was late submitting her report, this was potentially a threat to her Face (a fourth Trigger!). Normally this would have led to her feeling embarrassed but given that this was in no way Louise's fault, in this case it simply increased her annoyance and negative evaluation of the Graduate School (her Reactions).

To help you apply your learning on the GAAFFE risks to working situations, try working through Activity 2.1.

> **Activity 2.1: Reflecting on rapport Triggers**
> Look at the following incidents and consider which rapport Triggers were being undermined or supported. Remember that more than one rapport risk factor can be Triggered at the same time.
> Note down what rapport Triggers were at stake in each of these scenarios for the main individual concerned (i.e., for Christoph and Marie respectively). Then reflect on a recent experience of your own.
> **1. Promotion concerns:** Christoph works for a scientific consultancy company. He is an ambitious and hard-working young man, keen to perform well, get promoted and to earn more money. He has been given increasing responsibility and praised for his work. However, he found out that colleagues in a different division of his company were being promoted more quickly than in his division and were earning more money. He spoke to his boss about this. His boss acknowledged that Christoph was performing above his grade, but said that in his view, staff should not be considered for promotion until they had worked in their role for a set period of time. Christoph was not happy about this response from his boss.
> **2. Appointment difficulties:** Marie, a head of department, had recently chaired an interview panel for a new permanent member of her team. There were two internal candidates, currently on temporary contracts, who had different strengths and weaknesses. The panel could not reach an

Part 1 - Foundations

> agreement on which one to appoint. Marie therefore decided not to make any appointment on this occasion and to re-run the interview at a later date. A complaint of bias against Marie was submitted by a staff member who was personally close to one of the candidates; it was investigated by a senior manager and Marie was cleared of any bias or wrongdoing. However, the complainant then lobbied the senior manager, after which the manager told Marie that the interview should be held again without her involvement. Marie was offended and objected to his directive.
>
> **3. Your own example.** Think of an incident you have experienced at work where you felt annoyed or upset in some way. Which of the GAAFFE Triggers do you think influenced your reaction?

In Part 2 of the book, where we deal with specific relationship challenges in the workplace, we revisit the GAAFFE Triggers. For those would want to explore the topic in more depth, including delve more into the theoretical underpinnings of these concepts, see Chapter 9 in Part 3.

2.3   R - Reactions

'R' stands for the rapport-related reactions we have when one or more of our rapport Triggers have been activated. These reactions typically include:

- Our emotional responses to what we experience or desire;
- The evaluative judgements we make of the individuals involved;
- Our reflections on how best to respond.

These are represented diagrammatically in Figure 2.2.

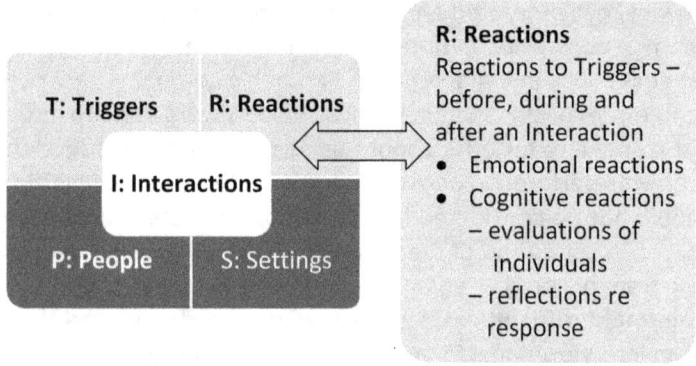

Figure 2.2: Types of Reactions to rapport Triggers

In terms of emotional reactions, these can be positive, such as when the individuals feel trustful of each other or feel supported and appreciated (i.e., there is rapport), or they may be negative, such as when individuals feel angry or upset with each other (i.e., where rapport is undermined). In Louise's case, her emotional reaction was negative – she felt annoyed. If we wish to maintain or build rapport, our aim should be to manage or minimise any negative emotions (ours and/or that of the other person) and to enhance positive ones. This is often difficult, though, so throughout the book we explore ways of promoting this.

Closely associated with our emotional reactions is the thinking that accompanies them – our cognitive reactions. Very often this entails making judgements of others. If we don't like what someone else has said or done (or when they have failed to say or do something we want), we tend to make negative evaluations of them, referring to them in terms such as rude, inconsiderate, obstructive. In making these assessments, we also often blame the other person for what happened. However, if our judgements are based on limited or one-sided information, these judgements may be unwarranted and unfair, and may thereby undermine rapport unnecessarily. In Louise's case, she made a strong evaluative judgement – that the other university's Graduate School was incompetent, inefficient, and unprofessional. The unfolding sequence of events consolidated her evaluation, and nothing that happened was able to change her opinion.

Another aspect of cognitive reactions is thinking over whether or not to respond, and if so, how and when to do so. For example, if the trigger event is minor, we may decide it is best simply to ignore it and say or do nothing. Even if it is more serious, we may judge it to be too risky or undesirable to let the other person know our reaction, perhaps for power or cultural reasons, or if we know the other person is going through a difficult time.

A key goal here is to use our cognitive reactions to try and manage our emotional reactions. Having a rule of thumb can be useful here; for instance, "never respond instantly to an annoying or upsetting email; try to wait a few hours." In the case study, Louise was provoked into writing an email in which she threatened to withdraw from her role as external examiner. However, this was not a spontaneous or impulsive reaction; it came after her conscious reflection on the situation and her decision that this was the best course of action. Her email led to a behavioural reaction from the Graduate School, and Louise was then able successfully to complete the examiner's report prior to the viva.

Reactions to rapport triggers – particularly when they are negative – along with self-awareness in understanding and interpreting them are crucial for rapport management. We explore them in more detail in subsequent chapters. Chapter 3 in particular focuses on them, including a framework for gaining insights into our emotions.

Meanwhile, look back at the mini case studies in Activity 2.1. Try thinking over how you would have reacted in each of those situations.

Part 1 – Foundations

Activity 2.2: Reactions to rapport Triggers
Look again at incidents a. and b. described in Activity 2.1. If you had been in each of those situations, how do you think you would have reacted? In the columns on the right, note down your thoughts.
Then revisit your own example and note down your reactions.

	Emotional reaction	Cognitive reaction – evaluation of individuals	Cognitive reaction – response reflections
Christoph and his promotion			
Marie and the appointment difficulties			
Reconsidering your own example			

Up to now, we've assumed that the Triggers and Reactions are ones that we ourselves are experiencing. However, it is also important that we pay close attention to the reactions of others, so that we can pick up on anything that we may have said or done that has triggered a reaction in others. We consider Reactions in more detail in Chapter 10, including the challenge of noticing subtle reactions during an interaction.

Next, we turn to the factors that can give rise to the rapport Triggers and Reactions in the first place – Interactions, People, and Settings.

2.4 I – Interactions

Typically, it is what people say and do that triggers our reactions. There are three key aspects:

- What is said or not said (the message content);
- How any message is conveyed (the communication style);
- How the dynamics of an interaction are co-ordinated (the communication dynamics).

Part 1 - Foundations

These three aspects are illustrated in Figure 2.3.

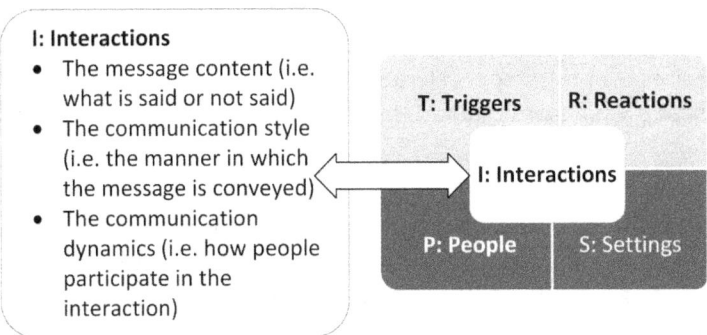

Figure 2.3: Aspects of the Interaction that can Trigger Reactions

To learn more about this, let's first consider another case study, Case Study 2.2. In this example, the team manager, Hera, is giving critical feedback to her team. She is clearly trying hard not to annoy them. As you read the extract, look out for the ways in which she tries to achieve this.

> **Case Study 2.2: Giving critical feedback[3]**
> Hera is a team manager in a Māori workplace in New Zealand. Below is an extract from one of her team meetings. XF is one of her team members.
>
> 1 Hera: which leads me onto one other item ... and that's the ... uhm ... issue of writing ... uhm [pauses slightly]
> 2 XF: mmh
> 3 Hera: uhm ... whenever you ... er ... are drafting I've noticed a couple of mistakes creeping into our work and that's stuff that ... that even I've signed out .... Suddenly as I'm re-reading, I spot a spelling mistake which I didn't see the first time round or a grammatical mistake
> 4 XF: yeah
> 5 Hera: I really make a plea for all of you to make sure that you take it to one other person at least [slight pause] to ... uhm ... to peer review
> 6 XF: I'm doing that eh [laughs]
> 7 Hera: before you before you sign it out
> 8 XF: yeah ...
> 9 Hera: it's so easy to overlook just a simple mistake

---

[3] Holmes, 2018, p. 44, transcription adjusted and simplified to make it easier for non-linguists to read

Part 1 - Foundations

> **Reflect**
> 1. What was the message Hera wanted to get across to her team?
> 2. Why do you think she hesitated so much?
> 3. Why do you think she admitted to sometimes being at fault herself?
> 4. How similar or different is Hera's style to yours when trying to persuade your team to act differently?

In this case study, Hera needed to convey some critical feedback – that her team had not been checking their written work carefully enough. In GAAFFE Trigger terms, her goal was to get them to reduce the number of mistakes by asking another team member to proofread their work. However, this message content – their work had too many mistakes in it – risked threatening the face of her team, thereby activating one of the GAAFFE triggers (Face) and leading to a negative reaction. So, another of her goals was to maintain positive rapport with her team. In order to try to achieve this, she adopted a particular communication style. On the one hand she avoided identifying any individual team member who was especially at fault, and on the other she adopted a modest, self-effacing style to try to reduce this risk of a negative reaction. She also used a lot of hesitation and understatement (e.g., a couple of mistakes) to soften the impact of her criticism – a feature called 'mitigation' by linguists. For a more in-depth exploration of Interactions, including mitigation, see Chapter 11.

Now let's return to Case Study 2.1 and consider how the Interaction affected Louise. When Louise received the automatic reply email saying urgent cases would be dealt with promptly, she initially believed that the documentation would be sent out soon. This is in line with the normal principles of communication – when one person sends a request, an answer of some sort is expected. However, when time went on and there was no reply, the other party's failure to communicate then triggered her reactions which became less positive. Here it was the communication dynamics (i.e., the process of one turn leading to another) rather than the message content or style that was the issue.

Later, however, when she was informed that her report was overdue by 10 days (message content) and saw a red alert against her name (a type of communication style), this triggered further reactions, including a written response.

Interactions can be synchronous or asynchronous, and ongoing or one-off. When interactions are synchronous (i.e., 'live'), there is usually little time to think through how to respond and so care is needed in such circumstances. This is particularly the case when the relationship is an ongoing or important one. When the interactions are asynchronous (as between Louise and the Graduate School), rapport (mis)management unfolds over time, with the previous interaction often

Part 1 - Foundations

affecting future interactions. For Louise, the relationship with the Graduate School was only short-term (Louise didn't anticipate doing further work for that university), but her relationship with the supervisor was longer-term and she actively took this into account in her interactions.

All this points to the other two elements of the TRIPS model: P-People and S-Settings. These are the sources of the background information that influence the TRI elements – how Interactions are carried out and whether any rapport Reactions are Triggered. They are core to understanding and interpreting the TRI elements and thus always need to be taken into consideration.

2.5 P – People

'P' stands for the 'People' or individuals involved in an interaction or those who are particularly relevant to it. They are often referred to as the participants. Three key features are especially important:

- The number of people present in an interaction,
  or copied into an email exchange;
- The characteristics of the people involved – their group identities and their individual identities, including:
    o their cultural backgrounds and how these have shaped their ways of seeing the world;
    o their expectations of what is normal/acceptable in specific situations;
    o their behavioural tendencies or preferences.
- The links or connections between the people involved, including their role responsibilities and their attitudes towards each other.

They are represented diagrammatically in Figure 2.4.

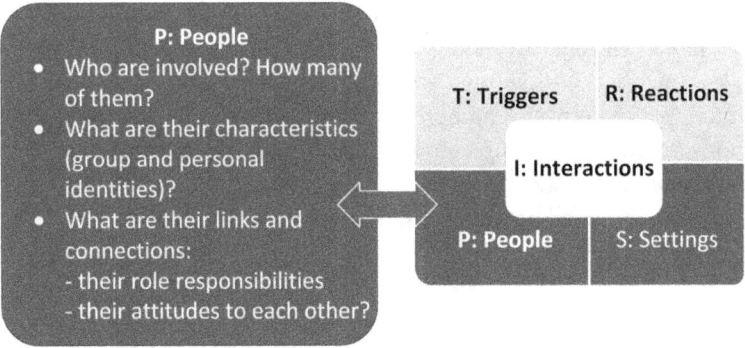

Figure 2.4: People factors that can affect how rapport is managed and interpreted

Making working relationships work   27

Part 1 – Foundations

Number of people
The greater the number of people present in an interaction, or copied into an email exchange, the greater the potential impact on rapport. If someone is criticised in front of others, this is likely to be much more face-threatening than if it takes place in private. So, in Case Study 2.2, Hera avoided criticising any individual team member, since it was a team meeting context.

If someone is praised in front of others, this can be face-enhancing for the individual; on the other hand, it can also be embarrassing for that person and others may feel resentful that they themselves have not been praised. In other words, the public nature of any communication, including the number of people who have access to it, always needs to be considered.

People's characteristics or identities
People's personal characteristics or identities are extremely important in rapport management. Psychologists often make a distinction between individual identities and group identities. Our individual identities refer to the wide-ranging features that are specific to us as an individual, such as our professional experience and expertise, working style, proficiency in a foreign language, and our beliefs, ideologies, and values. Our group identities come from the groups that we belong to and that are meaningful to us. These can include, for instance, fellow members of a department, or a sports team or religious group we may belong to. There can be an overlap between the two – for instance, our beliefs and values are often closely linked with the group(s) we are members of – but it's often a useful distinction.

In Case Study 2.2, Hera's working style could be regarded as high in empathy (see 'Working Styles' in Chapter 12) – an individual characteristic. On the other hand, Janet Holmes, who collected the extract, refers to this face-supportive style which avoids direct criticism as being a group characteristic of Māori people.

Our group memberships give us a sense of belonging and form a key part of our identity. However, they can also be a source of exclusion and discrimination, because there is a strong psychological tendency for members of one group to favour fellow members of their own group (known as the ingroup) and to give them preferential treatment over members of other groups (known as the outgroup).

Our individual and group identities can be multiple and various. Being aware of people's personalities, working styles, neurodiversity characteristics, group affiliations, and so on can all be important when interpreting interactions with them.

Links between people
People are linked with each other through their roles and attitudes towards each other.

People have workplace roles or positions, such as team manager (in Hera's case), external examiner (in Louise's case), director, junior doctor, and so on. These roles can influence what people regard as their 'rights' and hence what they believe they can say to others. In Case Study 2.1, Louise knew that in her role as external examiner she needed to evaluate the thesis, and she obviously could not do this without receiving the relevant documentation. She thus felt able to be critical of the Graduate School's failure to fulfil their responsibilities, and to label that as unprofessional. In Case Study 2.2, Hera was the team manager and therefore needed to maintain the quality of work. She thus had the right to criticise them but chose to do it in a face-supportive manner. Roles thus have responsibilities associated with them and, as we explain under S-Settings, people hold expectations of what everyone will say and do in particular communication settings. Breaches of those expectations can lead to rapport issues.

> **Activity 2.3: Roles and role responsibilities**
> Think of someone at work, such as your line manager or a colleague. Have you ever felt they failed to do what you wanted or expected them to do for you? If so, note down the circumstances, and think through what role responsibilities you were attributing to them. How might their sense of role responsibilities towards you differ from yours?

Furthermore, a range of other P: People factors affect the TRI of the TRIPS rapport management model. These include whether people are:

- equal or unequal (e.g., in terms of the work hierarchy);
- familiar or unfamiliar with each other
- close or distant
- biased or unbiased towards each other.

In Case Study 2.1, Louise did not know the PhD candidate's supervisor well, but he was part of her academic subject area network. This influenced her wording of her email, such that she included two apologies for her critical stance, one explicitly for the supervisor.

For more details on P: People, please see Chapter 12. Here we consider the final element of the TRIPS rapport management framework, Settings.

2.6 S – Settings

'S' stands for Settings – the contexts in which interactions take place. In order to handle rapport risks well and minimise the triggering of negative reactions, it is

Part 1 – Foundations

necessary to take the settings into account. This is because they affect people's expectations and interpretations of what is said and done, which in turn affect their rapport-related judgements and responses.

There are multiple layers to Settings, nested within each other. All of them affect (to a greater or lesser extent) what is said and done and their impact on rapport. This is because each of the setting layers has associated norms, rules and regulations, and values and beliefs, each of which interact to affect people's expectations, how they behave, and what triggers their reactions. Figure 2.5 illustrates four important layers. Chapter 13 provides a more detailed explanation.

The Interaction Setting
The most immediate (or local) settings are the Interaction Settings – the Settings in which an interaction takes place. This includes the 'where' (physical location), 'when' (time and timing), 'how' (e.g., online or face-to-face') and 'why' (the purpose) of the interaction, as well as the psychological atmosphere in which the interaction takes place.

Many interactions – known as communicative events – have a recognisable structure: a familiar set of features that individuals connected with that event can recognise. For example, if we think of a communicative event such as a business meeting, a sales encounter, or a training workshop, we typically have expectations over such elements as the following:

- The purpose of the activity;
- The 'normal' procedures for carrying it out;
- Who is expected to say or do what;
- Any features of the setting that are needed or important (e.g., a flip chart for a training workshop).

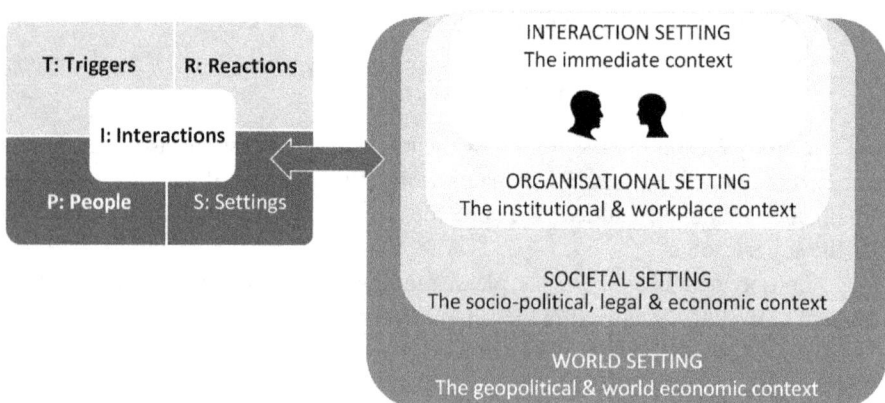

Fig.2.5: The nested layers of contextual Settings[4]

[4] Adapted from Spencer-Oatey et al., 2022, p. 187

With regard to Case Study 2.1, Louise – based on her prior experience of being a PhD examiner – had clear expectations as to how a PhD examination would take place and who is responsible for what. These included issues like how far in advance of the viva she would receive the thesis and forms, who would send them to her, when she needed to complete the forms, what outcome options she could select from, and so on. These procedural norms led to her having certain expectations for the interaction, and when these were breached, GAAFFE Triggers were activated, and rapport reactions ensued.

One of the challenges for managing rapport, especially in contexts of cultural diversity, is that people's expectations may differ. Different organisations may have different norms and procedures for handling a particular type of communicative event, and such differences can be even greater when the cultural context (e.g., national, organisational) is different. For instance, a PhD examination process in Scandinavia is extremely different from the process in the UK. So, misunderstandings can easily occur when the differences are not taken into account.

To help you gain further insights into the notion of communicative events and how they may affect your own workplace situation, Activity 2.4 offers some reflection opportunities.

> **Activity 2.4: Communicative events**
> Think of the way in which your organisation or department runs meetings.
> 1. What is your understanding of the purpose of those meetings, the procedures for conducting them, your role in them, and any important tools or settings?
> 2. How similar or different are any of these features to meetings you've experienced in a different organisation?
> 3. Have you ever felt annoyed or frustrated over unmet expectations; e.g., when you were not given the opportunity to contribute your ideas, or when the meeting did not achieve the goal you were hoping for? What do you think was the source of the problem?

As mentioned above, all interaction settings have a psychological atmosphere that accompanies the communicative event. This atmosphere is an important part of the interaction setting and links closely with notions of psychological safety. Psychological safety occurs "when employees [feel] safe and able to engage in their work cognitively, emotionally, and physically"[5]. We consider this further in Chapter 7 and in detail in Chapter 13. Here we simply note its importance and point out that it is closely associated with power. It can therefore stem from the attitude and behaviour of a leader (a People factor), who can influence the psychological aspects of the interaction. However, it can also be rooted in another layer of context – the Organisational Setting, which we turn to next.

---
[5] Kasumu, 2023, p. 85

Part 1 – Foundations

The Organisational Setting
The Organisational Setting zooms out a little from the Interaction Setting and considers the culture of the organisation and the workplace. It can include branding requirements and any procedural specifications, such as accepted or preferred styles of communication. Of particular relevance for rapport are the organisation's values, both deep and espoused (in other words what the organisation and its leadership explicitly say the values are), along with the workplace atmosphere associated with those values and how they are enacted.

If there are unhealthy levels of competition and distrust among senior management, the working environment is likely to be toxic and stressful for employees. This can permeate down to Interaction Settings, affecting the psychological atmosphere across the organisation. When psychological safety is low, the GAAFFE risks to rapport will be much higher, and careful attention will need to be paid to them in order to minimise those risks. Rather paradoxically, though, if employees are encouraged to take business-related risks, with mistakes and learning from them accepted (i.e., high psychological safety), some individuals may pay less attention to others' personal reactions and may need to be encouraged to still be mindful of the GAAFFE triggers.

The Societal and World Settings
All organisations function within a broader context. This can include:

- Societal and world issues, such as the Covid-19 pandemic, natural disasters, and wars, and their impact on the functioning of organisations;
- National rules, regulations and laws that organisations need to adhere to;
- Cultural values and principles that influence the practices of organisations.

In recent years, societal and world issues have had a huge and ongoing impact on organisations. Resulting uncertainties have often filtered through to employees, making relationship management particularly important, especially for leaders. Case Study 2.3 reports comments by Barbara, a leader in the travel industry – a sector particularly badly hit by the pandemic.

Case Study 2.3: The local impact of societal and world settings
As a leader, I needed to work out how to keep people focused in the midst of chaos, and optimistic in a time of darkness. In addition to the impact of COVID-19, there were other factors further impacting travel, plus fears of a recession and social and cultural change factors swirling around, making people fearful about their own place within and outside our business. My role, above all, was to keep people focused on their contributions to the business, so they knew their value and worth. That was a challenge – they

Part 1 - Foundations

> *were exhausted, anxious and under a lot of stress. The practical tactic was to break things down into digestible bits—it was the right solution for the right time. Every morning, we identified the one thing each person on the team needed to get done that day to feel good about themselves, and we regrouped later in the day to check-in on results. Every day we checked things off our list, congratulated ourselves for the win, and felt a sense of accomplishment that fuelled our readiness to it again the next day, and the next, and thereafter for several months. Instead of getting overwhelmed by the hundreds of things we needed to do each day, we forced ourselves to prioritize, and in doing so, shortened our horizon.*
>
> **Reflect**
> 1. How have societal and world setting affected you and your workplace?
> 2. Note the steps that Barbara took to help reduce people's stress.
> 3. How useful do you think they could be in your context?

The pandemic has also changed people's preferences and expectations around hybrid working, with the result that working patterns now need to be negotiated much more often in order to recruit and retain staff and maintain morale.

In terms of cultural values and principles, two that are particularly relevant to rapport are (a) attitudes towards hierarchy–equality (often known as power distance), which affect the way we relate to others if they are perceived to have more or less power than us, and (b) prioritisation of task versus relationship, i.e., to what extent we expect to be able to work effectively with someone without getting to know them first. These values can apply at the organisational level, but they can also be influenced by sectoral or societal level tendencies. We consider them in more detail in Chapter 13.

A summary of the TRIPS Rapport Management Framework is given in Table 2.2. In the chapters in Part 2 of the book, we illustrate the various ways in which the different factors need to be managed when handling different relationship challenges. The chapters in Part 3 of the book provide a more detailed exploration of each of the TRIPS factors and the theoretical underpinnings behind them.

2.7 Summary of the TRIPS Rapport Management Framework

T: Triggers	Rapport is easily threatened or undermined. This can happen when one or more triggers are activated because of a risk or hindrance to: • What each person is trying to achieve • How each person likes to be treated • What each person regards as 'good' or 'unacceptable' behaviour There are six key Triggers - the GAAFFE Triggers - Goals, Autonomy-control, Attention-inattention, Face, Fairness, Ethicality • Rapport can be enhanced when these sensitivities are addressed effectively and undermined when they are ignored
R: Reactions	When a Trigger has been activated, we may have three types of reaction (positive or negative): • An affective/emotional reaction • A behavioural reaction - what we do or say (if anything), in response • A cognitive, evaluative reaction - we may make judgements of the person or people involved, as well as of their behaviour
I: Interactions	Our perceptions of rapport are closely influenced by the interactions we have with others. This includes: • What people do or don't do • What people say or don't say • How people word what they say • The dynamics of an exchange, such as who speaks when and how often
P: People	Rapport - whether good or problematic - always exists among people and is affected by a range of features connected with the individuals involved. These include: • The number of people involved • The roles of the people involved • The links and attitudes between the people • Individual and group identities of the people
S: Settings	All exchanges take place in a setting and are influenced by that setting. The setting has multiple layers and includes: • The immediate setting in which the interaction is taking place • The organisational setting associated with the interaction • The broader societal setting that frames the interaction • The even broader world setting that frames the interaction

Table 2.2: An overview of the TRIPS factors that influence rapport

Part 2

RELATIONSHIP CHALLENGES AT WORK: TOOLS AND STRATEGIES FOR PROMOTING RAPPORT

Part 2 – Relationship challenges at work

Introduction to Part 2

In Part 2 of the book, we explore a range of relationship challenges that people may experience in the workplace and we introduce a set of recommended tools for dealing with each of them.

Three of the chapters deal with specific issues and how to handle them:

- Annoying or upsetting incidents – the Reaction Management Tool (Chapter 3)
- Conflict and disagreement – the Discord Management Tool (Chapter 4)
- Exclusion in meetings – the Participation Management Tool (Chapter 5)

The following three chapters deal with challenges associated with a given role:

- Colleagues working with colleagues – the Cooperative Colleague Tool (Chapter 6)
- Direct reports working with their line manager – the Upward Management Tool (Chapter 7)
- Line managers working with their direct reports – the Supportive Leadership Tool (Chapter 8)

Each of the tools recommends a set of strategies which are drawn from a suite of Relationship management strategies. We call these the RelATE family of strategies for handling rapport in interaction. The RelATE family of strategies comprises three 'superstrategies': Attend Think Engage, each of which has a number of component strategies, as shown in Figure P2.1.

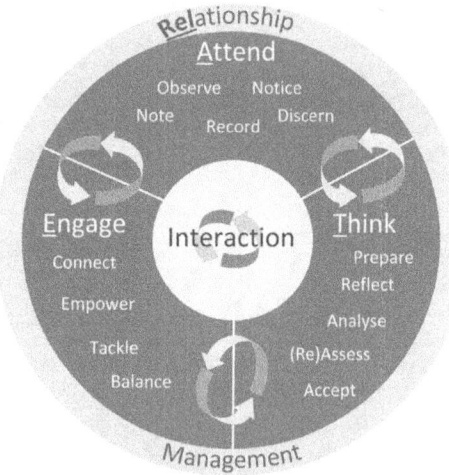

Figure P2.1: The RelATE family of Relationship Management Strategies

Attend (i.e., pay attention) identifies the need to be very observant, looking out for (potentially) significant features of the interaction, noting them mentally and, when appropriate, making some kind of record of what was said or what happened, such as in writing or by describing or relating it to someone else.

Think focuses on cognitive activities, especially reflecting on and analysing the features of the Interaction and factors affecting it. The TRIPS rapport management framework provides extremely useful guidelines for this, offering scaffolding (via its component features) to support Thinking. For this reason, many of the activities and tools in the Part 2 chapters encourage readers to think through systematically the issue at hand by referring to the TRIPS components. The Thinking superstrategy also covers any preparation (mental or information gathering) needed in advance of an interaction, and (cognitive) acceptance of any unresolved, ongoing challenges that may need further attention after any Engagement.

Engage refers to the purpose, need, and manner of the interaction. Connect and Empower both focus on the purpose. The aim of Connect is to build bonds with another person – bonds of care, appreciation, and understanding. It refers to the horizontal axis of the Interaction Compass (see Chapter 1). The aim of Empower is to support the other person in their work role, such as helping them when they need it and sharing (rather than withholding) information that will be useful to them. Tackle refers to the need to do something – to take some kind of action to address an issue, while Balance refers to the manner in which that action is performed. Balance is particularly relevant for the two axes of the Interaction Compass – achieving an appropriate balance (for a given context and relationship) between Autonomy and Control and between Attention and Inattention. It also applies to variation in communication style.

The three RelATE superstrategies are closely interconnected and do not always follow any particular sequence; moreover, they are not all necessarily utilised in all situations. How exactly they and their component strategies are deployed in any given context will vary according to the relationship issue at stake. For instance, with upsetting or annoying incidents (Chapter 3), the focus is on Attending and Thinking, whereas for promoting cooperation among colleagues (Chapter 6), the focus is much more on Engaging. In other words, both the selection and the sequencing of the RelATE superstrategies and their component strategies do not follow any set pattern; rather, they are chosen to address the challenge at hand in the combination and sequence that is best suited to that particular need.

Each of the chapters explains this in more detail.

Part 2 - Relationship challenges at work

Chapter 3: Upset or annoyed?

How to manage and learn from adverse experiences

3.1 Introduction

From time to time, all of us experience incidents that trigger some kind of negative reaction. We may feel annoyed, upset, or shocked; we may retaliate in some way through what we say or do; and we may make negative judgements of the people involved. Sometimes the incidents are minor; at other times they can be major. Either way, they can damage rapport, especially if our negative feelings and judgements are allowed to fester and if our responses exacerbate the situation.

This chapter addresses this common problem. Its key starting point is the R of the TRIPS rapport management model – Reactions – and it explores not only how we can control our emotions and judgements, but also the factors that give rise to them. This in turn can help us learn from our adverse experiences and deal with them more effectively.

First consider Case Study 3.1 and reflect on the questions that follow.

> **Case Study 3.1: A disagreement at work**
> Josh works for a global market research agency, with responsibility for a number of major accounts, delivering them insights into their customers' and consumers' viewpoints.
>
> One day he was working with a new, more junior member of staff, Phil, going through the presentation deck that Phil had prepared for delivering to a major client. Josh – who knew the client well – felt that the flow of the argument was not clear and that it wouldn't convince the client. So, he asked Phil to make adjustments. However, Phil refused, saying that he personally thought the current version worked really well. Josh tried to explain further, but Phil continued to disagree.
>
> As a result, Josh felt really annoyed with Phil and commented later to a friend, *"We've got a new guy at work who thinks he knows everything. He refuses to take any advice, even when it concerns a major client he's unfamiliar with. He seems so stubborn! I hope he won't ruin our reputation with that client."*
>
> **Reflect**
> Now consider the following questions:
> 1. How 'fair' do you think Josh's comments were about Phil?
> 2. How could Josh reduce his negative feelings towards Phil?
> 3. What might happen if he doesn't?

The types of questions raised in Case Study 3.1 are common in the workplace, and yet many people often fail to handle them well, and sometimes even to consider them. This can lead to ongoing relationship problems at work such as poor communication and lack of rapport, and this in turn typically results in low morale and poor staff retention. For these reasons, all employees, whatever their level of seniority, need to work hard at the following:

- Understanding and managing their emotional reactions;
- Becoming more aware of the sources or reasons for their feelings and reactions;
- Exploring influences or factors that they may have overlooked;
- Reflecting on their interpretations and judgements;
- Gaining new learning from their negative experiences.

These insights will not usually solve the relationship problems per se, unless they are particularly minor and not engrained, but they are an important first step. In fact, when we want to handle well our negative reactions to an incident or series of incidents, there are two key goals we need to achieve:

- Manage or regulate our emotions;
- Make sense of our reactions through systematic reflection.

Chapter 10 in Part 3 of the book explains this in detail. Here, in this chapter, we present a tool, the Reaction Management Tool, that is really helpful for learning from adverse experiences – in other words, from situations where an incident (or series of incidents) has resulted in negative reactions. The risk is that the person ruminates afterwards on what happened and may talk to others about it (as Josh did). If they are not careful, this can lead to an increase in their negative emotions and judgements, and sooner or later the relationship problem becomes deeply entrenched and more difficult to change.

The Reaction Management Tool offers a set of helpful steps for avoiding this danger and for handling such situations more effectively instead. There are three steps and in terms of our RelATE family of strategies, it involves Attending (i.e., paying attention) and Thinking:

> **Step 1**, Attend and Record, aims to start diffusing our negative reaction through (a) describing what happened objectively and factually, and (b) identifying as clearly as possible the emotions we are feeling and any evaluative judgements we have made of the other person(s).
> **Step 2**, Think and Reflect, aims to help us think through systematically (a) why we reacted as we did, and (b) why others may have acted as they did. Technically, this is known as cognitive sensemaking (see Chapter 10).

Step 3, Think and Reassess, aims to help us re-evaluate our reactions, including any judgements we have made of the other person(s), in the light of the insights gained from Steps 1 and 2.

Since emotions are such an integral part of the problem and a crucial element of Reactions, we first consider what emotions are and how to identify them.

3.2   Identifying emotions

The American Psychological Association[6] defines emotions as follows:

> Emotions are conscious mental reactions (such as anger or fear) subjectively experienced as strong feelings usually directed toward a specific object and typically accompanied by physiological and behavioral changes in the body.

This definition draws attention to several key features of emotions:

- Emotions are mental reactions;
- They are directed towards somebody or something;
- They are typically accompanied by changes in the body (e.g., sweating).

Some emotions are automatic reactions to danger of some kind, but they can also be influenced by our thinking. In fact, thoughts and feelings are very closely interconnected and there is actually a fuzzy line between what counts as an emotion and what does not!

There have been numerous attempts to classify emotions into different categories, but unfortunately, there is as yet no agreed framework. Many theorists have argued for a number of basic emotions, such as Love, Joy, Sadness, (Surprise), Fear, and Anger, with other emotion labels being fuzzy or indistinct variations or combinations of these basic categories. Many have also distinguished between positive and negative emotions, with some being opposites (e.g., Joy – Sadness). Other theorists emphasise how emotions can vary in intensity, from strong to weak. There are probably some nuances to these conceptualisations. For example, it could be that the context influences the valence of some emotions (e.g., 'righteous anger' when there is a major social injustice), or that some emotions could be regarded as potentially neutral (e.g., surprise or indifference). Nevertheless, the identification of basic emotions, the distinctions between positive and negative emotions, and their intensity are all useful 'handles' for increasing our understanding of emotions.

Building on this, the table below identifies one set of possibilities, worded in terms of how a person may feel, especially in a workplace context. The dotted lines are meant to indicate that the boundaries are fuzzy.

[6] https://www.apa.org/topics/emotions

	Love	Joy	Peace	
Typically Positive	• Welcomed included accepted	• Elated jubilant happy		
	• Honoured respected admired	• Exhilarated excited enthusiastic		
Neutral	• Supported cared for protected	• Triumphant proud pleased	• Assured hopeful expectant	• Serene peaceful calm
	Hate	**Sadness**	**Fear**	**Anger**
Typically Negative	• Ignored excluded rejected	• Depressed sad unhappy	• Terrified fearful frightened	• Furious angry annoyed
	• Despised disrespected disliked	• Humiliated shamed embarrassed	• Anxious worried uneasy	• Exasperated provoked frustrated
	• Exploited scapegoated used	• Alienated isolated lonely	• Despairing hopeless discouraged	• Envious jealous resentful

Table 3.1: A conceptualisation of different emotions

Most psychologists agree that paying attention to our emotions, and learning to label them with greater granularity (including learning new words to describe our emotions!), will be helpful personally and also for relating to people around us. One explains it like this:

> Being willing to understand your feelings will have two benefits in the long term. First, it will help you to discover some aspects of your life that trigger negative feelings. That is useful, because you don't want to misinterpret your negative feelings and attribute them to something else. ... Second, by understanding the sources of your emotions, you will become more expert in understanding the people around you as well.[7]

The Reaction Management Tool will support you in achieving this. We start by considering how we often react to an adverse experience and then consider the steps we need to take in order to handle it effectively. We use an authentic case

---

[7] Markman, 2017, p. 34

Part 2 – Relationship challenges at work

example – a relatively minor one – to help with this. We introduce the adverse experience in Section 3.3 and then apply the Reaction Management Tool to it in Section 3.4.

3.3 The Reaction Management Tool

The Reaction Management Tool applies in situations when some kind of adverse incident has occurred and there is a need to manage emotions. The tool recommends three steps, involving two superstrategies: Attend (pay attention) and Think (see Figure 3.1). The three steps are:

- Step 1: Attend and Record
- Step 2: Think and Reflect
- Step 3: Think and Reassess

You may wonder why there is no 'Engage' step. This is because we are focusing on incidents that have already happened, where the aim is to gain insights into a past incident and to manage our reactions to it. As we explained in the introduction to Part 2, not all superstrategies are necessarily utilised in all situations. In subsequent chapters, we deal with ways of responding to problematic situations, where engagement is of course vital. Here, though, the focus is on noting what happened previously, reflecting on our reactions, and reconsidering our reactions in the light of our reflections.

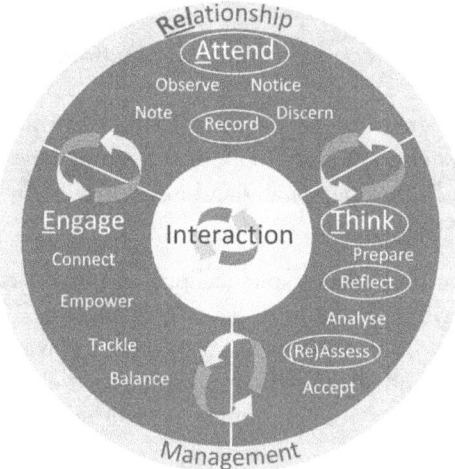

Figure 3.1: The RelATE strategies of the Reaction Management Tool

Part 2 - Relationship challenges at work

In explaining the tool, throughout the rest of the chapter we draw on a case study to illustrate. The case study concerns Becky – a volunteer at a community centre who had been leading a project to get solar panels installed at the centre. The project had been greatly delayed by a range of issues, but at last had been given the final go-ahead. She now needed to arrange installation dates with the solar power company but, as she reports in Case Study 3.2, things didn't go to plan, and she was highly frustrated.

Case Study 3.2: A manager's frustrating decision
Becky complained:
I was so frustrated last week. I'd been trying for ages to get a particular company to complete the installation at our Community Centre of a solar power system. They kept delaying the date, giving various excuses, until I complained. They then gave me a date for 7 days later. I was delighted and immediately emailed key people at the Centre (including my manager) to let them all know. Nobody replied so I thought all was well. Then, a few days later – really quite close to the installation date – my manager, Paul, emailed to say the dates were inconvenient and instructed me to cancel the agreed dates. He had only just realised that the installation would require the power to be turned off at some point – I mean, how stupid is that! It should have been obvious. He must be on a different planet!
He said he would let me know in a day or so's time which dates would be convenient and when he did, it was for 6 weeks later. I was so annoyed – people at the Community Centre had been fussing me to get the installation completed, and now there was this completely unnecessary delay! And what would the solar panel company think – especially after I'd been pressing them to give me an early date. It could be embarrassing having to backtrack on what I'd been pushing for.

Here we can see that Becky reacted to the situation in several ways:

- She was extremely frustrated and annoyed (an emotional response)
- She made negative comments about her manager – that he was stupid (an evaluative judgement)
- She felt embarrassed at having to backtrack on what she'd been pushing for (an emotional response)

The three steps of the Reaction Management Tool are extremely helpful for annoying or upsetting situations, such as this one.

Step 1: Attend and Record

Step 1 is to Record the adverse event – to pay attention to it and note down the 'facts' as objectively as possible. Becky's comments in Case Study 3.2 show clearly that her account of what happened was not simply a description, but rather was interspersed with evaluative remarks and interpretations: 'how stupid is that', 'it should have been obvious', 'he must be on a different planet'. In fact, her description of exactly what happened was rather brief.

Describe objectively what happened

So, the first task within Step 1 is to describe as objectively as possible what actually happened in the incident (the I – Interaction of the TRIPS framework), keeping only to the facts and avoiding evaluative comments. Doing this is actually more difficult than it might seem because our natural reaction is not simply to describe what happened, but also to explain and justify how we felt, and to make evaluative judgements of others involved. This, though, may hinder us in seeing the situation from different perspectives. So, the first key step in overcoming the negative emotions of a problematic incident is to try to separate the emotions and judgements, from the facts, describing exactly and objectively what happened; if possible, try to write it down.

Describe your emotional reactions

Next it is helpful to identify what emotions you're feeling and how intensely or strongly you're feeling them. Doing this – i.e., identifying and labelling emotions, including their level of intensity – is widely regarded as a second valuable step in managing emotional reactions. Again, this is not always as easy as it might appear. So, for support in this, refer to the Emotion framework given in Table 3.1. Try first to identify the main emotion family (e.g., anger, sadness), then the component grouping (e.g., exasperated – provoked – frustrated) and its degree of intensity. Activity 3.1 below offers some practice with this.

Describe any evaluative judgements you made of others involved

Finally for Step 1, note down any evaluative judgements you have made – either in your thoughts or in your comments to other people.

Part 2 - Relationship challenges at work

On our advice, Becky completed these three tasks, and her entries are shown in the table below.

Step 1: Attend and Record: Objective description of what happened & identification of emotional reaction	
I: Interaction (What happened)	*I (Becky) was asked to liaise with the solar power company to arrange installation dates. I spoke with Jane (an administrator) about the forthcoming work (before any dates had been fixed) who promised to give advance warning to clients who would be affected and asked me to let her know as soon as the dates were fixed. I had difficulty getting a timely booking from the solar power company, but after complaining to them I was given dates for the following week (7 days away). I immediately emailed all the people involved; I received no reply. Two days later, Paul emailed me to say he was concerned about the installation disturbing people who had booked the community's facilities, and especially any outage of power. He told me to cancel the installation for the following week. I did so. The next day he gave me dates that were six weeks away and asked me to arrange installation on those two dates. I did so.*
R: Emotional Reaction	*I felt moderately annoyed with Paul and a bit embarrassed to have to ask the solar power for a much later date when I had just complained to them about the delay in arranging installation dates.* *Emotion family 1: Anger - frustrated - moderate intensity* *Emotion family 2: Sadness - embarrassed - slight intensity*
R: Evaluative judgement	*I thought Paul was very stupid not to have realised in advance that the power would need to be turned off for a while. I felt Jane was not pro-active enough in talking to me about potential client issues.*

Table 3.1: Becky's objective descriptions

As can be seen from Becky's description of her emotional reactions (R – Emotional Reaction), she identified two main emotion families that she was experiencing, Anger and Sadness, the sub-components within those families, Frustrated and Embarrassed, as well as how intensive her feelings were.

Part 2 – Relationship challenges at work

When we label our emotions and consider their intensity, this is an important first step in managing them. When this is combined with an objective description of what happened, it can help build some distance from the incident, which in turn can help reduce the emotional rawness.

Now try working on this for yourself, by looking again at Case Study 3.1.

> **Activity 3.1: Practising Step 1 of the Reaction Management Tool**
> Look back at Case Study 3.1.
> 1. Drawing on the conceptualisation of emotions given in Table 3.1, identify what emotions you think Josh experienced and how intensively he seemed to experience them.
>
> 2. If you were to assess how fair you think Josh was in his judgements of Phil:
>   a. What additional information would you need to know? Think of the other two elements of the TRIPS framework: the People (P) involved and the links between them, and the Setting (S) in which the Interaction took place.
>   b. What specifically would you want to know about each?

As Question 2 in Activity 3.1 implies, despite the crucial importance of describing objectively what happened, labelling the emotions you experience, and identifying the judgements you've made, some additional information is needed to complete the first step, Record, and to be ready to move to the next stage of reflection. This is because in order to interpret incidents, we need to draw on relevant contextual information.

In line with the TRIPS framework, the Reaction Management Tool recommends noting the following additional elements:
   a. The people (P) involved, the links between them, and any information you have about their styles of working.
   b. The setting of the interaction (S).

The role of this information for handling adverse experiences will become clearer in Step 2 of the Reaction Management Tool.
   If you'd like more support on the P: People and S: Settings elements you may wish to consider, see the TRIPS Concept Tool templates in Chapter 15.

Part 2 - Relationship challenges at work

For Becky, her entries on this additional information are shown in Table 3.2.

Step 1: Attend and Record - Situational information, needed for interpretation purposes	
P: People	*Participants* • Becky (me) • Paul (community centre manager) • Jane (Paul's administrator) • Other members of the solar power working group at the community centre • Staff at the solar power company
	Role responsibilities: Becky: responsible for liaising with the solar power company Paul: responsible for all activities etc. at the community centre Jane: responsible for liaising with people who have booked the community centre facilities *Working Styles* • Becky - likes fast responses • Paul - often slow at responding to emails • Jane - efficient & well-organised
	Link attributes and attitudes: • Paul in line management role to Becky; Others all equal. Everyone knows each other well. • Warm and friendly relationships
S: Setting	*Physical setting* • Community building with several different rooms and facilities that are used and booked by members of the public *Purpose of communicative event* • Arranging contractual work *Organisational culture* • Important to respect and meet the needs of Community Centre users

Table 3.2 Becky's reflections on contextual influences

Part 2 – Relationship challenges at work

Step 2: Think and Reflect
Having laid the important foundation of Step 1 Attend and Record, the next step is to reflect on what happened. It's important to do this from two perspectives: firstly, from your own perspective, and then – as far as possible – from the other person's perspective.

Identify the source(s) of your emotions

First it is important to reflect on the source(s) of your emotions – what gave rise to them or triggered them. Use the GAAFFE rapport Triggers as a framework to help you with this, asking yourself questions such as the following:

G: Were you hindered in achieving your goal?
A: Did you feel inappropriately controlled in some way? (i.e., a threat to your autonomy) What caused you to feel like that?
A: Did you feel ignored or neglected? (i.e., a threat to your desire for attention). What happened (or didn't happen) that caused you to feel like this?
F: Did you feel unfairly treated? (i.e., a breach of fairness)
F: Were you made to feel embarrassed or disrespected in any way? (i.e., a threat to your face) What caused you to feel like that?
E: Did you feel there was anything unethical about the incident? (i.e., a breach of ethicality)

Becky's reflections on her own reactions

As Becky reflected in this way, she realised the following:

Goal: *"Getting the installation completed as soon as possible was an important goal for me. I wanted to reduce our sky-high Community Centre electricity costs as soon as possible."*

Attention: *"I felt that my manager, Paul, wasn't paying sufficient attention to the project, or to communicating with me about it. And what about Jane – why had she been silent too, when it was her job to liaise with clients?"*

Face: *"As I reflected, I realised that I had felt a bit uncomfortable with other Community Centre members repeatedly asking me when the project was going to be completed – it was as though they thought I was inefficient. In addition, I was also rather embarrassed about having to ask the solar power company for a much later date, when just a few days previously I'd complained to them about the delay and when a senior manager in the company had intervened to offer us an earlier date."*

These reflections show that the thwarting of Becky's goal (timely installation), the lack of attention she felt from Paul, and her concerns over other people's perceptions of her competence (a threat to her face) were all key causes of her frustration and annoyance. In other words, when these three GAAFFE Triggers (Goals, Attention, Face) were not attended to or mitigated, rapport with her colleagues was undermined.

Becky's comments on the Attention Trigger points to another layer of explanation – how other people failed (in Becky's eyes) to fulfil their role responsibilities and made her feel that they weren't paying sufficient attention to her and her project. This led her to start attributing blame to them.

The next step, then, is to try and consider things from other people's perspective to check how justifiable the blame is or whether additional perspectives throw new light on the situation.

Insights gained by Becky on the role of others

Becky exchanged a few more emails with Paul and the next day he emailed as follows:

> *I am just trying to be sensitive to all involved. I do want it to happen asap, but if it's not done carefully, any upset to those who've booked our facilities could linger long after the panels are installed – sorry I don't mean to frustrate. I know how much work you have put in.*

Here we can see that Paul explained why he wanted the installation to be postponed, that he acknowledged Becky's emotional reaction ("I don't mean to frustrate") and he addressed her face needs ("I know how much work you have put in."). This helped Becky understand his goals and reduced her frustration with him.

Meanwhile, Jane drew up a document to identify the potential health and safety risks associated with the installation (e.g., ladders blocking corridors), in relation to users of the Community Centre during installation. Like Paul, she was clearly concerned about the users of the facilities, from a welfare perspective in addition to keeping them happy. So, Becky could then understand Jane's goals more clearly and, by her doing this work, she felt Jane was giving the project the attention it deserves.

Part 2 – Relationship challenges at work

Table 3.3 below summarises these multiple perspectives of the key people involved and provides the foundation for Step 3 Re-evaluation.

GAAFFE Triggers + follow-up actions	Participant Perspectives		
	Becky	Paul	Jane
Goals	• Get the installation completed as soon as possible	• Ensure Community Centre users are not upset or annoyed & plan the installation with that in mind	• Ensure Community Centre users are not upset or annoyed • Ensure health & safety risks are planned for
Attention	• Wanted Paul and Jane to give appropriate attention to the issue	• Paul is regularly slow in responding to emails	• Only works part-time, so difficult to respond in a timely manner
Face	• Concerned that she would appear inefficient to solar power company & those wanting a speedy installation	• Showed appreciation for all the work Becky had put into the project – face supportive	
I: Interaction – Follow-up action	• Cancelled the original installation date and re-scheduled it for 6 weeks later	• Liaised with key Community Centre stakeholders • Gave Becky a suitable revised date for installation	• Drew up a risk assessment • Identified dates with least impact on users • Liaised with all users re forthcoming installation

Table 3.3: Different participant perspectives on the case event

Step 3: Think and Reassess
Having completed Step 1 Attend and Record and Step 2 Think and Reflect, this paves the way for Step 3 Think and Reassess. This is the stage when people can re-think their own emotional reactions, consider how self-oriented or otherwise they were, as well as think over how fair or unfair they have been in their judgements of others. In other words, this third step encourages us to re-evaluate the incident in the light of the insights we've gained from the previous steps.

Useful questions to ask are:
- What have you learned about yourself, your expectations, preferences etc.?
- What have you learned about possible factors affecting the other person's behaviour or the situation more generally?
- How far is it fair to 'blame' the other person(s)?

Becky came to the following realisation:

I realised that I had been very narrowly focused on the task of getting the solar panels installed as soon as possible, and that Paul and Jane were right to take a broader view of the situation. I still feel that both of them could have acted earlier – they had both known for weeks that the installation was imminent, and they never mentioned anything about agreeing on suitable dates. But I guess they were just too busy thinking about other matters, and I should have known that Paul would be slow responding, since he's regularly like that. I myself could have been more pro-active in talking with them about it. At the end of the day, a few weeks delay in the installation doesn't really matter and nor does any embarrassment with the solar power company. So, I feel much better about it now and am no longer annoyed with Paul. I've also learned a lesson for myself – the importance of not being too narrowly focused on the goal that's important to me, and the need to take steps to find out what other people's goals are.

As can be seen, Becky was able to re-evaluate her emotional reactions and initial judgements and gain a broader understanding of Paul's behaviour. By thinking these elements through step by step, she was able to overcome her frustrations and to take a more detached view.

3.4 The Reaction Management Tool and a diversity/intercultural perspective

The case study we've used in this chapter involved people from similar backgrounds and most of the sources to the rapport problems could be captured by reflecting on the rapport Triggers. However, this is not always the case. Characteristics of the people involved, and the setting in which the interaction takes place, can affect people's interpretation of the event and reactions to it. This is because expectations stem from People and Setting factors, so it is particularly important to think through their potential influence when diversity of any kind is at play.

The TRIPS framework and the Reaction Management Tool are especially valuable when the people involved have diverse identity backgrounds or have grown up in different socio-cultural settings. This is because any lack of shared background knowledge increases the likelihood of misunderstandings and misinterpretations.

In these cases, it's particularly important to pay attention to the IPS elements of the TRIPS rapport management framework, for example:

I: Interaction	Might differences in cultural background – e.g., organisational culture, national culture – affect how directly or indirectly people speak, how emotion is demonstrated (e.g., in body language) or suppressed, how opportunities to contribute to discussions are handled, and how shared meaning is accomplished?
P: People	Might any of the people's group identities give rise to any unfair stereotyping? Might differences in cultural background – e.g., organisational culture, national culture – affect people's expectations over how hierarchical differences are handled (e.g., how much deference should be shown to a boss), or how far someone's role responsibilities extend (e.g., whether a boss is expected to attend the funeral of an employee's family member)?
S: Settings	Might differences in cultural background – e.g., organisational culture, national culture – affect people's expectations as to what is required and/or what is acceptable behaviour in a particular setting? For example, what are the norms for small talk in meetings online or in professional emails and what judgements are made of those who do not follow these norms?

For more details on these elements, see Chapters 11–13.

3.5   Using the Reaction Management Tool

It's important to remember that the Reaction Management Tool is just one of several for use in the workplace. When an incident is minor, and the individual feels able to think the issue through without talking to the other person about it, working through the three steps can often be sufficient for resolving the issue. Becky felt able to do this and it helped her see things from Paul's and Jane's perspectives and rapport was restored. Sometimes telling the other person that you feel a bit annoyed, when you can resolve the issue in your own mind through the Reaction Management process, can create some tension unnecessarily.

However, this is not always the case, of course. The other party may be seriously at fault, and you may wish to take action about this (for example, reporting the issue to managers or HR), or the issues may need to be worked through systematically with the help of others (for example, mediators or facilitators). Working through the Reaction Management Tool is always a good starting point, but other steps may need to be taken. Chapters 4 – 8 illustrate this in relation to different workplace challenges. Chapter 4, the next chapter, explores how to deal with disagreement constructively.

It is also worth noting that successful use of the Reaction Management Tool requires good levels of self-awareness, openness, and ability to reflect, which is easier for some people than for others. Reflecting on our emotional reactions and the reasons behind them and being able to identify and report these insightfully is a particularly difficult thing to achieve at first and requires practice and good feedback to become more skilled. We would, therefore, highly recommend working with someone else, such as a trusted colleague, or with a coach or mentor, where possible.

3.6   Key takeaways

- Learning to make 'fair judgements' is an important foundational skill for managing rapport.
- A key element of this is learning to recognise and manage emotions.
- People are likely to interpret situations from different perspectives and so it is important to understand those different perspectives as far as possible. This in itself can help reduce emotional impact.
- The Reaction Management Tool provides a set of steps for handling annoying and upsetting incidents more effectively:
o Attend and Record
o Think and Reflect
o Think and Reassess
- The GAAFFE Triggers, along with other components of the TRIPS Rapport Management Framework, identify the key issues that need to be considered and reflected upon while working through the steps of the Reaction Management Tool.

The Reaction Management Tool template, with steps and prompts, is provided in Chapter 14.

Part 2 – Relationship challenges at work

Chapter 4: Divided by conflict?
How to handle disagreement constructively

4.1 Introduction

This chapter focuses on the issue of disagreement. All of us have disagreements with colleagues from time to time – sometimes they can be minor and short-lived but at other times they can be more serious and long-lasting. Either way they can undermine rapport as well as affect business effectiveness and employee morale, so it is important to handle them as constructively as possible.

Sometimes we may use the Reaction Management Tool (see Chapter 3) to think over a disagreement for ourselves and we may then feel we have resolved it sufficiently. On other occasions, we may anticipate that a forthcoming conversation or meeting is going to be difficult, and we get nervous about it. On yet other occasions, a disagreement may arise spontaneously during an interaction. In all these situations and others, we need to have some strategies at our disposal to help us handle them well.

Disagreements are widely regarded as something negative – something that upsets people and causes discord and antagonism between the individuals concerned. Studies in linguistics have found that if someone wishes to express disagreement with the previous speaker, they typically wait milliseconds longer before doing so than when expressing agreement. For this reason, many linguists label disagreement as a 'dispreferred' response.

However, from a business perspective, disagreement plays a vital role in bringing forward new and different ideas, thereby helping ensure that different perspectives are taken into consideration. This supports better decision-making, especially when ideas can fruitfully be combined in synergistic ways. As business executive, Patrick Dunne, put it, "if we go through a year and if everyone agrees with everything we do, then we're in really serious trouble. We need those different viewpoints."[8]

The key, of course, is in managing any disagreement in a constructive way so that negative emotions are minimised and openness to other perspectives are maximised. The slight delay that linguists have identified indicates that expressing disagreement is potentially sensitive. This is because the GAAFFE rapport risk factors are at stake and need to be handled carefully. This chapter explores how to do this, using the 3 stage, often cyclical, Discord Management Tool: Think and Prepare, Engage and Connect, Think and Accept.

First, though, it's important to think a little about disagreement itself, including factors that can affect people's reactions to it, and some models that have been proposed for managing it.

---

[8] Personal communication

4.2 Disagreement: key features

Various terms are associated with the notion of disagreement, including conflict, dispute and discord. They can reflect a range of differences, such as in the intensity of the disagreement, whether it is short-term or long-term, and whether it is ideologically-based or needs-based. Unfortunately, different scholars interpret and use the terms slightly differently. Here, we do not try to distinguish between the notions of conflict and disagreement; however, we label our tool a Discord Management Tool because of its connotations of concord and harmony and hence of its links to rapport.

It is useful to note that sometimes a disagreement is between two individuals or two groups, and the person handling the situation is a mediator or 'impartial' third party. On other occasions, the person wanting or needing to handle the situation constructively is a member of one of the disagreeing parties. It is particularly difficult when only one of the disagreeing parties wants to find a resolution; usually only limited progress can be made in such circumstances. So, while we take these different roles and stances into account to a certain extent in the chapter, if one party is completely unwilling to explore greater mutual understanding and potential reconciliation, this makes things extremely difficult.

4.2.1 The components of disagreement

When people disagree with each other or are in conflict, there are two key aspects to it:

- Divergences – the nature or bases of the disagreement
- Reactions – how people respond to the divergence, in terms of how they feel about the difference and the other person, how they think over the issue, and what they do (or do not do) about it.

In terms of divergences, the sources of these can be very wide-ranging but can be broadly thought of as falling into the following areas:

- ideological or value-based divergences, such as over abortion rights or euthanasia;
- transactional divergences, such as over strategic business decisions or contract negotiations;
- interactional divergences, such as over different working styles or management styles.

The type of divergence, as well as its level of seriousness for the people concerned, typically influences the way they react to it and best ways of dealing with it.

Part 2 - Relationship challenges at work

When people experience divergences of various kinds, they normally react in some way, especially emotionally and behaviourally. Stage 2 of the Tool, Engage and Connect, considers ways of handling both of these aspects, and Stage 1, Think and Prepare, identifies ways of preparing for this. Various conflict management strategies have been proposed by scholars, as we explain next.

4.2.2 Conflict management strategies

Research into conflict management has explored the strategies that people use when dealing with conflict. The work by Kenneth Thomas[9] is particularly well known. His original work identified two axes: desire to satisfy own concerns (high–low) and desire to satisfy other's concerns (high–low). These resulted in four main conflict management strategies (domination, appeasement, neglect, and integration), along with a fifth, compromise. Later, with Ralph Kilmann,[10] the axes were adjusted to assertiveness (high–low) and cooperativeness (high–low), with the four conflict management strategies labelled as competing, accommodating, avoiding, and collaborating, with compromise again identified as a fifth.

Figure 4.1 shows a combination of the original and subsequent work, presenting it in a manner that links with our notion of the Interaction Compass (see Chapter 1 and Chapter 9).

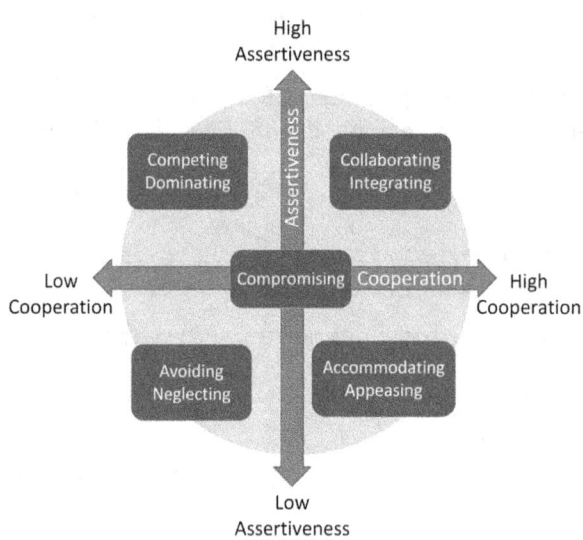

Figure 4.1: Conflict management strategies
(derived from the Thomas and Thomas-Kilmann frameworks)

[9] Thomas, 1976, 2002
[10] Kilmann, 2023

The four main conflict management strategies, identified by Thomas and Kilmann, along with the fifth, Compromise, can be explained as follows:

- **Dominating/competing:** the parties compete with each other, with each one trying to dominate the discussion, paying little attention to the interests or viewpoints of the other (i.e., high assertion, low cooperation).
- **Avoiding/neglecting:** one person avoids or neglects dealing with the divergence, even if the other person would prefer to address it (i.e., low assertion, low cooperation).
- **Accommodating/appeasing:** one person is particularly concerned about the preferences of the other person and defers to them (i.e., low assertion, high cooperation).
- **Collaborating/integrating:** both parties want to reach mutual understanding of each other's perspectives and seek ways of achieving both of their interests or viewpoints (i.e., high assertion, high cooperation).
- **Compromising:** both parties agree to a mutually acceptable solution, that partially satisfies their preferences/needs and provides an expedient resolution.

As we explain in Stage 2 of the Discord Management Tool, Engage and Connect, the ideal (from a rapport perspective) is to seek a synergistic solution (i.e., by collaborating and integrating) that meets the needs, desires, and preferences of both parties. However, when trust is low, it may not be feasible to work towards that immediately.

Many of you may have noticed that the two axes shown in Figure 4.1 are not only closely related to the High–Low Control and High–Low Connection of the Interaction Compass (see Chapter 1) but also to the two As of the GAAFFE Triggers: Autonomy (autonomy–control) and Attention (attention–inattention). This is understandable as the GAAFFE Triggers represent universal interpersonal concerns.

4.2.3 Disagreement, emotions and risk

Given that triggers give rise to reactions, and that emotions are core to reactions, it is inevitable that emotions are closely linked with disagreement and conflict. Our emotions, such as anger or fear, can occur at different stages of an interaction:

- Before an interaction: for example, if we are faced with a contractual dispute or need to talk with a colleague about a challenging issue, it is common to feel anxious about it in advance.
- During an interaction: for example, if someone says or does something that offends us, we may immediately have an emotional reaction that will need managing.
- After an interaction: for example, after we have had a disagreement with someone, our emotions may stay with us for a period of time and have the potential to influence our subsequent interactions with that individual.

In all these cases, we need to find ways of managing our emotions effectively (see Chapter 10 for more details on how to do this, as well as later in this chapter). This is important because if we fail to do so well, we not only risk seriously damaging rapport but also people's work performance. A study by two organisational behaviour scientists[11] yielded some interesting findings in relation to this. They studied the performance of international teams and found that the teams could be divided into three types, depending on how they handled disagreement and its impact on what they achieved.

- Some teams failed to manage their disagreement and became highly antagonistic towards each other. They found that these teams destroyed value rather than created it, so the researchers called them 'Destroyers'.
- Some teams covered up their disagreement, failing to explore each other's varying perspectives. Their achievements were just mediocre, and so the researchers called them 'Equalisers'.
- Other teams explicitly recognised, accepted, and even nurtured their differences, incorporating newly discovered perspectives into their work. The researchers called them 'Creators'.

In other words, disagreement can be positive, leading to synergistic, creative solutions to intractable problems. This only happens, though, if it is managed effectively. This means working through our disagreements constructively, not avoiding them or minimising them. Our Discord Management Tool offers guidance on how to achieve this.

As we noted earlier, sometimes a mediator or 'impartial' third party is involved in dealing with a disagreement. Clearly, their emotional involvement is very different from that of the disagreeing parties.

4.2.4   Contextual influences on disagreement

Looking at all this from a TRIPS rapport management perspective, it is important to bear in mind that the acceptability of overt disagreement can vary according to features in the context.

Disagreement is more acceptable in some communicative events than others. For instance, in a networking event, when a relationship is new, people tend to suppress verbalising any points of disagreement and instead seek areas of common ground. In a brainstorming meeting, on the other hand, sharing and evaluating ideas is central to the event and disagreement is thus much more likely to occur and be more acceptable.

A further influence is national and organisational cultural norms. In contexts where power distance is high, it is common for subordinates to be reluctant to share any contrary views – partly out of respect for superiors, and partly out of fear of the consequences. This also links with the notion of psychological safety – peo-

[11] DiStefano & Maznevski, 2000

Part 2 – Relationship challenges at work

ple need to feel 'challenger safety' in order to disagree with others, let alone with a more senior member of staff. (See Chapter 13 for more information on contextual influences, including cultural norms and psychological safety.)

Familiarity among the participants, and their mutual trust of each other, also plays an important role. Case Study 4.1 reports what happened when a British manager, Emily, attended a meeting at her company's German parent company. She found it difficult to express her views to her new German colleagues, especially as they seemed to be arguing so strongly.

> **Case Study 4.1: Arguing in meetings**[12]
> *I was in Germany for my first management meeting with my new colleagues from the German parent company. (...) There was a very heated discussion amongst the German colleagues about the best way to go ahead, which I felt was a real row. So I was rather insecure and nervous about putting my view across. But in the end, I said my piece and I think people understood. But I didn't join in the shouting. As it was our first international meeting, the German colleagues took us all out for a meal and a drink. I was extremely surprised by the fact that they all seemed to get on so well together and have so much fun.*
>
> **Reflect**
> 1. Do you identify more with Emily or her German colleagues?
> 2. How easy or difficult do you find it to express disagreement in meetings in your workplace? What do you think affects this?
> 3. How acceptable is it to shout in meetings at your workplace?

In this example, Emily was taken aback by the manner in which her new colleagues were expressing their disagreement. She interpreted it as conveying rancour and discord, yet all seemed to be well when they were socialising afterwards.

It is likely that in addition to potential differences in cultural norms, relational links had an influence. If Emily's new colleagues knew each other well and respected each other, the personal face threat from their arguing and shouting would have been much reduced. In contrast, if there had been a history of tension between the individuals, the situation might have been different – either reluctance to argue so strongly or a major deterioration in rapport between them.

In other words, the following contextual features (features of the S: Setting and P: People) influence how disagreement is perceived and managed:

- The type of communicative event
- National and organisational cultural norms for the given communicative event

---

12 Franklin, 2006

- Level of perceived psychological safety among the participants
- Relational history among the participants and their styles of communication

It is particularly important to remember these points when working in unfamiliar cultural settings.

4.3 The Discord Management Tool

We now explain in turn the three steps of the Discord Management Tool (see Figure 4.2):

- Step 1: Think and Prepare
- Step 2: Engage and Connect
- Step 3: Think and Accept

Sometimes a disagreement can be resolved with one iteration of the stages; if a business decision needs to be made, consensus may not be reached but a decision nevertheless made and the cycle finishes. In other types of disagreement situation, the stages will need to be cyclical – going through multiple iterations, while connection gradually increases, and resolution gets nearer.

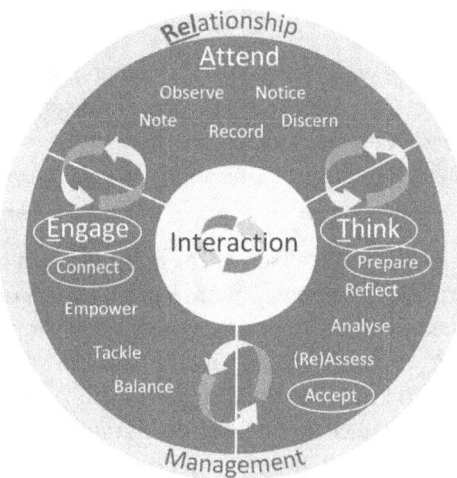

Figure 4.2: The RelATE strategies of the Discord Management Tool

Step 1: Think and Prepare
This stage particularly applies to situations where a disagreement is known about in advance or where differences could be expected to arise. It is vital for underpinning the Connecting stage.

Part 2 – Relationship challenges at work

However, even when you cannot be sure that a disagreement is going to arise, preparation is still very valuable. On the one hand, it enables you to have relevant information to hand, if any disagreement emerges over factual matters. On the other, it can help you plan best ways of handling the forthcoming interaction, thinking of the people involved, any relevant features of the setting, and preparing for any triggers that may occur.

The importance of preparation applies both to facilitators and individual participants.

Gather background information

One key aspect of preparation is information gathering – seeking out, clarifying, and noting down background information and relevant facts. Sometimes this may be desk research (e.g., checking legal documents), often it can involve asking relevant other people about the issue, and for facilitators it may also mean interviewing a range of people from different parties to learn about their varying perspectives.

Activity 4.1 provides a reflection opportunity on this.

Activity 4.1: Look at the following conflict situations and consider what type of background information the individual (manager, facilitator, or team leader) would need before attempting any kind of reconciliation and how they might obtain it.

Type of conflict	Brief description	Background information needed
1. Contractual conflict	A key account manager for a technical company responsible for servicing aircraft received a formal complaint from a customer airline over the slow speed with which a fault in an aircraft had been fixed.	
2. Business performance conflict	An inexperienced manager, Shane, was due to chair a cross-departmental meeting about production and sales, which the general manager of the company was also due to attend. Shane anticipated that the general manager might challenge his department's production performance.	
3. Decision-making conflict	A company board was very divided over an important strategic decision and so they asked you, a skilled facilitator, to help them reach agreement.	

Part 2 – Relationship challenges at work

In addition to background factual information, it is also important to think about the people and the setting (P and S in the TRIPS framework). For example:

- What do you know about the individuals involved and how might you need to take that into account when interacting with them in the Connecting stage? The Concept Tool for People in Chapter 15 provides you with some prompt questions to consider.
- What are the individuals' goals or what do you anticipate their goals to be? (Note: Goals is one of the GAAFFE Triggers)
- Are there any features of the setting that you need to consider? For instance, what kind of room and seating arrangements will there be or should you arrange? How can you make them most conducive for a constructive discussion? The Concept Tool for Settings in Chapter 15 provides you with some prompt questions to consider.

Reflect on information gathered
Having gathered relevant information about the (potential) conflict and its broader context, the next step is to think the information over. For instance, how can your insights on people and on setting shape your planning for the event, including how you might handle the interaction?

It is particularly important to consider whether any GAAFFE triggers underlie the (potential) disagreement and/or need to be handled sensitively when addressing the disagreement. Ask yourself questions such as shown below, when either thinking back on a conflict that has already occurred or when thinking forward to one that might lie ahead:

Goals	Thinking back: Were any of your (work-related) goals thwarted? Did you thwart any goals the other person(s) held? Thinking forward: How similar or different are your goals from those of the other person(s)? Are any synergies possible?
Autonomy	Thinking back: How far did you give the other person autonomy to express their views/do what they wanted? What impact might that have had? Thinking forward: How can you best manage autonomy–control when addressing any potential disagreement?
Attention	Thinking back: How far was the other person satisfied or dissatisfied with the amount of attention you gave them? Thinking forward: How can you manage this when addressing any potential disagreement?

Face	Thinking back: How far did you or the other person lose face through what happened? Thinking forward: How can you minimise face loss for the other person when addressing any potential disagreement?
Fairness	Thinking back: How far were you or the other person treated fairly? Thinking forward: How can you best maintain fairness when addressing any potential disagreement?
Ethicality	Thinking back: Were any ethical issues involved that concerned you or the other person(s)? Thinking forward: Are there any ethical issues that you need to take into account when addressing any potential disagreement?

Table 4.1: Reflection questions on the GAAFFE triggers

Clarify what conflict-related changes you want to achieve
Before engaging with any disagreement situation, it is very important to think through what you want to achieve; in other words, to think through your own goals (as facilitator or participant). It is common for people to be quite self-focused in this; for instance, for an ideological divergence, to change the other person's position; for a transactional divergence, to get one's own way; and for an interactional divergence, to get the other person to change.

However, a very self-focused orientation can easily antagonise the other party, risking a GAAFFE face threat which triggers a negative reaction. It is usually wiser to hold a more flexible attitude over goals; for instance, it is never easy to change someone else's ideological position or viewpoint, so a more realistic and helpful goal could be to understand more clearly the reasons for each other's stances. This can help both parties be more accepting of each other. Similarly, for an interactional divergence, rather than always expecting the other person to change, it may mean listening carefully to the other person's concerns and being willing to adjust your own behaviour.

Sometimes a shift in the focus of the desired goal may be necessary, as the following account from business executive, Patrick Dunne, illustrates:

I was coaching a young woman the other day who had had a big bust up with her boss – she wanted something, and they couldn't agree. I asked her what outcome she wanted, and she said she really wanted to get a particular thing done. I told her that's probably not a good enough outcome – since she had had such a major disagreement with her boss, I advised her that she probably needed to change the way he sees her now, that this was the next thing she needed to think of.[13]

---
[13] Personal communication

He went on to point out that when people think about goals, they tend to think about the issue they disagreed over rather than how they have left people feeling, or how they want to reposition themselves.

This brings out the close link between disagreement and reactions – how a disagreement can leave both you and the other party with negative emotions, as well as with negative evaluations of the other. This points to the importance of making emotional management a goal in its own right.

Manage your emotions
If you have had a strong emotional reaction to your experience of divergence with someone, it is usually wise to work through it in your own mind before engaging further with the person. If there has been a specific incident or series of incidents, we recommend that you use the Reaction Management Tool (see Chapter 3) to help you reflect on what happened and gain insights into the other person's possible perspectives. This tool is particularly helpful when you are angry and/or upset, and even identifying how you are feeling can be helpful in defusing your emotions.

With disagreement, the emotion of fear can be particularly common. This is fear of the consequences of facing up to the disagreement, such as the other person's anger or some kind of personal or project-related impact. Emotion control techniques will be needed here. These can include reducing your stress through managing your breathing, shifting your mindset so that you envisage the situation differently, and adjusting your expectations or desired outcomes for the encounter. The latter brings us to the next point – taking stock, personally and contextually.

Take stock – personally and contextually
Having gathered relevant background information, reflected on the potential impact of the various rapport triggers, clarified what you want to achieve, and started managing your emotions, it is then helpful to take stock of the whole situation. Self-reflection is extremely valuable here; for example, consider how open you are to appreciating or accepting different viewpoints or ways of doing things, how positive or negative your attitudes towards the other person(s) are, or how open you are to changing your own behaviour. This openness is an important foundation to a meaningful Connecting stage.

Taking stock can also involve deciding whether or not actually to proceed with the Connecting stage. For example, if relations are currently too strained for meaningful discussion, it could mean first doing more foundational work on building good collegial relations. We explore this in detail in Chapter 6. Often, of course, there is no option over this, but it is important not to avoid the situation out of fear; for example, out of fear that the other party will get angry and make you feel vulnerable, or perhaps because you fear not being able to control your own

Part 2 – Relationship challenges at work

anger. In these cases, it is important to face up to one's fears. Michelle Obama[14] has some helpful advice here. Drawing on her own experiences, she says we need to accept that our 'fearful mind is basically a life partner' we didn't choose and that we need to 'become more comfortably afraid'.

On the other hand, sometimes there can be a justifiable reason for not proceeding. For example, if you have had a disagreement with a colleague and you want to talk it over, it could be that you become aware they are facing many personal pressures at present. You may therefore decide it would not be helpful to talk with them at this point about the matter, especially if it is a relatively minor disagreement. Alternatively, you may decide that culturally or strategically it is wiser to address the situation in another way, such as through a third party. Failure to do this can exacerbate the situation, as Case Study 4.2 illustrates.

> **Case Study 4.2: The risk of raising a contentious issue**
> Eleanor was a British manager who had recently taken up a post in Singapore with a third sector organisation. The team she was managing comprised ethnic Chinese, Malay, and Indian members, with Chinese in the majority. She needed to recruit two new members of staff and the successful candidates (on performance grounds) were both ethnic Malays. A Chinese member of her team then wrote to her superior, claiming that she was racist. Eleanor's instinct was to bring the complaint out into the open and discuss it explicitly, but her husband (who was Chinese) advised her not to do so. However, she ignored his advice and spoke with the complainant saying, *"Look, I'll be absolutely frank with you; I'm rather hurt to be accused of racism; I don't think I'm racist, but I would like to hear why you have that perception"*. However, the individual denied accusing her of racism, making it impossible to talk the situation through. Then her Malay members of staff spoke out in support of her, making the situation even worse, because it began to look as if she really did have a closeness with the Malay staff and not with the Chinese staff.
>
> **Reflect**
> 1. Why do you think Eleanor's husband advised her not to discuss the criticism openly with the complainant?
> 2. Why do you think Eleanor ignored his advice?
> 3. What could Eleanor have done instead that might have been more appropriate?

This case study raises a further issue: for the Connecting stage to be fruitful, both parties need to be willing to acknowledge the discrepancy issue between them and

---
[14] Obama, 2022

be willing to try to work through it. Even if you are open, the other person may not be and without this, achieving your desired outcome is likely to be difficult. So, it will be necessary, whenever possible, to persuade the other party – either directly or with the help of an intermediary – of the value and need to engage with the issue. When this has been achieved, the next step is to arrange a suitable time and location – one that allows adequate time to talk things over and that can take place in a sufficiently neutral location.

> **Activity 4.2**
> Think back to an occasion when you needed to resolve a disagreement with someone.
> 1. What background information was helpful (or would have been helpful) for you to know prior to addressing the disagreement? Think particularly about P: People and S: Settings.
> 2. What GAAFFE rapport triggers did you need to take into account?
> 3. What were you hoping to achieve when addressing the disagreement?
> 4. How did you feel emotionally prior to engaging with the other person? What did you do to manage your emotions?
> 5. If you were to encounter such a situation again, what changes would you make in your preparations?

For more information on emotional reactions, see Chapter 10 on Reactions, which includes a discussion of the challenge of facing up to our fears and not avoiding difficult conversations when they are necessary.

Step 2: Engage and Connect
Step 2, Engage and Connect, refers to the period when Interaction takes place and when either a disagreement emerges spontaneously or when a known disagreement is addressed in some way. Here the 'how' of communication is particularly important. The Concept Tool for Interaction in Chapter 15 provides you with some prompt questions to consider dynamically throughout the unfolding interaction.

You might wonder why we are labelling this stage 'Connect' rather than 'discuss' or 'dialogue'. The reason is we want to focus on the fundamental aim of this stage, which is to find common ground and thereby promote mutual understanding among the parties. As we explained in the introduction to Part 2, we use the term 'connect' to convey this. Discussion or dialogue could simply be interpreted as talking – maybe talking over or across each other – rather than having a genuine interest in understanding the other party and interacting in a way that promotes it. In other words, there are different modes of interacting and the key is to engage in a way that promotes connection.

Part 2 – Relationship challenges at work

Figure 4.3 provides an overview of the different modes of interaction and the route that can help move an interaction from an unhelpful mode to a more useful one.

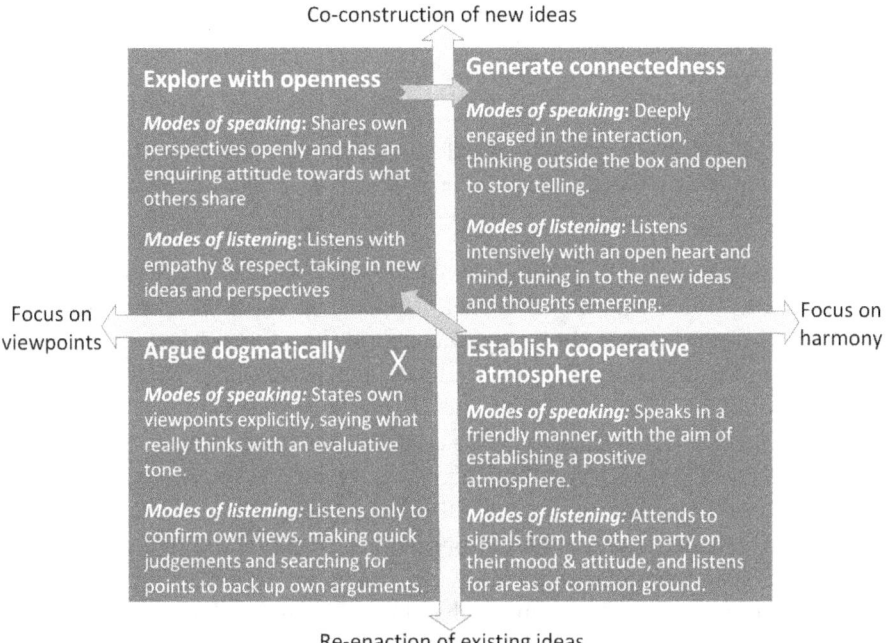

Figure 4.3: Modes of interaction[15]

In any meeting or interaction, where disagreement is known to exist or is regarded as a possibility, it is wise to start the conversation in a friendly manner in order to try to establish a positive atmosphere (see Figure 4.3: Establish cooperative atmosphere). If trust is low and emotional hurt and/or anger high, this may need to be an extended phase. Showing care and concern for the other can be very helpful here. Various strategies may be used; Case Study 4.3 illustrates an unusual strategy that was powerful in that particular context.

Case Study 4.3: The power of a meaningful gift[16]

In 2006, the British and Irish governments were trying to persuade Sinn Fein and the Democratic Unionist Party (DUP) to agree to a power sharing government. The talks were fractious and hostile and about to break

---

[15] This figure is loosely based on Hogan's (2007) interpretation of work by Kahane (2004) and Scharmer (2007)
[16] https://www.galwaydaily.com/news/how-a-spiddal-man-helped-secure-the-peace-process-in-the-north/

down. Towards the end, the Irish government presented DUP's Ian Paisley with a symbolically significant wooden sculpture as a personal gift to mark his 50th wedding anniversary. Paisley was deeply touched, and this overture became a turning point, paving the way for productive talks and eventually an agreement.

Reflect
1. What do you find helpful for establishing a cooperative atmosphere?
2. What are the pros and cons of giving gifts in your work context?

A danger to be avoided is allowing a conversation to stay at the preliminary stage even when it could move on. This often happens when people fear upsetting or annoying the other person, and – especially if they have not worked through their emotions and explored their strategies during the Think and Prepare stage – the conversation then stays at a superficial level. This is not helpful.

On the other hand, addressing the controversial issue with a critical or evaluative tone (see Figure 4.3: Arguing dogmatically), such as by criticising the other person and/or their views, is not helpful either. When people take up this mode, putting forward their own position firmly and showing little willingness to consider other perspectives (high control, low attention), this can easily upset or anger others. While it is important to know what they think, the problem with this mode of conversing is that it is not genuinely open. The individuals are primarily interested in getting their own ideas across, and instead of listening carefully to what others are saying, they are typically thinking about how they will rebut the views that don't accord with their own. This style of conversing is often referred to as 'downloading', as the individuals tend to churn out the same ideas over and over again, shutting their minds to anything contrary. From a rapport point of view, an 'Arguing dogmatically' style can be highly intimidating to others. The individuals can come across as arrogant and domineering and, as a result, others may stay silent, failing to challenge them, even if they disagree. This means that new or better ideas have little chance of emerging.

If rapport is to be maintained, if mutual understanding is to be achieved, if new ideas are to emerge, and if wise decisions are to be made, the style of conversing needs to shift to a different mode – to Exploring with openness (see Figure 4.2). This involves the mutual exchange of positions. In this mode, people are genuinely interested in each other's viewpoints (high attention) and they have the freedom and interactional space to express their own thoughts (high autonomy). Each person is genuinely interested in the perspectives of others and seeks to understand them.

This is in line with a form of psychological safety (see Chapter 13) mentioned by the psychologist Timothy Clark[17]. Referring to challenger safety (one form of

[17] Clark, 2020

Part 2 – Relationship challenges at work

psychological safety), he points out the importance of 'reducing social friction while increasing intellectual friction'. By this he means that we should not gloss over differences, but rather delve into them; however, we should do this in a supportive way – one that will minimise tensions and uphold rapport.

After people have had the opportunity to share their viewpoints, sometimes a decision needs to be made. Or in intractable situations, where positions are strongly entrenched and where one or more individuals have been deeply hurt, Exploring with openness does not bring any resolution in itself. In both such circumstances, another mode of conversing is needed: Generating connectedness. The aim here is to look at the issue from a significantly new angle – intellectually and/or empathetically. This enables the individuals or groups concerned to find a synergistic solution or to understand and appreciate each other at a deeper, affective level. Needless to say, this is challenging to achieve, but nevertheless extremely important because it is the most emotionally and intellectually satisfying to those concerned.

Given the importance of the modes 'Exploring with openness' and 'Generating connectedness', they are considered in more detail below.

Explore with openness
Listening is an important feature of this mode of conversing – not any kind of listening, though. What is needed is listening to understand instead of listening to respond or argue (as in Arguing dogmatically). Interestingly, the traditional Chinese character for 'listen' is made up of four components:[18] ear, ten eyes, one heart, and king (see Fig. 4.4). This illustrates that 'deep listening' involves not only hearing (ear), but also careful watching of people's nonverbal behaviour (ten eyes) and it needs to be underpinned by a sense of unity of purpose (one heart) and mutual respect (king).

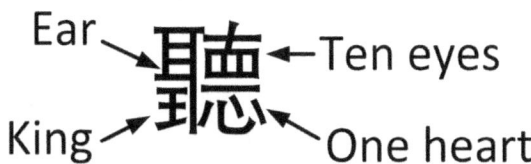

Fig. 4.4: Chinese traditional character for Listen (Ting)

---

[18] e.g., see https://www.linkedin.com/pulse/one-chinese-character-makes-you-better-leader-florian-vogel/

In line with this, business executive Patrick Dunne said:

> *It's very important to listen to what people say, but it's more important to 'listen' to what they think. I think the ability to perceive what might be in the thought bubbles of the people in the meeting can help a lot.*[19]

This, of course, is extremely challenging and requires ongoing practice, especially in culturally diverse contexts where norms around display of emotion and openly expressing what you really think may be very different.

The key is to enable the other person to feel understood and not judged. Sometimes it is helpful to be explicit over this, double-checking that you've understood what they've said by asking either for confirmation or for clarification. (For more information on this, see Chapter 11, as well as Table 5.8 when there are language code issues.) However, it can be unwise to make any kind of evaluative comment too soon – even if it is supportive – because this can steer the interaction away from a focus on developing mutual understanding towards one that is evaluative in nature, moving it closer to an arguing mode (Arguing dogmatically) which you want to avoid. Instead, it is better first to listen attentively, without saying anything, and then to ask non-judgemental open questions that will genuinely help you understand the other person's position more clearly. It is also important to pay attention to nonverbal features, including facial expressions, physical gestures, and silence, all of which can 'mean' different things to different people in different contexts.

Another key feature to be aware of is the distribution of talking time. When there are just two people, it is good if one person is given sufficient time to explain their views – in other words, with the other person keeping silent and not interrupting or commenting. However, sooner or later the other person needs to have the opportunity to take their turn. If there are several people, such as in a meeting, it is important for the chairperson to control how much time each person has to share their views, and to allocate it fairly. (For more details on this, see Chapter 5 on exclusion through turn-taking.)

Generate connectedness
When people 'Explore with openness', the focus is very much on sharing and understanding each other's ideas and perspectives. In the mode 'Generate connectedness', the focus turns overtly to finding connections. These can be intellectual connections, where new and innovative ideas emerge synergistically; they can also be emotional connections, where people come to understand and appreciate each other at a deeper level.

Case Study 4.4, reported by an Anglo-American conflict management facilitator,[20] illustrates one way that can help achieve this.

---
[19] Personal communication
[20] Cited in Hogan, 2007

Part 2 – Relationship challenges at work

> **Case Study 4.4: Owning racism**
> I was in a session in Canada where we were focusing on racism and there had been many comments about endemic racism between American Blacks and Whites. Then a small elderly woman began to speak. She talked of being from Quebec in French-speaking Canada, and the pain of arriving at a conference in another part of her own country and being expected to speak in English, which was for her a foreign language. She was profoundly hurt when her compatriots could not pronounce her name, and joked and suggested she should change the pronunciation so it would be easier to spell.
>
> Suddenly in a way that had not been clear to all before, the racial cultural divide was apparent. From that moment on we spoke of the racism in all of us, how I am living and how I own this issue as my own in my daily life.
>
> **Reflect**
> 1. Why do you think the elderly woman's words had such a profound impact?
> 2. Have you ever had an experience like this? If so, recall what happened and how you/others were affected?

In this case study, it was the elderly woman's personal story that opened other people's eyes and hearts to the issue of racism, so that they perceived it in a deeper and more personal way than previously.

Storytelling in fact can be a very fruitful strategy for overcoming differences and promoting mutual understanding and connection. This is because people's personal stories not only deal with the divergent ideas or goals, but also link them with people's emotions and senses of identity. If that can be done in a way that others can identify with, this can be extremely powerful in building bridges.

On the other hand, some people can feel uncomfortable when they hear a personal and emotionally sensitive story. They are not sure how to react – what to say or do. Similarly, those sharing their personal story can easily feel vulnerable when they open up in this way. So, trust among the individuals needs to be built up first, such as through 'sharing with openness'. If storytelling seems daunting for you, one option is to enhance your confidence in using this approach by practising it in different ways. For instance, you could share a relatively factual story, recounting the series of experiences that have helped form your current views; alternatively, you could practise sharing a more personal story with people whom you trust or feel close to.

Part 2 - Relationship challenges at work

Manage emotions
Throughout the Engage and Connect stage, it is important for everyone to manage their emotions, as it is easy to become annoyed or fearful or both, and such emotions can easily have a negative impact on resolving the disagreement.

As mentioned above in the Think and Prepare stage, useful strategies for handling personal fear and uncertainty, in addition to 'standard' anxiety management techniques, include modifying expectations and goals. If we have set our hearts on a particular outcome to a disagreement, difficulties in achieving it can cause significant stress and frustration. In such situations, taking a more flexible approach and appreciating, for example, small steps of 'progress' can be highly beneficial. If a disagreement emerges unexpectedly, preparation is also important. It could mean deciding in advance your preferred strategies for controlling emotion and honing them over time with practice. It could also mean accepting that sometimes emotions may run very high and that implementing 'time out' interludes can be helpful.

When negotiating transactional disagreements, such as a contractual dispute, a particularly useful strategy is to keep returning to the facts – the findings you identified during the Preparation stage – and turning the conversation to focus on those. A key account manager in the airline industry, referring to a contractual dispute that his company was having with a major client, explains this in Case Study 4.5.

> **Case Study 4.5: Managing emotions in a contractual dispute**
> *Contractually we were required to pay a very large penalty, but we were arguing that because of certain conditions we wouldn't pay anything. To succeed in this, first I had to sort out all the emotional. It's understandable – they were without an aircraft and so could not serve a certain route. So they were facing a financial loss and they were getting really emotional about it. Such situations can easily escalate up to top management level in both companies, so I needed to avoid that. My approach is to collect facts, focus on facts. When you speak about facts, they are somewhat undeniable. Emotions are subjective. Facts are rather objective. It won't prevent the discussion from getting emotional, but at least you have a path that you can follow in the discussion. Once you feel it's getting emotional, you bring the people back to the path. But the key is not to make it seem as though you are the winner – they need to feel our companies are partners.*
>
> **Reflect**
> 1. How can focusing on the facts help with managing emotions?
> 2. How can you make sure that you don't come across as the winner?

Part 2 – Relationship challenges at work

> **Activity 4.3**
> Think of a disagreement you experienced recently or one that you remember vividly.
> 1. Which modes of conversing did you and the other(s) use?
> 2. How satisfied were you with the way you each handled the disagreement?
> 3. How easy or difficult was it to manage your emotions? Why do you think that was the case?
> 4. How well did the other(s) manage their emotions? Why do you think that was the case?
> 5. How far did you stick with your original goal? Did you modify or adjust your goal and if so, in what way?
> 6. How far were you able to resolve your disagreement? What factors influenced that?

Stage 3: Think and Accept

After the Engage and Connect stage has come to an end (at least temporarily), all parties need to accept the (interim) outcome in some kind of way. What that acceptance means in practice can be very variable, though, as the following possibilities illustrate:

- Accept that the disagreement wasn't (fully) resolved and needs more work;
- Accept the synergistic solution proposed or decision made and start planning how to implement it;
- Accept the decision reached, even though it was not your preferred option;
- Accept that your understanding and empathy for the other party was inadequate, and that you need to work on increasing it;
- Accept that an aspect of your behaviour is perceived negatively by significant others and that you need to make some adjustments.

In many workplace situations, if a group of people (e.g., board members or senior managers) make a decision, any individuals who did not fully agree with a decision nevertheless have a responsibility to support it. Yet it is important that they are not left feeling dissatisfied or isolated. One executive coach recommends doing the following to help with this:

- Allocate 15 minutes at the end of the meeting for members to reflect on how they feel the meeting went (e.g., did we rush anything, did we take too long over something?) and for each person to share their feelings about any decision made.
- If chairing the meeting, acknowledge the reservations that some may have about a decision, express appreciation for their expertise, and ask for their support in mitigating any risks that they are particularly sensitive to.

Part 2 – Relationship challenges at work

- If anyone is really unhappy about a decision, again acknowledge that publicly, comment on their sound judgement, and arrange to meet with them individually to discuss it in more detail.
- Agree on a statement about the meeting, and the decisions made, which everyone will then email to their relevant network. This will avoid different individuals sharing potentially different versions or interpretations of the meeting.

All of these steps help to strengthen unity while addressing the face needs of those who may have some negative feelings for one reason or another.

4.4 Key takeaways

- Two key axes are at play in handling disagreement:
  - High–Low Assertiveness: how far each person dominates or controls what happens (linked to the autonomy–control Trigger and the high–low control axis of the Interaction Compass).
  - High–Low Cooperation: how far each person is mindful of the needs or wishes of the other (linked to the attention–inattention Trigger and the high–low connection axis of the Interaction Compass).
- Synergistic outcomes typically require high mutual attention and dynamically alternating autonomy–control.
- The Discord Management Tool identifies three key steps for managing disagreement.
  - Think and Prepare: Before addressing a disagreement with others, careful preparation is needed. This includes gathering of relevant background information, reflection on potential issues that will trigger rapport reactions, and taking stock of the whole situation, including personal emotions.
  - Engage and Connect: When addressing a disagreement through interaction, it is important to be aware of the different possible modes of conversing, and the ones that will best lead to finding common ground. 'Exploring with openness' and 'Generating connectedness' are particularly valuable once initial trust has been built.
  - Think and Accept: Even the most effective disagreement interactions do not necessarily lead to synergy or resolution. So, when the Engage and Connect stage has ended, some kind of acceptance is needed. Exactly what that acceptance means in practice will vary according to circumstances.

A template for using the Discord Management Tool, with steps and prompts, is given in Chapter 14.

Chapter 5: Silence(d) in meetings?
How to overcome sidelining and promote inclusion

5.1 Introduction

In this chapter we consider a very different type of challenge from disagreement – that of participating in meetings.

Have you ever found it difficult to join in a discussion at work or share your thoughts or ideas during a meeting, making you feel sidelined or excluded? Or have you noticed that some people are regularly extremely quiet, rarely sharing their opinions? The likelihood is that many of you will have answered 'yes' to one or both of those questions, especially if you have worked among a culturally diverse group of people.

How did you feel about these situations personally and how did you feel about the people who were excluding you or who were failing to talk? It is likely that your feelings were negative in both cases. In other words, it can be difficult for the person who feels unable to talk, but it can also be difficult for those who want them to participate more. Often both parties blame each other. In this chapter, we argue that enabling 'fair' participation in meetings is the responsibility of all, but that managers or leaders are particularly responsible.

Being sidelined or excluded is a challenging experience. This is because everyone has a fundamental need to belong to a group – to be accepted, included, and respected. Professionally, we want to be able to contribute to teamwork discussions and to explain our viewpoints at meetings. Socially, we typically want certain friends and colleagues to include us in informal chats and in invitations to events we enjoy. If we are prevented or excluded from these things in some way, we can feel treated like an outsider and feel a reduced sense of belonging. In other words, we feel sidelined or excluded, and as a result our rapport with those colleagues can be undermined.

We may also feel frustrated when certain members are particularly quiet, and we have difficulty finding out what they think or prefer. Consider Case Study 5.1, which reports comments from a former Australian ambassador to Vietnam.

> **Case Study 5.1: The challenge of silence in meetings**[21]
> *We were aware that the Embassy was not working as well as it might. We believe that everyone has something to offer and that you need to draw that out of people if you're going to really make the best use of your staff and get to where you want to go. We found that our usual way of doing this – you sit around, you talk things through, you brainstorm – wasn't*

---

[21] Byrne et al., 1996. For further discussion of this case study, see Spencer-Oatey et al., 2022, pp. 70-71.

Part 2 – Relationship challenges at work

> working here. We'd have a meeting with staff, we'd put some ideas and there would be silence. Then someone from the local staff would get up and say something and there would be more silence. Then perhaps someone else would say something. We'd ask everybody what they thought about those ideas and there would be no response. The meeting would then break up, not having got very far.
>
> **Reflect**
> 1. Why was the situation frustrating for the former Australian ambassador?
> 2. Why didn't the local staff participate actively in the discussion?

Silence and low levels of participation in meetings can be frustrating for all concerned. The Australian ambassador perceived the lack of participation as silence, while those who don't speak up can sometimes feel silenced by the way in which those around them are communicating.

Communication styles and the role silence plays in turn-taking differ across cultures. However, as the research findings reported in the next section indicate, participation problems in meetings are not only an issue of national culture. Multiple factors can be involved.

Whatever their source, these kinds of situation are very problematic for several reasons:

- Lack of inclusion has a negative impact on employee wellbeing, and as a result it may lead to absenteeism, burn-out, and problems in retaining talent.
- When some employees feel uncomfortable (for whatever reason) contributing to discussions, their expertise may be underestimated, leading to unequal opportunities for promotion and developmental possibilities; this in turn may affect the embedding of diversity, equity, and inclusion (DEI) initiatives and achieving a truly inclusive culture.
- Creativity and innovation may be hampered by failure to draw on the ideas and suggestions of all members of the workforce.

For all these reasons, it is always important to be sensitive to participation issues. Even if it is only a minority of employees who are experiencing such challenges, it is still very necessary to address the issue. In fact, it is particularly relevant and vital for those in leadership or management positions, because they have more opportunity than others to control it in formal settings and to set a good example in other contexts.

Part 2 – Relationship challenges at work

This chapter focuses on this issue of exclusion/inclusion in group discussions and meetings. We recommend the Participant Management Tool for this:
- Step 1: Attend and Discern
- Step 2: Think and Analyse
- Step 3: Engage and Tackle

First, we report some research findings of relevance to the topic.

5.2 Background information on participation and 'speaking up' issues

5.2.1 Research into anxiety over speaking up

Recent research in the USA[22] found that various demographic factors, including gender, age, level of seniority, and ethnic background, all affected the ease with which individuals felt able to contribute their thoughts. Take a look at the charts below that show the percentage of people who experienced high levels of anxiety over speaking in different contexts, according to gender, age, and race/ethnicity.

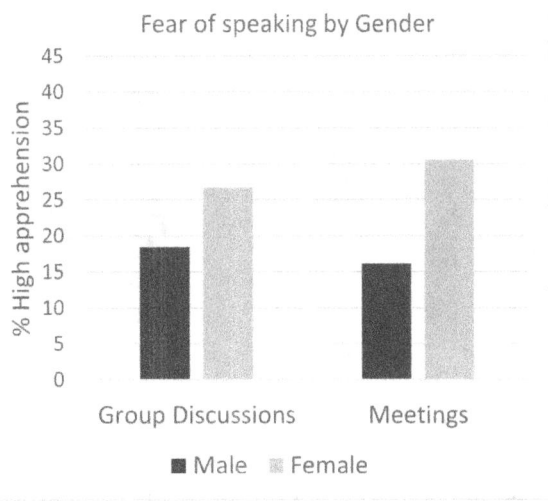

Fig.5.1: Percentage male and female employees who experienced high levels of fear over speaking in different contexts

---

[22] Cardon et al., 2022

Part 2 – Relationship challenges at work

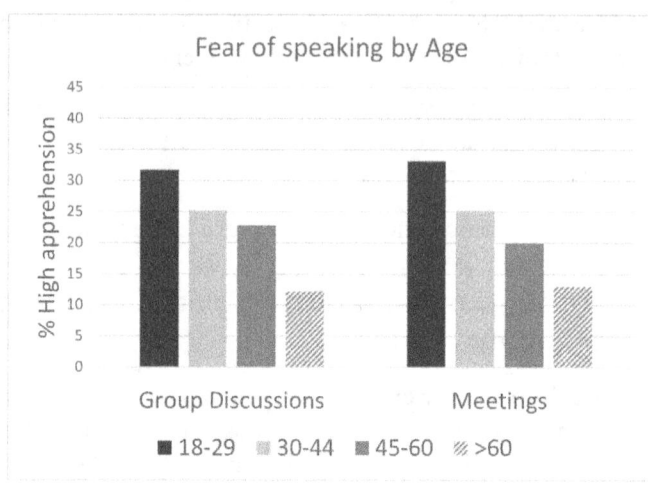

Fig. 5.2: Percentage of employees at different ages who experienced high levels of fear over speaking in different contexts

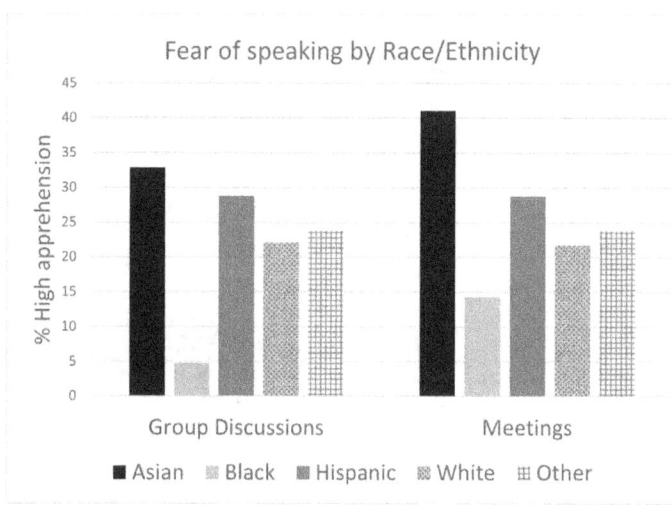

Fig. 5.3: Percentage of employees of different racial/ethnic backgrounds who experienced high levels of fear over speaking in different contexts[23]

What is very clear from these charts is the following:

- Employees' identity characteristics (e.g., gender, age, race/ethnicity) all affected people's level of comfort in participating in discussions, meetings, or social conversations.

---

[23] The low levels of anxiety reported by black participants seems surprising, although the authors comment that another study found similar findings

Part 2 - Relationship challenges at work

- Women and younger employees all experienced more difficulties in participating than other employees and this was also the case for many from non-dominant racial/ethnic backgrounds, especially Asians in meetings.

This data was collected only in the USA, so we cannot know for certain what the situation is in particular organisations or in different countries. However, it certainly indicates that it is an issue that needs careful attention.

5.2.2 Possible reasons for problems in speaking up

The authors of the study did not investigate why the survey respondents were anxious about speaking up; however, three broad categories of explanation seem likely, as shown in Table 5.1.

Potential sources of Speaking Anxiety and Speaking Reluctance	
1. Self-doubts or concerns over personal competence	• General lack of self-confidence • Fear of losing face • Shy personality • Doubts about competence/expertise • Difficulty in understanding the discussion/following the arguments (e.g., because of level of fluency in the working language) • Difficulty conveying ideas clearly or with suitable tone (e.g., because of level of fluency in the working language) • Insufficient time to prepare
2. Concerns or beliefs about others	• Think others are more expert/knowledgeable • Desire to listen to and learn from those with expertise • Importance of showing deference to leaders/those more powerful • Fear of annoying the leader/others • Reluctance to undermine harmony by raising a different viewpoint • Reluctance to waste other people's time • Lack of familiarity/common ground • Feeling unaccepted by others/regarded as an outgroup member • History of poor relationship
3. The dynamics of communication	• Others interrupt or people talk over each other • Difficulty finding a 'space' to take a turn • Others ignore one person's contribution or rephrase it as their own

Part 2 – Relationship challenges at work

	• Uncomfortable with the style of communication, for example the way people use their body language to emphasise their points, respond to others' points or how loud they are being • Features of online technology & its management

Table 5.1: Potential reasons for employees' reluctance to contribute ideas at work

This chapter focuses particularly on the third possible reason: the dynamics of communication. This can involve aspects from the other two reasons, but this chapter's main focus is on the ways in which people interact with each other from a process perspective. In other words, the key focus is the I: Interaction of the TRIPS acronym. For issues associated with psychological safety, which is closely connected with aspects of the second reason, see Chapters 7 and 13.

As an introduction to the challenge of managing the dynamics of communication, consider the following reflection, which is reported by an Indonesian, Bernie, about his teamwork experiences when he initially moved to Australia.

> *Personally, I found it very, very hard to express something, or even come into a discussion, when I was with my other marketing colleagues. There just wasn't any gap for you to come in – so I felt very, very threatened and very uncomfortable to express a point of view, because I cannot find any space, I cannot seem to find any opportunity to do that. The situation does not allow [sic], most of the time.*[24]

Here, Bernie maintains that he couldn't find the 'space' to make his points. It seems others were speaking one after the other very rapidly, and he couldn't find even a small gap to come in with his comments. In his eyes, if he had said something, it would have meant interrupting the others or talking over them, and he didn't feel able to do this.

Does this remind you of any situation that you have experienced personally or observed while working with other people? Use Activity 5.1 to help you reflect.

Activity 5.1: Reflecting on problems of participation
Think of a situation where you felt reluctant or unable to share your thoughts or opinions:
1. What kind of situation was it?
2. Why did you feel reluctant or unable to share your thoughts/opinions?
3. What could have helped you participate?

---

[24] Byrne et al., 1996

Part 2 - Relationship challenges at work

A key point about situations of exclusion is that everyone plays a role. Often the 'silent person' is blamed or looked down upon for not speaking up. Actually, though, responsibility for inclusion does not just lie with the individual experiencing exclusion – in fact, it can be particularly difficult for them to overcome the problem. Rather, responsibility lies with everyone who is taking part in the event, and especially those in leadership positions, or the chairperson, if the event is a formal meeting.

5.2.3 Why participation and speaking up are important

Participation and speaking up are important for three main reasons:

- Creative and synergistic thinking: If one or more individuals feel unable (for whatever reason) to contribute to a discussion, others will fail to benefit from their ideas and expertise. This can reduce the potential for identifying creative solutions to challenging problems.
- Discrimination and negative stereotyping: When individuals with certain identities (e.g., gender, ethnicity, nationality) have difficulty (for whatever reason) in participating in meetings/discussions, others will often stereotype them, attributing the problem to a feature of their identity. They fail to recognise their own roles in contributing to the problem.
- Interpersonal rapport: If one or more individuals feels unable to participate in a meeting or discussion, they may lose any sense of belonging, and may easily develop feelings of resentment against others in the group. This may result in them actively disengaging from their work, team and organisation and may lead them to start looking for another job, resulting in talent retention issues for the organisation.

To dig deeper into the second and third reasons, reflect again on the situation you identified in Activity 5.1. This time focus on the impact it had on your feelings or attitudes towards the other people present.

Activity 5.2: Reflecting on the impact of participation difficulties

Think again about a situation where you felt reluctant or unable to share your thoughts or opinions:
1. How did you feel about the whole situation and the people involved? i.e., What were your Reactions?
2. What were the likely sources of your Reactions? Use the GAAFFE Triggers to help your thinking:
    G: Were your goals affected?
    A: Did you feel unhelpfully controlled in any way?
    A: Did you feel you unduly ignored? Or was too much attention focused on you, making you feel put on the spot?

Part 2 – Relationship challenges at work

> F: Did you feel disrespected?
> F: Did you feel unfairly treated?
> E: Did you feel discriminated against?

Many people, it seems, experience participation problems at work and we maintain that all employees need to be caring towards others in this respect. Everyone needs to encourage their colleagues to contribute when they want to and to help them feel a valued member of the group.

The Participation Management Tool, introduced in this chapter, offers a valuable framework to support this.

5.3   The Participation Management Tool

The Participation Management Tool comprises three key steps:

Step 1: Attend and Discern – Discern whether anyone is being excluded because of speaking-inclusion issues.
Step 2: Think and Analyse – Explore the sources and consequences of any issues noticed.
Step 3: Engage and Tackle – Take steps to address any participation problems.

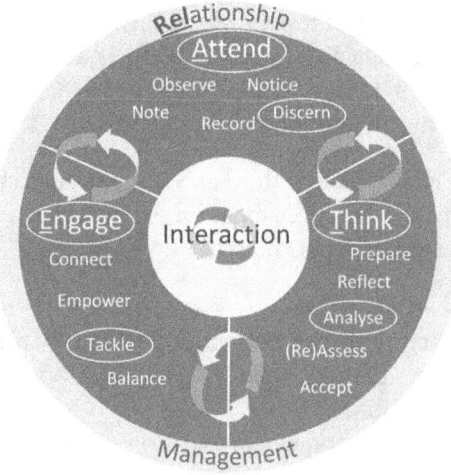

Figure 5.4: The RelATE strategies of the Participation Management Tool

In this section, with the help of some in-depth case study data[25], we explain each of these steps in turn. The authors explored the collaboration experiences of a 6-member MBA team who were working together on a series of projects over an

[25] Debray & Spencer-Oatey, 2019

Part 2 – Relationship challenges at work

8-month period. Here we focus particularly on the experiences of one member of the team, Alden, who was not a very fluent speaker of English and who had difficulty contributing to team discussions.

Step 1: Attend and Discern

Step 1 of the tool, Attend (i.e., pay attention) and Discern, entails perceiving whether anyone is being excluded. There can be two main kinds of exclusion, and both types need to be looked out for and noticed by paying close attention to what is said and done during the Interaction:

- Exclusion through difficulties in understanding;
- Exclusion through difficulties in taking a turn.

We deal with them in turn below.

Discerning difficulties in understanding

If anyone is new to a group, it can sometimes be hard immediately to follow all of their conversation or discussion. This can be for a range of reasons, such as: others are using unfamiliar acronyms or technical terms, they may be speaking with an unfamiliar accent, they may be speaking unusually fast, or they may be using a style that is difficult to interpret (e.g., very indirect). (See Chapter 11 for more information on how communication works).

So, it is important to check whether any participants (especially newcomers and less fluent speakers of the working language) are experiencing any difficulty in following the topic of discussion or flow of the argument. Table 5.2 provides a checklist of questions that you can usefully ask yourself to help ensure no one is being excluded due to difficulties in understanding. It can be face-threatening for an individual to admit that they don't follow an argument (i.e., the GAAFFE Trigger of Face is at risk), so others need to be helpful by noticing potential problems.

'Attend and discern' questions around communication understanding

1. Is any specialist expertise or background knowledge required in order to follow any arguments or discussion but that hasn't been explained clearly?
2. Are any unfamiliar abbreviations being used – ones that would not make sense to newcomers?
3. Do any of the participants speak with a strong accent that might make it difficult for others to understand?
4. Are any of the participants speaking very fast, or using slang or idiomatic expressions that might make it difficult for some to understand?

5. Do all participants have a shared understanding of key words or concepts that are being used, or might there be different interpretations?
6. Are any of the participants speaking in an indirect style that might make it difficult for others to interpret what they really mean? Or an overtly direct style that might be misinterpreted as rude, aggressive or personally threatening?
7. Is any comprehension checking being done (i.e., double-checking whether the message heard is what the speaker intended)?

Table 5.2: Helpful questions for noticing issues of communication understanding

Failure to do this emerged clearly in the researchers' study, as can be seen from some comments made by Alden, one of the MBA team members:

> *I was quite quiet at first, as I was trying to get used to their way of speaking. It was difficult, because they were speaking so fast and were using slang terms that I didn't understand very well. They didn't take the time to listen to me or explain things properly. After a few weeks I began to feel more comfortable and wanted to share my opinions. Somehow, though, they just ignored me. It seems they had made up their minds that I had nothing useful to say. I can't fit in because my point is always ignored or challenged. So, I don't have the motivation to this job.*

As these comments illustrate, Alden found other members' speech very fast and full of slang, often making it difficult for him to understand what they were saying. Sadly, other team members did not notice (or were unwilling to notice) the problem and did not take the extra time to explain things to him more slowly and thoroughly. Such challenges are not unique to people who are less fluent in the working language (although that often aggravates the problem); anyone who is an outsider of some kind (e.g., from a different profession) may experience difficulties.

Discerning difficulties in taking a turn
If someone is having difficulties in understanding and following a conversation, they will likely also be having difficulties taking a turn. However, even when there are no comprehension difficulties, there may still be difficulties joining a conversation.

There are several potential reasons for this. These can include: non-member of the ingroup, others' strong personalities, hesitation over how to word something, different turn-taking patterns, and desire or need to think over an issue before responding. In a recent workshop among a group of managers from different countries, this issue came up. When some highly fluent second language speakers of English suggested that they sometimes find it difficult to enter the conversation (in their case this was primarily because of the need to reflect on meaning and think about how to phrase what they wanted to say), some of the native speakers of English were rather dismissive of the matter, saying "But you know you can say anything you want … just don't hesitate to come in." In other words, fluent speakers who are also self-assured may overlook or dismiss the issue, often assuming that it does not require any action on their part. This is very unwise and will risk them missing out on valuable contributions from all attendees.

We strongly recommend paying close attention to the issue. Table 5.3 provides a checklist of questions that can help you discern whether anyone is being excluded due to difficulties in taking a turn.

'Discernment' questions about taking a turn

1. Are some members talking a lot? Are some members particularly quiet? Is anyone trying to encourage quiet members to participate? What happens when they do (i.e., what is the reaction?)
2. How does the turn-taking take place?
   a. Is the conversation speed fast or slow?
   b. Are there lots of overlaps (which some people may feel are interruptions) or are there long pauses between turns?
   c. Is someone (e.g., a chairperson) managing the turn-taking or is it a free-for-all?
   d. Where are people looking when talking? Are there individuals who are not included in people's 'gaze'?
3. Is anyone finding it difficult to take a turn? What evidence could you consider: e.g.,
   a. Are any individuals moving forward in their seat but not saying anything immediately afterwards?
   b. Are any individuals trying to catch the attention of the chair or other speakers in some way?
   c. Are any individuals often interrupted by others, especially if they are slow in expressing their ideas?
   d. Is anyone who has not spoken looking unhappy, concerned, or puzzled?

Table 5.3: Helpful questions for noticing turn-taking and participation difficulties

Part 2 – Relationship challenges at work

Step 2: Think and Analyse
The next step of the Participation Management Tool is to explore the sources and consequences of any participation issues discerned in Step 1.

In order to do this, it is useful to explore three of the TRIPS elements – T: Triggers, P: People and S: Setting – and combine insights from them with the I: Interaction information gained during Step 1: Attend and Discern. Table 5.4 suggests some aspects to think about (for additional ideas, check the concept tools in Chapter 15). Be aware, though, that some issues may be more relevant than others in any particular situation, and some may be more difficult to answer than others. In addition, since many features are subjective in nature, the aim is not so much to gain 'definitive answers' as to expand awareness of – and sensitivity to – possible influencing factors.

TRIPS Element	Key features to explore
T: Triggers	Which Trigger factors could be having an influence? For example: a. G: Goals – do members have shared goals? b. A: Autonomy – are members giving each other enough autonomy? c. A: Attention – are members paying enough attention to each other? d. F: Face – are members sensitive enough to each other's face concerns? e. F: Fairness – are members treating each other fairly enough? f. E: Ethicality – are members being discriminatory in any way?
P: People	Which People factors could be having an influence? For example: a. Participants' levels of seniority? b. Different levels of fluency in the working language? c. Greater familiarity among a sub-set of participants? d. A person's group identity characteristics? e. Any particular attitudes or feelings towards, or beliefs about, certain participants and/or their group identity?
S: Setting	Which Setting factors could be having an influence? For example: a. Are there any physical features of the setting such as the seating or the technology that could make participation more difficult for some members? b. How stressful is the atmosphere? c. Are there different norms for levels of directness/explicitness of communication? d. Are there different norms (e.g., organisational) for handling turn-taking in meetings?

Table 5.4: Potential explanatory sources to consider

Part 2 – Relationship challenges at work

Returning to the case of Alden, his team members made a range of comments about him, frequently in his presence, including:

- *Alden is 'silent'*
- *Alden is 'different'*
- *Alden is 'really Chinese'*
- *I know he is from a shy culture but …* (said with a sigh)

These comments had a tone of blame about them, indicating other team members' dissatisfaction with his behaviour. They linked this with his nationality and cultural background. In other words, they held certain attitudes towards him and stereotyped him. Partly as a result of this, they ignored him, treated him with token interest, dismissed outright many of the things he said, and treated him as someone they needed to carry. This was reflected in their interaction behaviour:

- Members often talked over Alden;
- They often interrupted him;
- They regularly displayed only token interest in what he said;
- They regularly positioned him as an outsider by talking about him in the third person (i.e., using he or him), as if he was not in the room;
- They sometimes dismissed what he said, for instance, once when he made a suggestion, one team member responded by saying, "Oh please … go away."

Alden repeatedly tried to counteract all their attitudes and positionings, but they were so intertwined that it was virtually impossible for him to do so.

Alden's challenge of being excluded – and the other members' challenge of having to 'carry' him – stemmed from many of the features of the Interaction; in other words, from the team's failure to pay attention to and discern the Step 1 signals. These included: the problematic way in which the others spoke (fast, with slang words), making it difficult for him to understand, and with overlapping turns, making it difficult to find a space to contribute his ideas.

Applying Step 2 Think and Analyse helps point to the sources and consequences of these difficulties. The problems were associated with Alden's level of proficiency in English (individual identity characteristic) and the other team members' insensitivity to this and their stereotyping of him (group identity characteristic). This changed the supposedly equal relationship (everyone was a professional on the same course) into an unequal one and undermined rapport for all concerned. All this made both parties feel that the situation was unfair and that their project goals were being affected (GAAFFE: Goals and Fairness). For Alden, it was also face-threatening to his sense of competence (GAAFFE: Face), an infringement of his freedom to contribute (GAAFFE: Autonomy) and his right (given the 'typical' norms of groupwork) to an appropriate share of attention (GAAFFE: Attention).

Part 2 – Relationship challenges at work

In other words, P-People issues influenced the interaction, and T-Triggers affected everyone's Reactions, including team members' annoyance and Alden's low motivation.

Ironically, all team members had the same goals – to complete their project to a high standard and within the required timeframe. If Alden's team members had paid attention to their own behaviour in their interactions rather than simply criticise Alden, they would have discerned their own role in the problem, because this is what was happening regularly.

Sadly, the team repeatedly failed to notice the issue and so the problem continued and, if anything, got worse. Alden remained a minimal contributor across all of the meetings over the 8 month period, and actually he said less and less as the project progressed. As he explained, he had lost motivation for their teamwork project. Rapport between him and the other team members had been damaged.

Step 3: Engage and Tackle

When Step 2 Think and Analyse has been completed, the third step is to tackle the sources of any exclusion or negative positioning by taking some form of action. Although everyone in a meeting may need to do something differently, leaders and managers have a particularly important role to play and so they are considered first.

Actions for Leaders and Managers

Leaders and managers need to demonstrate inclusive behaviour themselves. In addition to raising their own understanding and awareness of the issue, valuable steps they can take are explained below.

Varying the procedures for chairing meetings

When an event has a chair, it can be very helpful for this person to try out different ways of handling the chairing. Table 5.5 suggests a number of different possibilities, along with pros and cons for each. The suitability of each one is likely to vary according to factors such as the type of event, the issue at stake, and the make-up of the participants. However, many chairpersons tend to stick with the same procedure, varying it very little across events or types of events. This can make it difficult for those who are uncomfortable with that particular way of handling a meeting. So, to reduce the risk of discomfort and reluctance to participate for some, the chairperson or facilitator can usefully vary the procedure, deciding on the most suitable options, based on the context and what needs to be achieved.

Part 2 - Relationship challenges at work

Option	Procedure	Pros	Cons
Chairperson selects	Chairperson invites key participants (e.g., those responsible for the issue at hand) to speak.	Helps maintain focus and manage the conversation, particularly when there is little time.	May create disengagement among those who are not asked to contribute. As a result, key points and insights may be missed.
Participants self-select	Each participant speaks when they wish Each participant indicates their desire to speak and the sequence in which they do so is controlled by the chair or where there is no chair by the participants themselves.	All those who choose to speak feel they are listened to. No-one feels they are 'forced' to speak.	Those who are less confident, unsure of their language ability or new to the organisation or the group may hesitate to put themselves forward (some of the best points, ideas or insights are never shared as a result).
All participants speak in order	Chairperson invites every participant to speak in turn, for example in the order they are seated (or the group decide they will speak in order).	Everyone gets the opportunity to participate, contribute, and be listened to (equitable turn-taking). Helps others realise that those who do not normally speak may have valuable insights and ideas.	May put extra pressure on those who feel reluctant to share for a number of reasons. May be particularly stressful for those 'at the end of the line' as they have to wait their turn while they feel it would make more sense to build on someone else's comment when it is made. May make the conversation unnecessarily cumbersome, particularly if some people end up talking for a long time when their turn comes and/or if people keep repeating the same point because they feel they must say something.

Table 5.5: Indicative range of options for handling participation within meetings

Part 2 – Relationship challenges at work

When there is a need to generate new ideas, to gain feedback on a sensitive issue, or to overcome reluctance to talk within a meeting, it can be helpful to move the discussion outside of the meeting. Thinking back to Case Study 5.1, this is what the Australian ambassador to Vietnam reported doing when she and other leaders wanted to find out the opinions of their local staff about a certain issue. The local staff were reluctant to speak out in the formal meeting and asked that instead they be allowed to talk about it in small groups outside of the meeting context, discuss among group representatives, and then feed back to senior management.

Table 5.6 presents some more ideas around this.

Option	Procedure	Pros	Cons
Preliminary small group discussion	Participants encouraged to discuss issue in small groups (in advance or at the beginning of the session) and group representatives feed back ideas to everyone.	Encourages those who are unwilling to speak up in larger groups to share and be listened to. A bigger pool of more diverse ideas and insights are likely to emerge	Requires more time and space and some thought in how the sub-groups are selected. Depending on who is selected to give feedback and how good the group is in deciding and prioritising their feedback, the quality and diversity of the small group level conversation may be lost when it is shared with the bigger group (so thought needs to be given to how the small group discussion is documented in some way).

Part 2 - Relationship challenges at work

Option	Procedure	Pros	Cons
Initial 'silent' 'brainstorming'	Before a discussion begins, the group is encouraged to write down their thoughts, ideas, opinions, questions etc. and post them on a physical or electronic wall (there are several tools to help teams do this). The group is then invited to work in small teams and sort out, prioritise and discuss the various contributions.	Easier to contribute anonymously in the first instance. Allows everyone 'safe space' and time to articulate and post their thoughts and questions.	Requires extra time and possibly some investment in technology. Could create too much data to manage comfortably. Requires careful management of the follow up discussion to avoid people feeling their contributions are being unfairly rejected or marginalised without proper consideration.

Table 5.6: Indicative measures for encouraging idea generation outside of (the main part of) a meeting

Promoting psychological safety

Leaders and managers have an important role to play in fostering an atmosphere of psychological safety and modelling positive inclusive behaviour. When chairing and/or participating in meetings, they need to watch out for any excluding behaviour that occurs (as per the elements identified in Tables 5.2 and 5.3), including in their own behaviour, and actively take action to rectify it. If any individuals (or any particular individual) display this regularly, it will mean talking with them privately about the matter, as well as being explicit in the team about the behaviours that are expected and the consequences if these expectations are not met. (See Chapter 13 for more information on psychological safety.)

Arrange training

Since everyone plays a role in the inclusion or exclusion of others, it can often be helpful for leaders or managers to arrange training for groups of people. One set of activities that we have found particularly helpful is raising awareness of turn-taking; in other words, to draw people's attention to the way in which the changeover between one speaker and another takes place. This is particularly relevant for workplace discussions or brainstorming meetings and is something that many people have not paid conscious attention to previously.

Part 2 – Relationship challenges at work

Trying out different ways of handling turn-taking can help everyone become more aware of different turn-taking patterns, of the challenges that some may experience when faced with a pattern they are less familiar with, and can give everyone practice at flexing their interaction style. Most people are familiar with having to speak in order (e.g., see Table 5.5), but trying out the alternatives listed in Table 5.7 can significantly raise people's awareness.

Option	Procedure	Why useful	What to look for as a facilitator/trainer
Speaking with gaps	Participants must leave a three-second silence gap between turns. This needs to be adhered to very carefully.	Creates awareness of the importance of reflection time and or the 'space to come in' needed by some people. Allows people to experience the importance of reflecting on someone's contribution before responding. Gives individuals the opportunity to reflect on their own turn-taking behaviour and the impact it has on others.	Although 3 seconds does not sound long, normally those who are not used to this turn-taking pattern (for example overlappers) find it very uncomfortable. Watch out for people trying to 'fill in the silence' as they inevitable will. Watch how people deploy their body language to show their discomfort during the silence. Discuss this with the group when you debrief the exercise. Why did they find it so uncomfortable? But also, what were the benefits of the silence for them/for others?

Part 2 – Relationship challenges at work

Option	Procedure	Why useful	What to look for as a facilitator/trainer
Speaking with recap	Participants can speak at any order but before they say what they want to say they must reflect back on what the previous person said. Ideally, they should link their point to the previous point.	Promotes active listening and encourages deep understanding and collective sensemaking.	Encourage individuals to really listen without interrupting. Some people may feel very nervous having to summarise other people's points and may need some tips to help them do so effectively, particularly if they are not native speakers; consider providing tips and examples. People may be tempted to disengage once they have had their say. Think about how to encourage everyone to continue to pay attention throughout, for example by giving them a topic to discuss in which they feel they have a real interest/stake or requiring the team to make a joint decision at the end of the discussion.

Table 5.7: Different options for enhancing awareness of turn-taking

People need to be encouraged to reflect on their feelings and reactions to these different options. Re speaking with gaps, this often reveals how useful silence is for those people who want or need time to reflect on what has been said and then to respond thoughtfully. This can be particularly helpful for people less familiar with the topic area and/or those less fluent in the working language. It also helps those who need more space to come into the conversation, either because they are used to larger gaps between turns for cultural reasons, or because they need more time to put their thoughts into words, perhaps because of their personality. Speaking with recap 'forces' people to put much more effort into listening deeply to others, enabling the previous speaker to feel more truly heard.

Part 2 – Relationship challenges at work

Actions for Everyone
If Step 1 has revealed that one or more members have difficulties following the discussion, it is particularly important for everyone to pay attention to the clarity of their communication. People's difficulties could be due to a lower level of fluency in the working language or because of weaker background knowledge of the topic being discussed. In either case, it will be particularly helpful and important for the more fluent members and those with greater background knowledge to adjust various aspects of their language use. Table 5.8 lists a number of strategies that will help others follow the conversation and thereby aid inclusion. It is best to do this as proactively and naturally as possible, choosing the most suitable level of adjustment needed for the context, in order to avoid any potential face-threat.

Problem-preventive strategies		Problem-focused strategies	
Speed	Speak at a speed that is suitable for the less fluent speaker.	Checking	Ask questions to check that the other person has understood what you said; e.g., *Am I being clear?*
Pausing	Allow more pauses and (learn to) be comfortable with others' pauses.	Repetition	Ask for repetition of something not heard or understood properly; e.g., *Sorry, could you say that again?*
Choice of words	Choose vocabulary that the less fluent speaker is more likely to know, and avoid slang, idioms, and specific cultural references that they may have difficulty understanding.	Clarification	Ask for further explanation of something that is not clear, e.g., *What do you mean by …?*
Number of words	Use shorter sentences and omit unnecessary words.	Confirmation	Ask for confirmation that you have heard or understood something correctly, e.g., *Do you mean …?*
Structuring	Use discourse markers, e.g., *Firstly, secondly*, to show your sequence of points/arguments.		

Table 5.8: Strategies for enhancing mutual understanding

In addition, the steps explained above for leaders or managers could usefully be adopted by 'regular' members. As mentioned several times, everyone needs to take their own responsibility for promoting inclusion. So, for instance, the ideas given in Table 5.6 are options that everyone could usefully try out and gain familiarity with.

On the one hand, this means engaging actively with the issues identified in Steps 1 and 2, monitoring one's own behaviour as well as that of others. For teams or groups, it can also mean explicitly talking through the issue of participation and turn-taking and may even entail agreeing some flexible 'rules' of interaction. (See Chapter 6 for more information on this.)

One difficult issue is whether to talk with others about any excluding behaviour they exhibit. It can be very face-threatening to the other person if any challenge is not handled sensitively and can easily lead to resentment and lower rapport. So, before saying anything, it's important to think through what you want to gain from raising the matter, setting realistic expectations, and acknowledging that any required change is likely to take place gradually. It's particularly important not to be (or be perceived as) confrontational. For further discussion of this issue, see Chapter 6 on microaggression and ways of handling it.

5.4 Key takeaways

- This chapter has focused on problems of participation and associated exclusion in meetings and group discussions.
- People's identity characteristics (e.g., their age, gender, ethnic background) can significantly affect their inclusion.
- It is common for the blame to be put on individuals for not participating, but in fact all participants affect the inclusion or exclusion of others. In other words, the Interaction is 'co-constructed'.
- The Participation Management Tool identifies steps for addressing the problem.
  o Step 1 Attend and Discern identifies the need to pay attention to the issue and discern whether any exclusion is taking place.
  o If any exclusion is occurring, Step 2 Think and Analyse helps identify the source(s) of the problem.
  o The TRIPS framework provides conceptual guidance for both of these steps.
  o After Step 2 Think and Analyse has taken place and the key problem areas have been identified, Step 3 Engage and Tackle needs to take place.
- Leaders, chairs of meetings and facilitators have particular responsibility for taking appropriate action, but everyone needs to play their part.

A template for using the Participation Management Tool, with steps and prompts, is given in Chapter 14.

Chapter 6: Troubled by colleagues?

How to reduce divisions and foster cooperation

6.1 Introduction

Relationships with colleagues is an extremely important aspect of workplace life, as colleagues are a key source of both support and challenge. When our relationships with them are going well, we typically feel a sense of belonging and team spirit, we feel able to ask others for advice or help when needed, and we offer the same in return when others are in need. Yet when our relationships with colleagues are problematic, we may feel isolated and excluded, frustrated, sad and stressed, and may positively dislike life at work.

Consider, for instance, the following comment from a mid-career engineer, Edwin, who was talking about his previous job:

> *I really disliked my previous job. We very much worked on our own, perhaps because of the lack of management and disorganisation. We mainly just looked after our own customers, and there wasn't any real cross-functional team feeling of supporting one another. The department was not supportive, you really just watched other people struggle. I was very unhappy and demotivated working there and decided to leave.*

This chapter considers how to improve the situation – how to encourage a supportive and collaborative culture between colleagues.

We start by considering some common challenges that can undermine cooperation. Then we introduce the Cooperative Colleague Tool (Engage and Connect, Engage and Empower, and Engage and Balance) that is useful for fostering collaboration among individuals and project teams.

6.2 Challenges from colleagues

We may experience a range of challenges from colleagues that undermine our sense of rapport with them. We have selected just a few of them to consider here.

6.2.1 Colleagues who are unreliable

One quite common problem is colleagues who don't pull their weight and who cannot be relied on to fulfil their responsibilities on a particular task. There could be a variety of reasons for this, including:

- Lack of interest in the task
- Commitment to other tasks
- Overwork
- Poor time management
- Sense of alienation from colleagues and/or the organisation
- Personal problems

The problem can be very frustrating for the colleagues who are affected. Consider Case Study 6.1, which is reported by Sarah, who works for a research consultancy.

> **Case Study 6.1: Unfulfilled responsibilities**
> *One of my colleagues, Ervin, invited me to help him with a project for an external client that entailed writing a 'state-of-the-art' report on a topic we were both familiar with. At first, things went well, and we had some fruitful discussions, planning what to put into the report and how to organise it. Later, though, the situation became very problematic. Ervin kept saying he was busy with all kinds of different things, giving one excuse after another as to why he couldn't work on the report. So, he made little or no progress with the sections he had promised to write. I too was very busy, but we had a deadline to meet and our line manager was pressing us to complete it. I felt all I could do was to keep writing as much of the report as I could – it was so frustrating! In the end, I had written the vast majority of it myself and was able to submit it on time.*
>
> *The report was extremely well received by our line manager and the client, which was very pleasing. However, Ervin then took a lot of the credit for it – after all, his name was on the cover as well as mine. I didn't feel I could tell people that he had actually contributed very little, so I just had to accept things. But it completely undermined my trust in Ervin – I can't see how I can collaborate with him again on a project like this.*
>
> **Reflect**
> 1. Why do you think Ervin didn't keep to his writing responsibilities?
> 2. Why do you think Sarah did most of the work on the report?
> 3. What different emotions did Sarah probably go through from the very beginning to the end of the project?
> 4. Do you think it was wise for Sarah to write so much of the report? Why/why not? If not, how could she have handled the situation better?
> 5. What advice would you give to Sarah about working with Ervin in the future?

Part 2 – Relationship challenges at work

6.2.2 Colleagues who are critical and complain

Another type of problem is when colleagues are publicly critical of us, as in Case Study 6.2.

> **Case Study 6.2: A public criticism**
>
> Olivia had recently started a new job with a PR company and soon after she started, her line manager, Amy, made her responsible for producing a monthly report for a particular client. Amy would set her a deadline for each month's report and Olivia did her very best to keep to it. She divided up the work among the various team members and kept checking in with them as to whether they were on track to meet the deadline.
>
> One of the team members, Rima from Syria, more junior to Olivia, was unhappy about this and tension started developing between Olivia and Rima. Then, in a face-to-face meeting involving the whole team – also attended by Amy – Rima queried in quite an aggressive manner why Olivia should be managing this monthly report. *"She's only new, why should she be in charge? I don't agree with that!"* complained Rima. Amy explained that she had given Olivia that responsibility and also advised her that she was coming across as rather aggressive.
>
> Afterwards Amy advised Olivia to try and put the matter behind her and to improve her relationship with Rima. Olivia was keen to do this and emailed Rima, saying she hoped they could both put the issue behind them and work well together going forward. Rima didn't reply.
>
> **Reflect**
> 1. Why do you think Rima was unhappy with Olivia being responsible for the monthly report?
> 2. How might the problem have been avoided?
> 3. How do you think Olivia felt about Rima's public complaint?

6.2.3 Colleagues who indirectly insult

A third type of problem may be less overt but can still be extremely damaging. This occurs when a colleague insults another colleague indirectly – either deliberately or inadvertently. This is frequently known as microaggression, or sometimes called micro-incivility. In this book, we use the term microinsults. Such comments are subtle ways of signalling negative messages, such as that the person does not belong, is incompetent in some way, or is not worth being listened to, because of the social group they belong to. In other words, they are treated as an outgroup member – an outsider.

Part 2 - Relationship challenges at work

One of the difficulties is that such comments – because they are so subtle and indirect – can be interpreted differently. One linguist explains it as follows:

> Microaggressions can lie anywhere between conscious/deliberate and unconscious/unintentional. Consequently, they may be intended in some cases to cause offence and challenge rapport, and perceived as such or not, while in other cases they could be intended to create or maintain rapport and perceived as such or not.[26]

This is because language use always requires interpretation and is influenced by features of the Setting and the People concerned, as well as the actual wording and manner in which the comment is conveyed.

Case Study 6.4 provides an interesting example of a (potential) microinsult . The interaction took place in New Zealand between Isaac, a Chinese accountant and a work colleague, Leo. Isaac was an intern at Leo's organisation and Leo had been allocated to him as a workplace mentor. One day, after they had both been in the cafeteria, the conversation shown in Case Study 6.3 took place.

Case Study 6.3: An indirect insult?[27]
Leo: I noticed you in the cafeteria just now. They didn't have chopsticks!
Isaac: [Laughs]
Leo: Do you use knife and fork at all?
Isaac: Err .. just a few times
Leo: Just a few times
Isaac: A few times, yeah
Leo: Oh right. So that would have been quite challenging. So, you know you might want to work on that,

Reflect
1. Was Leo being insulting towards Isaac? Why/why not?
2. What evidence do you need to help you decide?

When one of us (Helen) was in China, she was frequently asked at Chinese meals by hosts who did not know her well whether she could use chopsticks. This was asked as an expression of concern – if she said 'no', they would have provided knife, fork and spoon. On another occasion, when she first lived there, a Chinese colleague told her that the way in which she held her chopsticks was incorrect and made the colleague feel uncomfortable! On both occasions, Helen was certainly treated as an outgroup member – but in that case Helen was not offended because

---

[26] Holmes, 2023, p. 37
[27] Holmes, 2023, p. 44

she knew that she was indeed an outsider and accepted that. She responded by practising hard how to hold chopsticks in a more acceptable way!

Yet when the setting is different – such as when an ethnic Chinese person has been born and brought up in the UK or lived in the country for a long time – the interpretation and reaction is likely to be different. In such situations, it is likely to be experienced as a microinsult, whether the other person intended that or not.

For more details on communication and potential microinsults, see Chapter 11.

> **Activity 6.1: Interconnections between people challenges and GAAFFE Triggers**
> Look back at Case Studies 6.1 – 6.3. Reflect on the GAAFFE Triggers that led to the rapport challenges and note them in the space provided.

Case Study	GAAFFE Triggers associated with the rapport challenge
Case Study 6.1	Sarah:
Case Study 6.2	Olivia: Rima:
Case Study 6.3	Isaac:

Having considered some of the challenges that can undermine rapport among colleagues, we now explain a tool that is useful for building rapport instead.

6.3 The Cooperative Colleague Tool

The Cooperative Colleague Tool comprises three key steps, which can often usefully be applied cyclically. They are represented diagrammatically in Figure 6.1.

Step 1: Engage and Connect – Initiate and foster interpersonal links with colleagues

Step 2: Engage and Empower – Support and empower colleagues in achieving their goals

Step 3: Engage and Balance – Manage key tensions by balancing them supportively

Part 2 – Relationship challenges at work

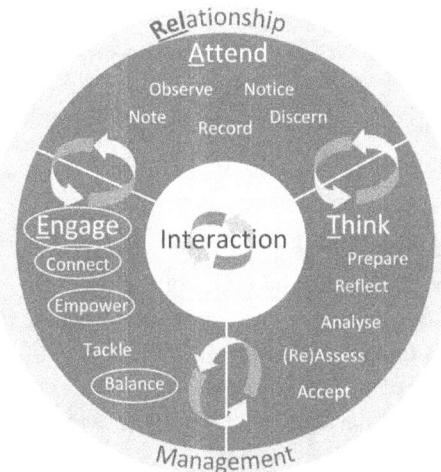

Figure 6.1: The RelATE strategies of the Cooperative Colleague Tool

Step 1: Engage and Connect
A first key step in building cooperation with colleagues is to focus on interpersonal connections. In the Interaction Compass, this is the horizontal axis. In many cultural settings, a focus on interpersonal connections is given top priority and time is spent on that before dealing with task-related matters. Case Study 6.4 illustrates this. It is reported by Helmut, a German key account manager for an engineering company who was trying to negotiate a new business relationship with a client in the Middle East.

> **Case Study 6.4: An agenda ignored**
> *I went on a three-day trip to the Middle East. I sent an agenda in advance and on arrival I tried to get them to discuss the agenda items. But the response was, 'My friend, first we drink tea.' For three days, we talked about nothing but the weather, our countries and our families. When I got back to Germany and told my boss, he was very angry that I had seemingly achieved so little. I made two more trips and almost the same thing happened – only about 10% of our talk was business related. They visited my company in Germany, and very little time was spent in the office; instead, we took them sightseeing, driving them around the area. Despite the 'wasted time' from my boss's perspective, we signed the contract after six months and with only minor negotiation.*

Part 2 – Relationship challenges at work

> **Reflect**
> 1. Why do you think the client was reluctant to discuss Helmut's agenda items?
> 2. Why was Helmut's boss angry?
> 3. How could this relate to the GAAFFE Triggers?

Within the home workplace, it is also extremely important to put time and effort into establishing good connections with colleagues. Why, though, is it so vital? One key reason is that interpersonal rapport acts as 'glue' to keep colleagues collaborating when task-related problems or differences of opinion arise (which they inevitably do). This is particularly important in contexts of diversity in order to help minimise the risk of descent into factionalism and 'othering' when disagreement and conflict occurs.

Highly experienced international project manager, Sue Canney Davison, argues as follows regarding the relative balance between time spent at the start of a project on building relationships and working on the project task:

Start slowly and end fast; start fast and maybe not end at all.[28] (p. 171)

In other words, she strongly recommends spending time at the beginning of a project on getting to know your team and not immediately focusing on the task. Research has shown that if you ignore interpersonal relationships, or rush too quickly into the task at hand, things may fall apart when differences of opinion emerge.

This also applies to dealing with disagreement more generally. In Chapter 4, we pointed out that having completed the Think and Prepare stage, it may not always be wise to proceed to the next stage and try to talk through your differing viewpoints. This is especially the case when a relationship is particularly strained. So, if time has been taken to build as much trust and cooperation with a colleague as possible, this helps smooth the way to more productive discussions.

Step 1 of the Cooperative Colleague Tool, Engage and Connect, addresses this need. The following subsections illustrate ways it can be carried out and issues to pay attention to.

Connect by initiating conversations

Initiating conversations is the starting point for connecting; without it, colleagues can easily feel excluded. Yet many people find it very difficult to take the initiative to start a conversation with a stranger, as it can require them to move out of their comfort zone. Even something as supposedly easy as greetings can be problematic, especially when there are language and/or cultural differences or changes. For example:

---

[28] Canney Davison, 1996, p. 171

- We may be unsure what nonverbal behaviour to use. When do we shake hands, kiss on the cheek, or simply greet the other person verbally? The Covid-19 pandemic brought this issue to the fore, with people in the UK and elsewhere starting to elbow-bump, but then feeling uncertain what to do as the pandemic waned.
- We may be unsure how to respond. For example, if someone greets us with a religious greeting, such as 'Peace be upon you', what should we say in response?
- There may be different conventions as to who should initiate the greeting. For instance, in both Iran and Nigeria, it is the person of lower status who should initiate the greeting.[29]

In many contexts, both at work and at conferences or networking events, it is common for people who know each other (well) to gather in small groups, catching up on each other's news. This makes it difficult for a 'newcomer' to start a conversation with any of them, unless they are particularly extrovert. It is easy in such circumstances to stick with the people you know, or even just spend the time checking your own emails. This results in lost opportunities and can also give rise to a sense of personal disappointment, dissatisfaction, and loneliness at work. So, what can be done?

If you are the one feeling isolated, one way is to work on your own hesitations: to be clear what you want to achieve, to set yourself small achievable goals (e.g., to go up and start a conversation with two new people), and to actively work on improving in this way. Another way is to accept that certain events, such as large networking events or social spaces are not the most productive for you. In line with this, there's a growing trend for small networks of professionals, both within organisations and within sectors, to be established to offer mutual support. These may be more appealing and productive for some.

If you are a person with lots of contacts, look out for people who are on their own and make a point of initiating contact with them. Even just a few exchanges could be really helpful in reducing their sense of exclusion. Without doing this, colleagues can easily feel excluded or even discriminated against. This was the experience of a young Chinese woman who was an intern in a British company. She talked about this afterwards to a Chinese friend, as shown in Case Study 6.5.

Case Study 6.5: Ignored at work
Intern: *I found it difficult to integrate with the staff. The white people stuck together, and the Asians stuck together. We were discriminated against – just subtle discrimination.*
Friend: *Perhaps it's because we are newcomers.*

---

[29] Fawole & Rammala, 2021

Part 2 – Relationship challenges at work

> Intern: No, I don't think so. Do you know why? Because in the coffee room, in the kitchen they don't know each other because different departments all go to that one kitchen room, but they say "hello," "hi," or just have a small talk, but they don't have a talk with us.
>
> **Reflect**
> 1. Why do you think the local staff didn't talk to the intern?
> 2. Do you think she was discriminated against? Why/why not?

For further exploration of exclusion at work, please see Chapter 5 which focuses on exclusion in meetings.

Connect by engaging in small talk
After exchanging greetings, it is not always easy to know how to build on them and continue the conversation. There can be some tricky issues to navigate.

In social contexts in the UK, asking the other person where they come from is quite common, yet can be highly problematic in certain circumstances. If both people are white, it will be interpreted in terms of their geographical region of origin and will not usually cause offence. But if one person has a different ethnic background, asking this could imply they don't belong and hence be a microinsult, especially if followed by 'No, where do you really come from'. One author gives the following advice for potentially sensitive situations, such as when race or gender issues could affect interpretation:

> In all these potentially awkward situations, don't stop asking the questions. Instead, think about how to ask them well. Think about how to discover people's stories with genuine interest rather than implied judgement. ... The more aware we are of how our questions feel to others, the more those questions will open doors rather than put up defences.[30]

Another potentially tricky issue is getting people's names right, especially pronouncing them when they are unfamiliar to us. Getting the pronunciation (almost!) right – and remembering it later – can mean a huge amount to people, or even just attempting to say their name. One writer, Mark Murphy,[31] gives a revealing example of this. He had ordered an Uber and found the driver's name very unusual – Ogoguantua. So, he practised it a few times before the driver arrived, and when a car pulled up, he asked 'Ogoguantua?' They drove off and shortly afterwards, the driver asked Mark to say his name again, which Mark did. The driver then said, "Thank you. I moved here from Africa a little over a year ago. I've been driving for Uber for six months and you're the first rider who has actually said my

[30] Fanshawe, 2022, p. 15
[31] Fuller et al., 2020, p. 85

name." Names are an important part of people's identity and so always need to be attended to carefully. They address two of the GAAFFE Triggers – Attention and Face – helping boost rapport when handled well and threatening it when ignored or handled badly. In fact, repeatedly failing to use or pronounce a person's name correctly can also be perceived as a microinsult.

Connect by seeking common ground
Any relationship needs points of common interest or shared experiences to be meaningful and sometimes it can take a little time and effort to find them, requiring engagement and participation. This inevitably requires a certain amount of sharing of personal information and a key challenge here can be deciding what and how much to ask about or share. Cultural factors (as well as individual factors) can have a major impact here, as there can be noticeable differences in what kind of information it is appropriate to ask about or disclose. For instance, when Helen was working in China, she was regularly asked on first encounters how old she was, how many children she had, and how much she earned, which she found disconcerting initially. (See Chapter 11 for further discussion of the issue of self-disclosure.)

Finding common ground with colleagues can also be tricky when there are unfamiliar practices to get used to, or ones that you feel uncomfortable with (e.g., for financial reasons or personal principles). These can act as barriers to finding common ground and need to be overcome in some way. Case Study 6.6 was reported by an American employee, Anna May, who had recently started working in a British company.

Case Study 6.6: Adjusting to an unfamiliar office culture
I do not come from a big tea drinking culture and was not familiar with the practice of drinking tea in an English office. Every morning about an hour after we arrived, Vicky, or one of the other ladies would ask if I wanted a cup of hot water or some tea. I hated to impose on them, so I told them I was alright. After a while I felt I was being antisocial so I accepted their offers for tea a couple of times but felt badly because, to me, I should have been making them tea. I was younger than they were, and in my culture (be it American or Asian-American) this is the way things are done. The main problem, however, was that I was not sure how to brew proper tea and was concerned that I would serve a cup either too weak or too strong. Finally, I got up the courage to offer to prepare the beverages even though I did not actually want one that early in the morning. After a bit of practice, I figured out the right amount of time to steep a tea bag and felt better accepting when others offered to make me a beverage.
Although I may have had a difficult time adjusting to the office's tea

Part 2 – Relationship challenges at work

culture, coffee culture in fact helped me to bond with my co-worker Vicky. Things felt a bit awkward in the beginning when Peter was out of the office, as Vicky and I were alone, working in silence. At one point, my love of coffee and exploring new cafés came up and suddenly we were exchanging ideas about the best places to get cappuccino in Leamington Spa and beyond. She wrote down a list of spots she thought I should check out during my lunch breaks, and I told her about my favourite café in Birmingham. This initial talk opened the door to other chats about topics including career paths, working in the non-profit sector and even relationships. On the last day at our old office before the move to new premises, Vicky actually took me on a 'coffee crawl,' sipping caffeinated drinks at several wonderful local spots.

Reflect
1. What challenges did Anna May experience in finding common ground with her colleagues?
2. How did she try to overcome them?
3. How did Vicky also help build common ground?
4. What challenges and successes have you experienced in finding common ground with your colleagues or clients? What strategies have worked well for you?

As this case study indicates, finding common ground can take time. It often requires courage and persistence to establish it but can be very worthwhile for both parties when it occurs.

Once a certain degree of a relationship is in place, further bonding can often occur through engaging in troubles talk and humour.

Troubles talk refers to interactions in which people jointly complain about a perceived source of trouble, which could range from mildly inconvenient to serious. One longitudinal study of an MBA team[32] found that this formed a powerful bonding mechanism for the members. Certain features, though, were key for it to have a positive rather than a negative impact. Firstly, the problem is not blamed or attributed to any of those present. Secondly, care is taken to ensure the troubles talk does not continue for too long or become too negative. Thirdly, advice-giving is avoided so that no member is perceived as more capable than another. When these features were met, it functioned very effectively as a means of fostering connections. However, if any of them are missing, it could have the opposite impact and undermine connections.

Another informal way of potentially increasing bonding is through humour. Light-hearted interactions can function powerfully as a means of constructing ingroup solidarity and promoting a sense of community. However, unfortunately, the opposite can also occur with humour creating divisions and offence. Banter, for example, can be treated as humour by one person and interpreted as 'othering' and offensive by another. So, in contexts of diversity, it is particularly important to be mindful and cautious over engaging in supposedly humorous exchanges.

Opportunities for chatting have recently been impacted significantly by hybrid working and an increase in geographically distributed teams. While both have brought noticeable personal convenience to people, a potential downside is the negative impact it can have on establishing and maintaining connections. When someone is new to a workplace, it can be extremely hard if colleagues are rarely around. Once relationships are established, it's easier to maintain them online, but when someone new joins, it's important for existing colleagues to make a special effort to get to know them. That's why particular attention has to be paid to onboarding processes, where new employees joining an organisation or a team where at least some hybrid working is the norm, are given extra support, for example through buddying and mentoring schemes, to facilitate connections and build relationships.

Many organisations have adopted remote or hybrid working because of the benefits to them, such as being able to attract and retain global talent. This means that colleagues may work in teams that are located in different parts of the world, where the vast majority of interaction is online. In these situations, it is particularly important to pay attention to establishing and maintaining interpersonal relations.

To address this need, some teams and organisations are intentionally creating virtual 'touch points' or 'human moments' to encourage people to connect and share and get to know each other online, over and above coming together to work on a task over Teams or Zoom. The US branch of the Chinese company, Alibaba, for example, celebrated its annual Aliday – a celebration of the values of community and collective activity – by having an online quilt making event.[33]

Even simple things like occasionally getting team members to choose an online background of a place that's important to them, or that they'd like to visit, and spending a few minutes in which members explain their choices can be really helpful. Various books[34] are available that suggest different activities for promoting rapport online, and we recommend consulting them if this is relevant to your work situation.

Connect by caring
Another facet of connecting is the positive impact that caring can have. One way of doing this is by giving practical task-related help when needed – we consider that under Step 2 Cooperative Colleague Tool. Here we focus on showing care though empathy and concern for others. Often this simply means offering a listening ear at relevant times, being willing to spend time listening to others' (personal) concerns. It can also mean 'giving others slack' when they are having a difficult day,

---

[33] Hinds & Elliott, 2021
[34] e.g., Littlefield, 2020

disregarding it rather than complaining to someone else or gossiping about them. Now consider your own experiences of connecting with colleagues by reflecting on the questions in Activity 6.2.

> **Activity 6.2: Connecting with colleagues**
> 1. How easy or difficult do you find it to initiate a conversation in a work context with someone you don't know? What factors influence you? How often do you do it and how could you improve (if needed)?
> 2. How easy or difficult do you find it to draw out points of shared interest or common experiences with your colleagues? Why do you think this is so?
> 3. To what extent has hybrid working affected your ability to form connections with colleagues?
> 4. Have you ever experienced any microaggression/microinsults at work – either personally, or observed between others? What was said and how did you react?
> 5. How often do you spend timing being a 'listening ear' when a colleague is experiencing some personal issues and needs someone to talk to? How could you be more open and available for this?

In this section we have focused on establishing and maintaining interpersonal bonds and rapport with colleagues. In the next section we turn to supporting and empowering others to achieve their goals.

Step 2: Engage and Empower

Step 2 of the Cooperative Colleague Tool, Engage and Empower, is complementary to Step 1 Engage and Connect, and is the other side of the coin. While Engage and Connect focuses on interpersonal (i.e., non-work specific) links, Engage and Empower promotes links through work-related matters. Both are needed for a cooperative relationship. In this section we explain ways in which cooperation can be built by supporting each other on work-related matters – empowering others to achieve their best.

Empower others by collaborating

For many tasks at work, we can benefit hugely from working as a team and drawing on the insights and ideas of others. One engineer, Joe, who works on resolving car faults that have been reported to them, commented as follows on the importance of collaboration:

> As a team, we'll have people from different departments. We all work to try and fix whatever has gone wrong. That information either comes from the dealerships or

> *from calls to roadside assist. We analyse that data and where there's a pattern, we create a project and put a team together to try and understand and fix that problem. We've all got knowledge we can share. So as a team we can all support each other.*

In other words, in many projects different skills are needed such that project success requires effective collaboration among multiple individuals. If one member does not give the support needed, the whole project suffers, and it can be particularly problematic for the project leader.

Project leaders can often be in a difficult position because they have no formal 'power' over other members. As we saw in Case Study 6.2, some project members may resent the position of the project leader, feeling they have no right to set deadlines and standards. As a result, they may not cooperate well. On other occasions, there may be pressures and demands from other projects, such that certain members genuinely have little or no spare capacity. If their other project is high value, there will be pressure from senior management to prioritise it. In such cases there may be little that the leader of the smaller project can do, other than find workarounds.

In yet other circumstances, certain colleagues may not fully value or grasp the need for mutual collaboration. For instance, Joe went on to comment that sometimes (new) colleagues needed persuading on the importance of working collaboratively – in this case, to gain hands-on experience.

> *I have a couple of graduates that are working with me. I've learned a massive amount from them. For the younger ones, it's a matter of pulling them away from their desks, getting them to feel the parts and to talk with people. They're students who've finished their degrees in a very different environment. They're very good at quietly working on their own, and probably incredibly happy working from home. We're making them feel a bit uncomfortable by saying we actually want you to come to the plant.*

This points to the need for universities and other training organisations to promote collaborative working – a challenge that many have taken up.

Sometimes, of course, it's not necessary – or even helpful – to work collaboratively, and so a balance needs to be maintained on this. We explore that further in Step 3 of the Cooperative Colleague Tool, Engage and Balance.

Empower others by helping them

Another facet of building cooperation is helping other colleagues when they need it. Sooner or later, this will actually be beneficial to the helper, as one engineer explained:

> *In my experience, if you really help somebody out, it comes back to you tenfold. Because if I have a problem, say, I help somebody out because their machine is*

broken, and I help them figure out what the problem is. Then my machine breaks in an area that they work on. I'm much more likely to get parts that I really shouldn't have gotten, or somebody's got time to come and look at it when they are not being allocated for that. So I think it really does pay you back much more than the time you put in to help people.[35]

In other words, this engineer argues that sooner or later you'll need someone else's help and that there is therefore payback over time. If one individual cannot provide the help needed, it's good if they can find or suggest someone else who can.

Of course, helping in this way can run the risk of the other person taking advantage and not returning the favour. We consider this in Step 3 of the Cooperative Colleague Tool, Balance.

If the help involves advice-giving, it's important to pay attention to wording in order not to imply arrogance or to come across as a 'know-it-all'. In some cultural settings, little phrases like the following can help with this:

- One of the things that might help is …
- You could perhaps try …
- What I like to do is …
- There may be lots of ways to do this, but …

This can help make a message less direct. In this way, it can address the GAAFFE Triggers of Autonomy and Face and thereby reduce the risk of triggering a negative rapport reaction. For more details on directness–indirectness, see Stage 3 Engage and Balance, as well as Chapters 8 and 11.

Empower others by sharing and adjusting
A third facet of promoting cooperation through empowerment involves sharing and (if need be) adjusting.

Information is a form of power (see Chapter 12) and so unfortunately it can be used as a tool for personal advantage and as a weapon to disadvantage, disempower, or discredit others. This happens when information that would be useful to others is deliberately withheld. Such a situation needs to be addressed whenever possible as it activates the GAAFFE Trigger of Fairness, and thereby undermines people's sense of justice. Often this leads to lack of trust among the individuals concerned.

It can be difficult for colleagues to deal with the issue directly, unless the person is unaware that they are acting in this way. However, sometimes they may simply not realise the relevance of the information to others, or they may be so focused on their own tasks that they overlook it. One way of handling such a situation is to arrange or ask for slots in meetings where individuals are explicitly required to share information relevant to a given topic.

[35] Fletcher, 1999, p. 67

Part 2 – Relationship challenges at work

Another aspect of sharing is less about information and more about processes. People may have different styles of working (see Chapter 12) and team members may need to co-ordinate their preferences. Many authors[36] have recommended that teams agree on their ways of working together, such as by agreeing on ground rules. This can be handled with different degrees of explicitness, but in all cases, it can involve a certain amount of mutual adjustment. For instance, people may agree rules about listening to others, speed of speech, and handling of deadlines, which may mean personal adjustments for the sake of the group. (See also Table 5.8 on language adjustment.)

Sometimes individuals may feel the need to make clear their needs to customers as well as colleagues, as illustrated in Case Study 6.7, posted publicly on LinkedIn by Lea[37], who has ADHD (Attention deficit hyperactivity disorder).

Case Study 6.7: "I have ADHD"
Asking for our needs for ADHD shouldn't feel like we're being unreasonable. And yet, adding this short paragraph to my emails feels like a bold move that people will find uncomfortable or inconvenient.

But you know what's more inconvenient?

Having to chase me for a response because you buried three questions in 6 paragraphs, and when I opened the email, I felt overwhelmed, ignored it to do later, and never went back (avoidance procrastination).

Having ADHD makes life extra complicated. It means doing things in a way that often doesn't make sense to other people.

"Why can't you just get on with it?"

"Just do it now and get it over with."

How many times have I heard that in my life?

So, for the benefit of both myself and the people who grace my inbox, I'm attempting to create a simple solution, meaning we both get what we want without a drama.

Message at the bottom of Lea's emails
Please note: I have ADHD, which can mean I find large blocks of text overwhelming and struggle to process them. Please ensure that if you have a question, these are at the TOP of your email, and multiple questions/requests are clearly summarised in bullet points. This will ensure I can respond comprehensively and save us both time! I appreciate your effort in accommodating my request.

---

[36] e.g., Vigier & Spencer-Oatey, 2018
[37] https://www.linkedin.com/posts/lea-turner_adhd-neurodiversity-inclusivity-activity-7138104187438919681-CNDK?utm_source=share&utm_medium=member_desktop

Part 2 – Relationship challenges at work

> **Reflect**
> 1. Why might people feel uncomfortable or inconvenienced when reading Lea's message at the bottom of her emails? What GAAFFE Triggers might it activate for recipients?
> 2. Why might Lea feel a little apprehensive about including such a message? What GAAFFE Triggers might it activate?
> 3. Why did she feel the need to include a message like this? What GAAFFE Triggers was she trying to address?
> 4. How would you react to Lea's message if you received her email? How easily do you think you would be able (to remember) to adjust to Lea's request? Give your reasons.

Empower others by being courteous and acknowledging fault when needed
It's important not to forget, of course, that people need to treat each other with basic courtesy – to compliment others when they've done something particularly commendable, to convey appreciation to others when they have worked especially hard on a particular project, and to apologise to others when mistakes or errors of judgement have been made. It is often particularly difficult to admit fault and apologise to another person, yet this is vital for a fruitful and cooperative relationship. It is important, though, not to upset or annoy people inadvertently by mishandling such messages in some way, such as when a man repeatedly compliments a woman on her appearance and not on her work!

Now consider your own experiences of building work-related links with colleagues by reflecting on the questions in Activity 6.3.

> **Activity 6.3: Supporting colleagues on task-related matters**
> 1. When collaborating with colleagues on a task or project, what went well in your collaboration and what went less well? What factors helped it go well and what factors undermined it?
> 2. How often do you help your colleagues on a work-related task or project that isn't actually your responsibility? What factors influence your decision as to whether to help or not?
> 3. Has a colleague ever offered you help when you needed it? What impact did it have on your relationship?
> 4. Have you experienced a colleague withholding or simply not sharing some information that would be relevant to you and others? If so, how did it make you feel and what did you do (if anything) about it? Going forward, might you do anything different?
> 5. Have you ever withheld information or simply not shared some information that you knew or thought would be helpful to someone

else? Why did you do this, and what impact do you think it had on your relationship?
6. To what extent have you and colleagues talked over your working style preferences? How have you been adapting to colleagues' different needs, such as those related to language proficiency or neurodiversity?

Step 3: Engage and Balance
Much of life is about achieving an appropriate balance between too much and too little of something. Here we explain several issues that we need to balance, starting with autonomy–control. In Chapter 1, we introduced this continuum – one of the GAAFFE Triggers – and this is one facet of a relationship that always needs balancing.

Balancing autonomy–control
In Case Study 6.2, we reported a problem that Olivia was having with Rima. In a follow-up interview with Olivia about three months later, Olivia reported that her relationship with Rima was now very good. Asked to explain how that had come about, Olivia reported making two adjustments.

One was around autonomy–control. Now, when her line manager, Amy, gives her a deadline for the monthly report, Olivia checks with her team whether they feel this is realistic. If it is, then fine; if it isn't, she tries to renegotiate the deadline with Amy. Moreover, instead of dividing up the work on the report herself, she now asks each member which parts they would prefer to do for the current report. In other words, Olivia is giving her team much more autonomy and negotiation rights. Rima is much happier working in this way.

Balancing directness–indirectness
Closely connected with the continuum of autonomy–control is directness–indirectness and this was the other adjustment that Olivia made. She started watching Rima's interactions with other staff in the office and realised that she used the same direct style – which came across as somewhat aggressive – with everyone. It wasn't only with Olivia. Olivia also realised that much of it was a language problem – that Rima was having difficulty expressing her real meaning in English and was getting frustrated over it. In this case, Olivia didn't change the level of directness of her own language, but rather adjusted by accepting the directness level of Rima's language and by not getting offended by it.

Different patterns and expectations over the use of directness–indirectness in language use can lead to two types of problems – offence if the communication is more direct than expected or desired (as Olivia experienced), and miscommunication if the communication is more indirect than the hearer is used to. Consider Case Study 6.8, where the latter problem arose.

Part 2 – Relationship challenges at work

> **Case Study 6.8: Interpreting a request** [38]
>
> A British university lecturer, Shirley needed a second opinion on some students' work, and she asked a colleague, Anke, if she would mind helping. Anke was very happy to do so, and the following conversation took place:
> Anke: *When do you need my comments?*
> Shirley: *Oh no hurry. Perhaps the middle of next week.*
>
> The following Wednesday, Shirley asked Anke how she was getting on preparing her feedback:
> Anke: *Oh why? Do you need it this week?*
> Shirley: *Well yes, I mentioned the middle of this week.*
> Anke: *I didn't realise that, Shirley. You really need to speak more clearly.*
>
> **Reflect:**
> 1. Why do you think Shirley said, "Oh no hurry"? What did she mean by it?
> 2. Why did Anke regard Shirley as unclear?
> 3. How do you think they each felt about the incident?

In this example, Shirley thought she was being very clear, but Anke felt the opposite. The problem stemmed from differences in directness–indirectness.

So balancing directness–indirectness is another continuum that always needs careful attention in order not to cause unintentional offence on the one hand or unclear messaging on the other.

For more information on directness–indirectness and strategies for handling it, see Chapters 8 and 11.

Balancing cost–benefits and reciprocity

In Step 2 of the Cooperative Colleague Tool, Engage and Empower, we referred to the value of supporting others through helping them. The engineer quoted there referred to the payback that comes from doing this; in other words, that the 'cost' (e.g., in time and effort) of helping a colleague is balanced out by the benefits (e.g., in return help) that are gained at a later stage. This is very positive for building a sense of community.

However, what if time goes on and someone does not give any help in return? This leads to feelings of resentment and unfairness (i.e., activates the GAAFFE Trigger of Fairness), and colleagues may stop helping that person. This is what happened to Sarah, in Case Study 6.1, in the light of Ervin's ongoing behaviour.

The reason for this is because there is a fundamental principle of reciprocity that applies in all societies. It requires one person to repay, in some way or other,

---
[38] Spencer-Oatey et al., 2022, p. 63

what another person has provided. (See Chapter 9 for further discussion of reciprocity.)

One of the key issues here is how long it is appropriate to keep helping someone, without receiving some kind benefit in return. There is no fixed answer to such a question. Rather it is important to bear the balance in mind – not just in terms of your own behaviour, but how truly beneficial it is for the other person to keep giving them help. It could, in fact, hold back their development and willingness to engage with new tasks, so in such cases, it is wise to push back and try to explain the reasons for doing this.

Balancing individual and collaborative working

Another continuum that needs balancing is that between individual and collaborative working. Sometimes the work that a team must do is divided up between the different members – as we saw with Olivia's team. However, there will always be occasions – whether in a team, in a group, or in a department – when members need to come together to talk things through and decide what to do.

So, try to balance the following:

- Be sensitive to people's time by not discussing things that can easily be handled individually, yet also be sensitive to some people's need to discuss their individual work with others.
- Don't overload individuals or cause them too much stress by failing to organise small-group work when that would be most helpful, yet don't exclude people by building small-group silos that certain individuals cannot join and/or the whole group doesn't know about.

Activity 6.4: Managing key tensions

1. Think of an occasion when a colleague was too controlling or too direct. What happened / what did they say? How did you feel?
2. Have there been any occasions when you omitted to consult colleagues on a decision that affects them? If so, how did they react?
3. To what extent do you adjust the level of directness with which you speak to colleagues? What factors influence you in this?
4. Think of a situation when someone failed to repay the help you gave them. How did you feel and what did you do? Have you ever done that to others?
5. How successful do you feel you are in distinguishing between individual tasks, small-group tasks, and all-group tasks? How feasible do you feel it is to divide them in this way?

6.4 Key takeaways

- This chapter has focused on building rapport and fostering collaboration with colleagues.
- A range of different types of relationship challenge can arise, including failure to fulfil their responsibilities, personal criticism or complaint, and indirect insults (i.e., microinsults).
- The Cooperative Colleague Tool identifies three key steps for addressing these issues:
  o Step 1, Engage and Connect, explains the value of initiating and fostering interpersonal links with colleagues. This can provide the 'glue' to maintain a spirit of cooperation when differences of opinion and tensions arise.
  o Step 2, Engage and Empower, explains the importance of supporting and helping empower colleagues in achieving their goals. This will almost always be mutually beneficial in the longer term.
  o Step 3, Engage and Balance, explains the need to balance several key tensions, including autonomy–control, directness–indirectness, cost-benefit and reciprocity, and individual and collaborative working.

A template for using the Cooperative Colleague Tool, with steps and prompts, is given in Chapter 14.

Chapter 7: Problems with bosses?
How to 'manage up' and enhance alignment

7.1 Introduction

This chapter focuses on managing rapport with a boss/line manager, especially when there are problems of some kind. In many respects it is linked with the next chapter, Chapter 8, which deals with the converse – managing direct reports or 'managing down'. In any relationship, it is important to see the other person's point of view, as well as one's own. So, we try to incorporate this dual perspective in both chapters. For managers and direct reports, this is particularly important because both are supposed to be working towards a common workplace goal (e.g., a project goal), while building and maintaining each other's wellbeing. In reality, though, they may have different goals, have little shared understanding of each other's goals, prioritise their goals differently, and have little interest in each other's wellbeing. This can be a significant challenge for both parties in building and maintaining rapport.

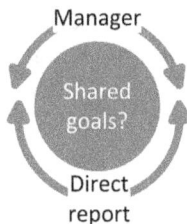

Figure 7.1: Managers, direct reports, and workplace goals

Although much of our focus in this chapter is on problems of working with bosses, in line with the 'challenge' theme of this section of the book, effective 'managing up' is actually useful in all circumstances. So, what does it refer to? One leadership development consultant explains it as follows:

> Managing up is about consciously and deliberatively developing and maintaining effective relationships with supervisors, bosses, and other people above you in the chain of command. It is a deliberate effort to increase cooperation and collaboration in a relationship between individuals who often have different perspectives and uneven power levels. It is about consciously working with your boss to obtain the best possible results for you, your boss, and the organization.[39]

In other words, 'managing up' is not about (inappropriately) going over your boss's head, not about being rude or disrespectful, nor about being sycophantic. On

---
[39] Abbajay, 2018, p. 1

Part 2 – Relationship challenges at work

the contrary, it is about finding ways of working as smoothly and effectively as possible with your boss. This, of course, can sometimes be extremely difficult, so we start by considering some different types of boss behaviour that can be problematic for their direct reports. After that we introduce the Upward Management Tool (Attend and Discern; Think and Reflect; Engage and Tackle) that can help address them.

7.2 'Boss behaviour' challenges

We recently collected data from a range of respondents on their attitudes and experiences of working with their line manager. The research instrument, the Relationship Management Profiler (RELMAP)[40], is designed around the GAAFFE Triggers, and participants rated the importance to them of each of the triggers and the extent to which they were experiencing them being upheld in their workplace.

A noticeable proportion of direct reports were particularly dissatisfied with their manager's handling of goals, autonomy–control, and ethicality so we consider them further below.

7.2.1 Goals

The respondents almost universally rated goals as important (or very important) to them, yet well over one quarter reported that they were not handled well. Some of them gave very low ratings indeed, indicating very high levels of dissatisfaction.

This can be seen from Figure 7.2 which shows the distribution of ratings for Goals. While all but one of the ratings are in the two right-hand quadrants, indicating that Goals are important (or very important) to those respondents, 28% of the responses – a very noticeable proportion – lie in the bottom right-hand quadrant, showing that these people were dissatisfied.

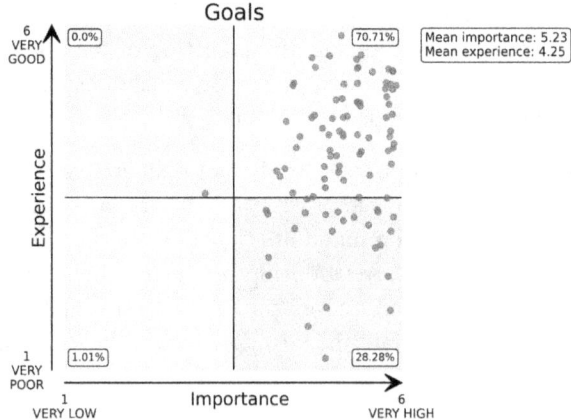

Figure 7.2: Scatterplot of responses to the GAAFFE Trigger of Goals

[40] https://globalpeopleconsulting.com/the-relationship-management-profiler-relmap

Part 2 – Relationship challenges at work

To explore what this might mean in practice, consider Case Study 7.1. It concerns a university lecturer, Conrad, who comments on difficulties with his course director, Jasmine.

> **Case Study 7.1 A thwarted personal goal**
> *I've been granted a sabbatical for the spring term, and I need my manager, Jasmine, to arrange teaching cover for the courses I teach. I've been trying to talk with her about it for over two months, but I haven't yet succeeded in having a proper discussion with her about what needs to be done. I'm getting increasingly worried about it, as I have no authority to recruit anyone myself.*
>
> *The trouble is that Jasmine has become increasingly absent in the department. In the summer she was appointed to a more senior role in another department – one that deals with some strategic university plans. It's only a part-time role, but ever since her promotion, she rarely comes to our department – she seems to be spending her time across the campus with the senior management. Strangely, she's kept her management responsibilities here in our department – it seems she doesn't want to give them up!*
>
> *I'm getting really anxious about the situation, as it's now only about 6 weeks away. Will she be able to arrange cover for my teaching at such short notice, or will I end up having to give up my sabbatical – or even teach during it? That would really have a negative impact on the research publications I need to write during my sabbatical. It's so frustrating and annoying!*
>
> **Reflect**
> 1. Identify explicitly what Conrad's goal is and why he's getting anxious and frustrated.
> 2. Why do you think Jasmine is not addressing Conrad's goal?
> 3. What advice would you give to Conrad? What workaround to the problem might there be?

This case study raises a fundamental question: what can or should a direct report do when their line manager is problematic in some way? It's not usually wise (although very occasionally necessary) to go above the line manager's head, so creativity is often needed in finding workarounds. We consider this further later in the chapter.

It's also important to bear in mind that sometimes middle managers do not have the power or influence to meet a direct report's goal. For example, one middle manager commented as follows in our survey:

Part 2 – Relationship challenges at work

> *I think at middle management level it can be hard to have much influence over the [career] pathway of direct reports when decisions are often with division heads.*

This can be particularly the case for issues such as promotion or pay increases, where company policy may limit what middle managers can or cannot do to meet an employee's goals. So, direct reports need to be mindful of what is realistic for them to expect from their manager in terms of achieving their personal goals.

7.2.2 Balance of autonomy–control

A second GAAFFE Trigger that emerged from the survey as problematic for a noticeable proportion of people was autonomy–control. The vast majority regarded this factor as important, yet almost one quarter felt the balance between the two ends of the continuum was not as they wanted. Once again, some of the respondents gave very low ratings, indicating very high levels of dissatisfaction.

This can be seen from Figure 7.3 which shows the distribution of ratings. While almost all of the ratings are in the two right-hand quadrants, indicating that the balance between autonomy and control is important (or very important) to the respondents, the noticeable proportion – almost one quarter – in the bottom right-hand quadrant shows that many were dissatisfied.

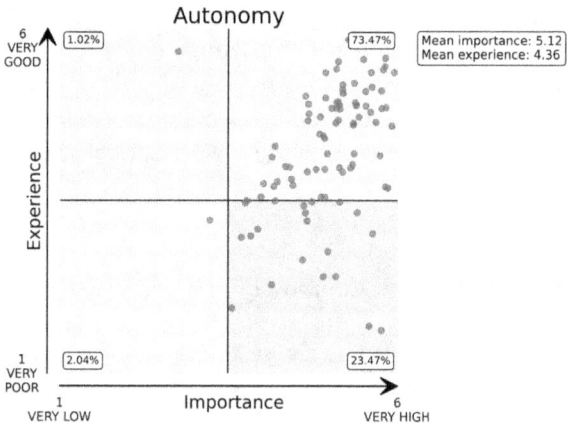

Figure 7.3: Scatterplot of responses to the GAAFFE Trigger of autonomy–control

To explore what this might mean in practice, consider Case Study 7.2. It concerns a relatively junior PR consultant, Melanie, who was working for a very small company that had two directors, Nigel and Angela. Nigel was responsible for creative development while Angela was responsible for operations. Melanie was struggling to deal with the situation, as she explains in Case Study 7.2.

Part 2 – Relationship challenges at work

> **Case Study 7.2: Inadequate direction**
> *It's so difficult working for this company! Angela, my boss, is almost never here – literally! For personal reasons, she spends most of her time out of the country, only coming into the office two or three times a month, and then just for a day on each occasion. We all dread her days in the office, as it's nothing but a string of complaints from her – "Why haven't you done this? Why did you do it this way?" But she gives us no guidance whatsoever – no priorities, no explanation as to how she wants things done. Just criticism! And not only that – often Nigel will sign off a project for a client, but Angela will complain it wasn't good enough and then blame us. And she's so blunt and rude in the way she criticises as well! We're all feeling stressed and anxious, but also angry and resentful – after all, she ought to be here more often and give us proper direction.*
>
> **Reflect**
> 1. Melanie has a number of complaints about Angela. List them all.
> 2. In addition to the GAAFFE Trigger autonomy–control, what other Triggers are likely to be affecting Melanie?
> 3. What advice would you give to Melanie?

Angela is a co-director of the company and so has considerable power; however, in Melanie's eyes she does not give the guidance required and then complains when the work does not meet her requirements. Angela, on the other hand, may be assuming (realistically or otherwise) that Melanie and her colleagues should be able to work independently to a high standard, and should not need much guidance. However, when this repeatedly wasn't the case, Angela should have taken steps to address the situation, rather than just criticise negatively.

In fact, for many managers it can be difficult to find an appropriate balance between autonomy and control. On the one hand, they may need to adjust that balance to suit different individuals, which isn't always easy, and on the other they may find it difficult to gauge how much direction any staff member actually wants or needs, especially if there are performance issues. The following comments by managers from our survey illustrate this:

> *I've always been quite hands-off giving a lot of freedom and very open on sharing information. I'm finding that I need to be more involved with one of my current direct reports than I've been in the past, so that is an adjustment.*

> *It is difficult to give my team freedom to do their work because without close scrutiny, things tend to get missed. It is difficult to know how much strategic input they'd like or would benefit from.*

Part 2 – Relationship challenges at work

7.2.3 Ethicality

A third GAAFFE Trigger that emerged from the survey as problematic for a noticeable proportion of people was Ethicality. Almost all respondents regarded this factor as important, yet for just over one fifth of them ethical issues were not handled as they wanted. Once again, some of the respondents gave very low ratings, indicating very high levels of dissatisfaction.

This can be seen from Figure 7.4 which shows the distribution of ratings. While all but one of the ratings are in the two right-hand quadrants, indicating that Ethicality is important (or very important) to the respondents, a noticeable proportion – about one fifth – is in the bottom right-hand quadrant, showing that many were dissatisfied.

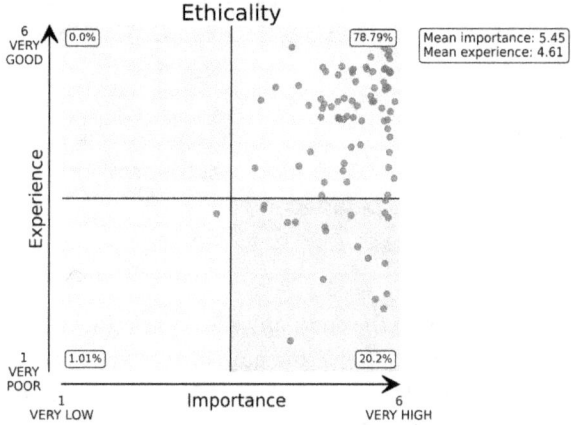

Figure 7.4: Scatterplot of responses to the GAAFFE Trigger of Ethicality

To explore what this might mean in practice, consider Case Study 7.3. It concerns a Chinese employee, Jingli, who has been living and working in the UK for many years. After taking up a new post in a different organisation, she started having difficulties with her boss, Arya. She describes her problems in Case Study 7.3.

Case Study 7.3: A bullying line manager
My line manager piles so much work on me that I regularly have to work both evenings and weekends. Sometimes she even gives me a major task on a Friday afternoon and says I need to have completed it by Monday morning. That's really unfair and unreasonable.

She's always criticising me for poor performance, but a few weeks ago she was more specific, saying I need to pay more attention to quality than quantity. I tried to explain that the problem is the volume of work

Part 2 – Relationship challenges at work

she is giving me, but she just shouted at me, denying that she had given me so much work.

Then, to my huge surprise, the next day I received a very one-sided written record of the meeting, with the heading showing that yesterday's meeting was the first of a 4-week formal underperformance review. I was shocked as she hadn't mentioned anything about that at the time. Also, in her account, there was no mention of the issues I would be assessed on.

Is this allowed? I thought staff were entitled to be told in advance of any such formal meetings. Now, when she puts meetings into my calendar labelled 'catch-ups', I don't know whether they are underperformance reviews or genuinely simply catch-ups.

I'm extremely upset by all this and also really confused because several senior managers have praised me for the work that I've done for them. So, I don't believe there's a real problem with the quality of my work. Another issue is that she's now started excluding me from meetings, saying there's no need for me to attend and that she'll attend instead. Yet the content of those meetings is directly relevant to the tasks she's set me, and when I ask her for a report or account of what was agreed, I never receive it.

I really don't know what to do. The previous postholder had exactly the same problems and that's why she left. In fact, she said to me, "Arya is horrible. She treats people – her direct reports – like slaves." I try to be less emotional and stressed, but it's difficult. I'd like to complain, but my line manager is very good friends with the senior staff and I'm afraid it would make the matter worse. In any case, when the previous postholder complained, Arya simply denied it all and nothing further was done. It's so upsetting – I can hardly sleep I'm so stressed.

Reflect

1. List the various problems that Jingli is experiencing with her line manager, Arya.
2. Look at Table 7.1 (further below) on types of toxic culture. Which (if any) of the categories seem to correspond to Arya's behaviour?
3. What GAAFFE Triggers are probably activated for Jingli through Arya's behaviour?
4. What advice would you give to Jingli?

We cannot know what Arya's perspective is, but there is clearly a serious problem here – at least from Jingli's perspective. Her boss doesn't seem to be following standard HR policy on underperformance management and employee rights, and several features of Jingli's experiences correspond to common designations of bullying.[41] Once again, there is a gap between manager and direct report in interpretations of who should do what and to what standard, a failure to achieve mutual understanding of each other's perspectives, and a disrespectful style of communication.

Sadly, issues of bullying and toxic workplace cultures have been reported several times in the press recently. It is not clear how widespread it actually is, partly because people are reluctant to report it for various reasons. In our survey, two of the comments were as follows:

- *I, of course, promote staff welfare as much as I can; however, I can't say the same for those higher up.*
- *On the rare occasions when these issues [of bullying] arise, HR are weak and not prepared to be robust in a response.*

7.3 Power and psychological safety

Fundamental to the manager–direct report relationship – and reflected in the case studies we've just considered – is the issue of unequal power. This is a core P: People issue.

The manager–direct report relationship is intrinsically unequal, which means that the manager has the power to control many positive outcomes and negative outcomes. As a result of this, anxiety and fear can frequently occur during interactions between boss and direct report, making it difficult for the latter to negotiate on issues with their manager or to convey any kind of disagreement.

If a manager takes a strongly hierarchical position, this affects the psychological atmosphere of all interactions, known as the level of psychological safety. When psychological safety is low, the direct report is always very conscious of the potential risk of negative outcomes and therefore will usually feel constrained in how open and honest they can be with the manager in sharing their viewpoints and concerns. (See Chapter 13 for a more detailed discussion of psychological safety.)

Although the manager–direct report relationship is inherently hierarchical, individuals (for personal or cultural reasons) can differ in the extent to which they regard and treat the relationship as unequal. Both parties will always need to find comfortable ways of handling the power differential between them, but when there is a mismatch in their perspectives, this can make managing rapport particularly tricky. Given that direct reports normally have to adapt more to their line manager than vice versa (because of the power difference in the role relationship), this makes it particularly incumbent on the direct report to find ways of relating to the manager in line with the latter's preferences.

There are no easy fixes for this, but the Upward Management Tool can be a helpful guide.

---

[41] e.g., see Hetrick, 2023

7.4 The Upward Management Tool

The Upward Management Tool comprises three key steps, which can often usefully be applied cyclically: Attend (i.e., pay attention) and Discern, Think and Reflect, Engage and Tackle. They are represented diagrammatically in Figure 7.5.

Step 1: Attend and Discern – Discern the ways in which you and your line manager are or are not aligned in your preferences and experiences.
Step 2: Think and Reflect – Think through the sources and impact of what you have noticed.
Step 3: Engage and Tackle – Seek out ways to address the issues that have emerged.

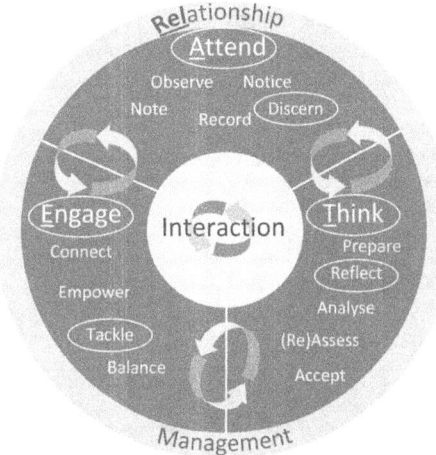

Figure 7.5: The RelATE strategies of the Upward Management Tool

Step 1: Attend and Discern
The first step is to notice and discern things about your manager and things about yourself. There are two main aspects that need paying attention to:

- Your line manager's preferred ways of doing things, and how similar or different they are to your own;
- Any challenges you are experiencing in working with your line manager.

Discern work-related preferences
Sometimes relationship problems can arise because of different ways of working and mismatches in expectations. So, the first features to pay attention to are the behavioural preferences of you and your line manager.
    In order to gain such insights, it will mean paying attention to the I: Interaction of the TRIPS framework, since it is features of the interaction that will yield

clues to these preferences. For instance, if you have a quick question you want to ask your manager, and have received a brush-off on previous occasions, it can be helpful to pay attention to your manager's behaviour at different times of day and try to discern whether or not there is any pattern. That might guide you over the best time of day to catch them or when not to approach them.

This relates closely to people's working styles, including the issues listed in Activity 7.1. This activity can help you notice how far your preferences are – or are not – aligned with those of your manager. For more detailed information on working styles, and a related task, consult Chapter 12.

Activity 7.1: Discerning working style alignment/non-alignment

Working Style issue	Discernment questions	Your manager's tendencies	Alignment with your own style
Attitude to deadlines	• How strict is your manager about keeping to deadlines? And you?		
Management of time	• Is your manager a last-minute person? And you?		
Speed of working	• Does your manager expect a fast turnaround of work? And you?		
Attitude to detail	• Is your manager very fussy about detailed things? And you?		
Degree of organisation	• Is your manager well organised? And you?		
Communication mode	• What is your manager's preferred way of communicating (e.g., email, face-to-face)? And yours?		
Communication style	• Is your manager's communication style direct and to the point or more indirect and implicit? And yours?		

Part 2 – Relationship challenges at work

Discern your work-related challenges with your boss
The second feature that you need to pay attention to are any challenges you are experiencing in working with your boss. These often extend beyond working style preferences and relate to broader aspects of your interactions. The GAAFFE Triggers offer a useful framework for noticing these features. These insights will then feed into the next step of the Upward Management Tool, Think and Reflect.

Work through Activity 7.2 to help you think through your challenges.

Activity 7.2: Identifying your challenges and their main sources		
GAAFFE Trigger	Discernment questions	Your experiences with your line manager
Goals	• Are you and your line manager aligned on work goals?	
Autonomy-control	• Do you get the amount of direction or autonomy you want from your line manager?	
Attention-inattention	• Do you have a suitable amount of access to your line manager?	
Face	• Is your line manager suitably respectful towards you?	
Fairness	• Does your line manager treat you fairly?	
Ethicality	• Is your line manager's behaviour towards you ethical?	

Step 2: Think and Reflect
Having gathered the information from Step 1: Attend and Discern, the next step is to reflect on that information. There are three key areas to reflect on:
- Reflect on your reactions
- Reflect on your attitudinal alignment with your line manager
- Reflect on the seriousness and impact of your challenges

Reflect on your reactions
We can all feel upset or angry with our manager from time to time – that is natural. To help with specific instances, we recommend using our Reaction Management Tool, explained in Chapter 3. Here we're focusing on more frequent and enduring

Part 2 – Relationship challenges at work

patterns of challenge to working effectively with your boss. Activity 7.3 is designed to help you think through your Reactions.

Activity 7.3: Reflecting on your Reactions		
	Indicative questions	**Notes**
Emotions experienced	What emotions do you often experience when interacting with your boss?	e.g., see Table 3.1
Disclosure of emotions	How far do you disclose your emotions and concerns, either verbally or nonverbally, to your boss?	e.g., Do you cry or lose your temper? Do you pull faces? Are you explicitly critical?
Physical symptoms	What physical symptoms, if any, are you experiencing that could be related to stress?	e.g., Frequent headaches; stomach upsets; difficulty sleeping
Sense of wellbeing	What impact do you think your boss's behaviour could be having on your sense of identity?	e.g., Level of self-confidence; sense of self-esteem; ability to function effectively; satisfaction with life

It's important to consider the manager's perspective, especially in terms of disclosure of emotions. It is not easy being an effective manager, and if direct reports are perceived to be rude or disrespectful this can be face-threatening for the manager and is likely to undermine rapport. One of the managers who participated in our survey referred to this challenge in one of their comments.

> *I always try to treat staff with empathy, but it can be challenging when someone is very rude or disrespectful to me/other staff members. I am not typically an angry or stressed manager, I'm quite laid back, but I sometimes feel managers have to be superhumans in terms of emotional intelligence.*

Reflect on your attitudinal alignment with your manager
A second issue to reflect on is the attitudinal alignment you have with your manager. Consider the following:

- To what extent do you usually feel some kind of positive bond with your manager?
- To what extent do you usually believe in and trust your manager's professional expertise?

Part 2 – Relationship challenges at work

There is both a task and an interpersonal side to the manager–direct report relationship, and this gives rise to different working alignment situations, as illustrated in Figure 7.6.

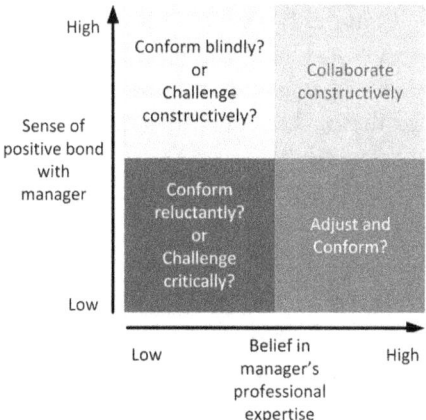

Figure 7.6: Different types of working alignment situations

The most positive situation is where someone feels able to support their manager from both task and interpersonal perspectives (top right-hand quadrant); i.e., the direct report feels the manager handles work issues effectively, making good decisions, and the two get on well together. Here there are no real issues and it's likely that they will be able to collaborate constructively.

The next most positive situation is where there is high interpersonal support for the manager but not necessarily task-based support (top left-hand quadrant); for example, they get on well together but may have different opinions about the best way of carrying out a particular project. In these circumstances, the direct report may either follow the manager's plans without questioning them (perhaps for personality reasons or their beliefs about hierarchy) or alternatively they may challenge their manager constructively, providing valuable critical feedback. Their positive relationship will typically help them feel comfortable doing this; in other words, the direct report will probably perceive enough psychological safety to bring up issues that the manager might otherwise react to negatively.

The bottom two quadrants both reflect more challenging situations – ones where a direct report may have difficulties interacting with their line manager. The most negative situation is where a person has low levels of positive feelings for their manager and little respect for their professional expertise for the task at hand (bottom left-hand quadrant). In this situation, if a direct report expresses any disagreement over an issue, it risks being interpreted negatively. So, very often in these circumstances, the person simply conforms, reluctantly and silently, in order to minimise conflict. There is little or no psychological safety, and the individual conforms out of fear, which in turn takes its psychological toll over time. Alternatively, if the direct report is brave enough to speak out, they risk being branded as a troublemaker, especially if it happens frequently.

The fourth quadrant (bottom right) is an interesting one. In terms of managerial decision-making, the direct report has confidence in the line manager's professional expertise but feels little interpersonal connectivity with them. Here it could be particularly important for the direct report to think through the underlying reasons for that low level of connectivity and consider ways of improving it. An exception to this would be if the manager's interpersonal behaviour is truly unacceptable – an issue we take up further below.

At this point we should probably mention a fifth type of situation where the direct report becomes a colluder. Colluders are significantly different from conformers, as one researcher has explained:

> Conformers comply with destructive leaders out of fear whereas colluders actively participate in a destructive leader's agenda. Both types are motivated by self-interest, but their concerns are different: conformers try to minimize the consequences of not going along, while colluders seek personal gain through association with a destructive leader. The vulnerability of conformers is based on unmet basic needs, negative self-evaluations, and psychological immaturity. In contrast, colluders are ambitious, selfish and share the destructive leader's world views. [42]

In other words, colluders are opportunists – they support an unethical leader for personal gain, just as a means to enhance their own financial, political or professional success. They tend to emerge when a leader is deeply problematic and toxic. Leaders themselves may be unaware of their direct report's ulterior motives, but colleagues usually notice it. This can have a detrimental impact on collegial relations and can also undermine people's respect for a leader's judgement.

Activity 7.4: Reflecting on working alignment situations

1. What dilemmas have you faced around responding to your manager's instructions or decisions?
2. Which quadrant do you feel reflects your alignment situation most closely?
3. If it's one of the bottom two quadrants, what steps could you take to improve your sense of connectivity with your manager?
4. Have you ever experienced any colluders? How did they operate and how did you feel?

---

[42] Padilla et al, 2007, p. 183

Part 2 - Relationship challenges at work

Reflect on the seriousness of the challenges
Having noticed and reflected on the issues and experiences considered so far, the next step is to reflect on the seriousness of the challenges you are facing – for you personally and possibly for others too.

At this point, it could be helpful to consider what manager behaviour has been identified as toxic by researchers. Table 7.1 lists a wide range of types of problematic leader behaviour found in one research study.[43] We suggest you look at this list and then work through Activity 7.5.

Type of Toxic Behaviour	Examples
Manipulations	• Creating conflict, e.g., by having favourites, pitting subordinates against each other • Deception and lying, e.g., presenting subordinate's work as own • Inappropriate personal relationships with junior staff members
Intimidation & bullying	• Autocratic management style, e.g., 'my way or the highway'; bullying, overbearing, control freak; • Swearing & use of intimidating language • Targeting of dissenters, e.g., systematically try to get rid of them
Abuse & emotional volatility	• Abuse, tantrums and threatening behaviour • Very erratic behaviour towards staff, with peaks and lows of mood
Narcissism	• Arrogant demeanour • Constantly seeking and needing praise • Lapses into numerous and time-consuming self-praising anecdotes • No regard for needs of others – has to win at all costs
Micromanagement	• Workplace interactions treated as fault-finding exercises • Needs to know exactly what staff are doing every minute of the day
Passive aggression	• Agrees to take action but later negates this • If people persist in raising issues, will ignore them, not even greeting them

Table 7.1: Types of toxic culture behaviour in the workplace

[43] Webster et al, 2016

Part 2 – Relationship challenges at work

> **Activity 7.5: Reflecting on the seriousness of boss behaviour**
> 1. Have you experienced any of the behaviour listed in Table 7.1? What happened?
> 2. How often did they occur and how did they make you feel?
> 3. Have you witnessed any such behaviour (as listed in Table 7.1) towards one of your colleagues? What happened?
> 4. How did the recipient react?
> 5. In light of the above, and your other reflections in this section, how serious do you regard your challenges with your boss?

Step 3: Engage and Tackle
Having carried out Step 1, Attend and Discern, and Step 2, Think and Reflect, with regard to your relationship with your boss, gathering your thoughts and perspectives, the next step is to engage in ways of addressing the situation.

Wherever possible, it's best to start by talking with your boss about your concerns. However, some bosses may be very closed to this. If that is the case, we suggest three steps you could take to tackle the issue(s).

Seek support
One important step is to seek support, partly to help manage your emotional reactions and partly to receive some advice. Talking with family and friends can provide important and necessary emotional support. Trusted colleagues may also fulfil this role, but if they also have the same line manager, there could be a risk of inappropriate gossiping and breaches of confidentiality. Relaxation techniques can be useful for reducing stress and anxiety. (See Chapter 10 for more detailed suggestions on this.)

A more senior or more experienced professional can be particularly helpful in providing mentoring support. For example, Jingli (Case Study 7.3) contacted her former supervisor at a different organisation and was able to talk through her concerns and experiences at length with this person. On the one hand, this helped her emotionally; on the other, she obtained some helpful advice, such as on ways of interacting with her line manager and on considering things from her line manager's perspective. HR personnel are usually in the best position to give contractual advice.

Seek alignment
If at all possible, it is good to seek alignment with your line manager and ideally to work together on issues. Activity 7.1 above provides some guidelines on working style issues that you or both of you could work on.

Nevertheless, not all bosses will be open to this and, as mentioned previously, it is usually wise to assume that you will be the one who needs to adapt more to your line manager than vice versa. This can be uncomfortable as it may mean moving outside your comfort zone and acting in unfamiliar ways. It is uncomfortable because this kind of adjustment can activate two of your personal GAAFFE Triggers: your Face and your sense of Fairness.

- Changing your working style may be difficult and may undermine your self-confidence in your ability to perform in the way your manager wants. This threat to your competence is typically face-threatening and thus activates the GAAFFE Trigger of Face.
- Moreover, any need to change can activate another Trigger: the GAAFFE Trigger of Fairness. This is because one common reaction to personal change is resentment – 'Why do I have to change and not my line manager? It's not fair!'

When this happens, it is important to work through your reactions and seek ways of resolving them. For Jingli (Case Study 7.3), she found it difficult to negotiate in any way at all with her line manager, so when her manager gave her one task after another, she didn't respond at all. For instance, she didn't even comment politely that it seemed rather a lot to do, as she felt that would be disrespectful. Instead, she just wrote down all of the tasks and accepted (at least outwardly) her manager's instructions. In talking with her former supervisor, she realised she needed to change over this but didn't know how to do it. How could she negotiate with her manager in a polite and respectful manner? She wasn't sure and so she and her former supervisor talked through ways of achieving this. For instance, they agreed that she could ask her line manager to prioritise the tasks she was giving her, in case she couldn't get through them all in the time allowed. Later, when she had begun getting used to discussing the tasks with her manager, she could say more explicitly that she felt the tasks were too many – but not until she had built up less explicit negotiation strategies.

Building up confidence and competence in changing behaviour takes time and needs to be worked on step by step, gradually stretching closer and closer to the manager's preferred and desired working style. It is important to understand and accept that this is a process that does not happen overnight. This is needed in order to avoid self-blame, disappointment and resentment.

In terms of resentment and the GAAFFE Trigger of Fairness, it is helpful to try and reframe the situation; for example, to see it as an opportunity for gaining new skills and to keep that goal in mind while adjusting to a different style or set of requirements. (See Chapter 10 for more information on reframing.)

Seek alternatives

Sometimes, however, no matter how much effort is put into seeking alignment, things don't improve and alternative steps need to be taken. At this point, it is very important to document every incident. The first two steps of the Reaction Management Tool – Attend and Record, Think and Reflect – can provide a helpful framework for this (see Chapter 3).

One possibility is to submit a formal complaint, but many people find that this does not help significantly and in fact may even make matters worse. Often the situation is ignored by senior management and/or HR don't take any meaningful steps to address it. The boss may then react by being even more difficult.

Another possibility is to resign – to find another job or to take a redundancy package (if one is available). Obviously, this entails weighing up the pros and cons and (normally) having alternatives available. Jingli (Case Study 7.3) did this by discussing her options with her former supervisor. By doing this she was able to clarify for herself that she likes several aspects of her job so much that she would prefer to continue seeking ways of aligning with her boss's style of management.

Another way of seeking alternatives is to find some kind of workaround, such as bypassing the boss. This is not always feasible, but one research study[44] found that several interviewees used this strategy. One person, for instance, commented as follows:

The section in which I worked tended to work around the person, forming our own informal work groups to solve problems and make the work happen.

Case Study 7.4 illustrates how a medical safety officer, Raymond, was able to find a workaround to overcome the challenge of an uncooperative boss.

> **Case Study 7.4: Finding a workaround**
> Raymond works as a medical safety officer in a large hospital in the UK. He doesn't get on well with his line manager, Richard, who barely communicates with him. Richard is planning to retire before too long and mainly wants a quiet life during his last years of work.
>
> One of Raymond's roles is to investigate unusual deaths and to explore whether there are any unexpected patterns that should be looked into further. For this, he needs speedy access to ward-level records of deaths, which are provided by the relevant consultants. Unfortunately, for quite a while the consultants have been too busy to complete the necessary forms – even though they are allocated work time to do this. So, Raymond asked his line manager, Richard, for support in obtaining them by talking with the consultants. However, Raymond's manager was very unhelpful and refused to do anything to help – he is friends with many of the consultants and didn't want to upset them.
>
> Raymond has faced numerous challenges like this with Richard – sometimes he sounds friendly but does nothing; on other occasions he is actively obstructive. However, knowing that Richard is likely to

[44] Webster et al, 2016

Part 2 – Relationship challenges at work

retire soon, Raymond has decided to 'wait it out' and not try to look for another job. He therefore tried to find a workaround for obtaining the data he needs for this aspect of his job. He commented as follows:

I enjoy the challenge of solving a puzzle, of finding my way round things. In this case, I built relationships with administrative staff in different parts of the hospital who keep their own records on deaths. It has taken me a year to find a way round this particular problem, but now I've almost solved it!

Reflect
1. Explain the situation that Raymond faced.
2. If you had been advising him, what would you have recommended?
3. What was your reaction to his workaround?

It might seem strange – or inappropriate – to suggest finding a workaround or resigning from a post for relationship reasons, when the focus of this book is on 'making relationships work'. However, realistically it is important to recognise that, despite every effort, sometimes some working relationships cannot be improved significantly. Most relationships require effort from both parties. So, for wellbeing reasons, it is best to accept the unfortunate situation and find the most suitable resolution for the situation at hand.

Nevertheless, finding solutions is important, so we end this chapter with a further reflection activity.

Activity 7.6: Reflecting on your options and strategies
If you are currently experiencing problems with your boss, consider the following questions. Or if everything is fine now, think of a situation in the past when you faced such problems.

1. What steps could you take/did you take to obtain support?
2. How, and to what extent, could you/did you try to seek alignment with your boss? What aspects could you/did you focus on?
3. What alternatives could you/did you seek? How acceptable do you think they are or could be?

If you have a positive relationship with your boss:
4. What can you learn from your current relationship with your boss that you could apply to interactions with your direct reports, either now or in the future?

7.5 Key takeaways

- This chapter has focused on the manager–direct report relationship, taking the perspective of direct reports.
- Direct reports can face a range of challenges in interacting with their bosses. These can include lack of attention to personal or professional goals, too much or too little direction, and problems of unethical behaviour, such as bullying.
- The manager–direct report relationship is intrinsically unequal, with the manager having the power to control many positive and negative outcomes. This has a major impact on the level of psychological safety that the direct report experiences.
- The Upward Management Tool identifies three key steps for addressing these issues:
  o Step 1, Attend and Discern, helps direct reports to discern how far their working styles are aligned with those of their line manager and to identify what types of challenges they have in working together.
  o Step 2, Think and Reflect, encourages direct reports to reflect on their reactions to the challenges of working with their line manager, their attitudinal alignment with their manager, and the seriousness of the challenges they are experiencing.
  o Step 3, Engage and Tackle, explains the need to take steps to address the issues that have emerged. These include seeking support, seeking alignment, and seeking alternatives.

A template for using the Upward Management Tool, with steps and prompts, is given in Chapter 14.

Part 2 – Relationship challenges at work

Chapter 8: Exercised by leadership?
How to manage supportively and bravely

8.1　Introduction

In this chapter we continue our focus on handling the direct report– leader/manager relationship. In Chapter 7 we looked at it from the direct report perspective; in this chapter we consider it from the boss/manager's perspective. In both cases, we encourage each to try to look at things from the other's point of view, in addition to their own.

It is widely argued that relationships are key to leaders' success. For instance, a Forbes Council Member maintains that in leadership, relationships matter most. He explains it like this:

> Without relationship, there is no trust. Without relationship, there is no extra effort. Day after day, people do not come to work for a time clock. They come to work for a person. And for them to give anything other than the minimum, they must have relationships with that person. … Let me clarify: I am not an advocate of being best friends with those on the same payroll, and especially not with those who work for you. However, as managers or leaders, if we want to have productive employees, we need to make an effort to build relationships with them.[45]

This makes it very clear that good relationships with the people who work for them are vital to leaders. As with all relationship management, this can be challenging, especially since leaders face numerous demands. However, much of the initiative and responsibility lies with them, since they typically have more power than their direct reports. This means that leaders play a key role in influencing the workplace culture, including the promotion of psychological safety.

In this chapter, we start by considering some of the challenges that leaders often face. We then explain the tool we recommend, the Supportive Leadership Tool: Think and Reflect, Engage and Connect, Engage and Balance. The first step is designed to enhance your self-awareness as a leader; the second and third steps provide you with some valuable strategies for managing supportively and bravely. We use the term 'brave' because 'doing leadership' can be hard and requires courageous decisions and actions.

8.2　Challenges to providing supportive and brave leadership

Leaders face a wide range of challenges that can affect how well they can provide supportive and brave leadership to others. Some of these are external to them (organisational and societal changes) while others are internal (issues that challenge

---
[45] Molinario, 2018

Part 2 – Relationship challenges at work

their comfort zones and leadership skills). In this section we explore several of those challenges.

8.2.1 The skills needed for the demands of leadership

A position of leadership can be both exciting and daunting. If it results from a promotion, it can feel like a successful step up the promotion ladder and a just reward for previous hard work. Yet it typically requires a wide range of skills and ongoing adjustments to new and changing situations.

Table 8.1 lists the skills that are particularly relevant to the management of people and suggests some potential links with the GAAFFE Triggers – i.e., behaviour that can trigger a rapport reaction when handled either noticeably badly or noticeably well.

Management skills and work values	Potential links with GAAFFE Triggers
Delegation	Autonomy-control
Performance management	Autonomy-control, Goals
Coaching and feedback	Attention, Face, Goals
Rewards and motivation	Fairness, Face
Communication and climate setting	Attention, Ethicality
Relationship building – up, down, sideways – for the unit's benefit	Attention, Face
Fostering the success of direct reports	Attention, Goals
Self as manager	Face
Visible integrity	Ethicality

Table 8.1: People-management skills and values for managers and their potential links with the GAAFFE triggers[46]

This is quite a long list of requirements of people managers, and since they all can be linked in various ways to the GAAFFE Triggers, any mishandling of them can easily trigger a negative reaction in the direct report.

Let us take delegation as an example. This often means letting go of doing things that the manager has previously handled personally and, instead, passing over the responsibility to another person. If that person has problems performing well, it is very tempting to micromanage or simply do the work yourself. This is not good, partly because it deprives others of the opportunity to learn and grow, and partly because it will overburden the manager with too much work. Key GAAFFE Triggers here are Autonomy in association with Goals. The temptation is for the

[46] Derived from Charan et al., 2011

Part 2 – Relationship challenges at work

leader to use too much control and not give enough autonomy, for the sake of achieving the project goal. However, when doing this, the leader is overlooking another important goal for leaders – developing the skills of their direct reports and giving them the feedback and support to perform the job well themselves.

Let us take rewards and motivation as a second example. Rewards, such as bonuses, can be motivating for direct reports, enhancing their sense of competence and professional identity; in other words, they support the person's Face needs. On the other hand, if any of the rewards are perceived to be unfair, such as if they are allocated to the manager's friends or ingroup (maybe their previous close colleagues), this will trigger a negative reaction because of the Fairness GAAFFE trigger. Motivating direct reports is also associated with engagement and connection; in other words, with the need to handle well the GAAFFE trigger of Attention.

We pointed out in the previous chapter that Goals, Autonomy and Ethicality were three of the GAAFFE Triggers that a noticeable proportion of direct reports rated their managers as not handling well. In that survey we were also interested in finding out how confident leaders felt about handling each of the GAAFFE Triggers. Interestingly, more than half of them rated each of the triggers as not challenging, although a minority rated Goals, Autonomy, Ethicality and Fairness as somewhat challenging to handle. In other words, there was a certain amount of correspondence between managers and direct reports in their perceived competence in handling the GAAFFE Triggers, but not a huge amount. This draws attention to the importance of self-awareness in assessing one's own skills and performance.

8.2.2 The identity challenge of new responsibilities

When people take up new leadership responsibilities, this can often challenge their sense of self-identity. Their new responsibilities can give rise to nervousness, worry, and imposter syndrome thoughts, as the following quote from a new leader[47] illustrates:

When you first go into a managing role, you are quite nervous by the whole process of leading people and think 'I am not going to be very good at this'. ... It is doing something that I have never done before; it feels quite daunting because it will be very obvious whether you have done a good job.

As can be seen from this quote, the individual experienced self-doubt about their competence to fulfil their roles well.

Another challenge can come from their 'sandwich status'. Leaders can often be put under pressure from senior management to achieve higher performance targets, yet they may feel reluctant to impose these targets on their people for achievability and wellbeing reasons. As a result, they can feel caught in the middle between the demands of senior management and the needs of their staff. In such

---

[47] A female logistics leader, 32 years old, cited by Hay, 2014, pp. 515-516

cases, personal values are particularly important. Leaders need to think through for themselves how best to navigate such dilemmas, balancing the needs of the organisation with those of their staff. (Case Study 8.1, further below, illustrates this scenario, although it is written from the direct report's perspective.)

8.2.3 The management challenge of remote and hybrid working

When the Covid-19 pandemic forced most office-based work to move online, many managers realised that their work had become much more challenging overnight.

While technology made it possible to meet and discuss work and performance with their teams, many realised that what was missing were the informal, serendipitous meetings that inhabiting the same office made possible. Importantly, even those managers who realised that their team was happy working remotely and independently (and in many cases had already been doing that successfully) still felt that it was important to invest in maintaining connection to enhance wellbeing. This meant finding alternative ways to connect, listen and create community.

Many also became aware that remote working presented them with new control and communication challenges. It is much easier to set clear objectives and expectations, monitor performance, share feedback, and be a role model when working in the same space than it is when interacting on a screen, via phone and even worse via asynchronous electronic messaging. In fact, the two aspects – relationship and task– are intertwined. Each either supports or undermines the other.

8.3 The Supportive Leadership Tool

Having considered these various challenges, we now turn to ways of addressing them via the Supportive Leadership Tool. The three key steps of this tool, which can often usefully be applied cyclically, are: Think and Reflect, Engage and Connect, Engage and Balance. They are represented diagrammatically in Figure 8.1.

> Step 1: Think and Reflect – Reflect on your personal qualities, values, and sources of power and privilege as a leader.
> Step 2: Engage and Connect – Build bonds with your staff in a range of ways.
> Step 3: Engage and Balance – Manage key tensions between autonomy and control, and between directness and indirectness.

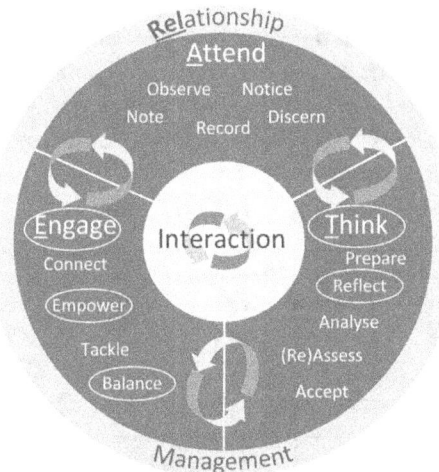

Figure 8.1: The RelATE strategies of the Supportive Leadership Tool

Step 1: Think and Reflect
A well-known research professor[48] who writes on leadership, vulnerability and shame, argues that 'who we are is how we lead'. This means – and as the challenges identified in the previous section suggest – self-awareness is of key importance. One business executive argues for it like this: "Groups of highly self-aware people are roughly twice as effective when it comes to the quality of their decisions, their ability to successfully complete co-ordination tasks and in managing conflict."[49] So, a fundamental starting point for leaders and managers, whatever the stage of their career, is to think through who they are – their sense of identity, their values, and the power that they hold – as well as gain insights into the ways in which their direct reports regard them.

We have already introduced the P: People of TRIPS in previous chapters, along with notions of identity. Here we focus on aspects particularly relevant to leadership; for a broader perspective, please see Chapter 12.

Reflect on your people management strengths
First, consider your leadership qualities for managing people and work through Activity 8.1.

---

[48] Brown, 2018
[49] Dunne, 2021, p. 91

Part 2 – Relationship challenges at work

Activity 8.1: Reflecting on people management strengths
- Rate each of the items below, according to your own opinion.
- Then, whenever possible, choose two or three trusted people you manage (or have previously managed) and ask them to rate you for these characteristics too.
- Finally, share and discuss your respective ratings.

People management strengths	How closely does this describe you? Not closely → Very closely					
a. Caring and considerate	1	2	3	4	5	6
b. Good listener	1	2	3	4	5	6
c. Approachable	1	2	3	4	5	6
d. Accessible/available for consultation	1	2	3	4	5	6
e. Encourages professional development of staff	1	2	3	4	5	6
f. Gives helpful feedback	1	2	3	4	5	6
g. Gives critical feedback sensitively	1	2	3	4	5	6
h. Explains things clearly	1	2	3	4	5	6
i. Gives an appropriate amount of guidance	1	2	3	4	5	6
j. Delegates tasks well	1	2	3	4	5	6
k. Consults before making decisions	1	2	3	4	5	6
l. Treats staff fairly	1	2	3	4	5	6
m. Treats staff respectfully	1	2	3	4	5	6
n. Acts with integrity	1	2	3	4	5	6

1. What do you regard as your top five strengths?
2. How similar or different are they from the ratings of your trusted people?
3. What do you regard as your least strong characteristics?
4. How similar or different are they from the ratings of your trusted people?
5. What have you learned about your management strengths and weaknesses through this activity?

Part 2 – Relationship challenges at work

Reflect on your leadership values
In addition to reflecting on your people management strengths, it is also important to think about your leadership values and how they compare with the values of your organisation and direct reports. Values are typically regarded as guiding principles in life, and from a leadership perspective they can be seen as guiding principles within the workplace. Some key issues around values include the following:

- The extent to which hierarchy is valued, compared with egalitarianism [HIER];
- The extent to which authority is valued, compared with freedom [AUTH];
- The extent to which regulatory standards are regarded as fixed, or variable according to circumstances [REGS];
- The extent to which traditional values are upheld and promoted, or new principles welcomed [TRAD];
- The extent to which care for self is prioritised over care for others [SELF].

(For additional information on values, see Chapter 13.)

Consider the items listed in Activity 8.2.

Activity 8.2: Reflecting on leadership values

Look at the items below and rate them according to the extent to which you agree with them. If possible, use the same activity with your colleagues and direct reports.

	Strongly Disagree					Strongly Agree
a. Leaders should have special privileges	1	2	3	4	5	6
b. Leaders should consult with staff before making decisions	1	2	3	4	5	6
c. Leaders should be flexible over the implementation of rules and regulations	1	2	3	4	5	6
d. Leaders should ensure contractual agreements are fully implemented	1	2	3	4	5	6
e. Leaders should recruit new staff completely objectively, not on personal recommendations	1	2	3	4	5	6
f. Leaders should allow staff a lot of freedom in carrying out their work	1	2	3	4	5	6

Part 2 – Relationship challenges at work

g. Leaders should prioritise staff welfare over their own personal benefits	1	2	3	4	5	6
h. Leaders should be a role model for others	1	2	3	4	5	6

1. How do each of the items map against the five value issues listed above [HIER, AUTH, REGS, TRAD, SELF]?
2. What do your ratings reveal about your own values?
3. Have you noticed or experienced any differences between your values and those of your organisation? If so, what were the differences?
4. Have you noticed or experienced any differences between your values and those of your direct reports? If so, what were the differences?

5. How do each of the items map against the five value issues listed above [HIER, AUTH, REGS, TRAD, SELF]?
6. What do your ratings reveal about your own values?
7. Have you noticed or experienced any differences between your values and those of your organisation? If so, what are the differences?
8. Have you noticed or experienced any differences between your values and those of your direct reports? If so, what are the differences?

Reflect on your power and privilege

The third important area for leaders to reflect on is their power and privilege: the extent to which they can control or influence the behaviour or reactions of others on the basis of various factors. (For a more detailed discussion of power, see Chapter 12.) This is extremely important because, along with your leadership values, it affects the level of psychological safety you are likely to foster and that direct reports will experience.

Power and privilege can stem from many elements, but they can be broadly divided into three categories, as shown in Table 8.2: demographic features, skills and work experience, and workplace role. Each of these categories has various component elements, examples of which are given in the table.

Part 2 – Relationship challenges at work

Sources of power and privilege	Elements	High power ←――――→ Low power
Demographic- and group identity-based power and privilege	Age	How much power and privilege does this person have on the basis of their age?
	Sex/gender	How much power and privilege does this person have on the basis of their sex/gender?
	Ethnicity/skin colour	How much power and privilege does this person have on the basis of their ethnicity/skin colour?
	Nationality	How much power and privilege does this person have on the basis of their nationality?
	[Other feature; e.g., religion, educational level, neurodiversity]	??
Skills & work experience-based power and privilege	Leadership experience	How much power and privilege does this person have on the basis of the amount of their leadership experience?
	Network of contacts	How much power and privilege does this person have on the basis of the strength of their network of contacts?
	Time in organisation	How much power and privilege does this person have on the basis of their length of time in the organisation?
	Fluency in working language	How much power and privilege does this person have on the basis of their level of fluency in the working language?
	[Other feature]	??
Role-based power and privilege	Power to reward	How much power to reward others does this person have on the basis of their job role?
	Power to punish	How much power to punish others does this person have on the basis of their job role?
	Authority over others	How much legitimate authority over others (e.g., for decision making) does this person have on the basis of their job role?
	Expertise	How much expertise that others want or need does this person have?
	Respect from others	How far do others look up to and emulate this person?

Table 8.2: Indicative factors affecting perceptions and attributions of power

Each of the elements in the table has the possibility of enhancing a person's power and privilege or of limiting it.

This means that it's very important for leaders to reflect on the level of power they have with regard to each of the elements. The more elements that are associated with high power in their working context and that they fulfil, the greater their overall level of power. This in turn will lead to a greater risk of low psychological safety for their direct reports, with them being more likely to defer to their leader and maybe fear them.

How far an element enhances or limits someone's power and privilege will typically depend on the workplace/organisational/societal settings. For example, suppose a leader is a white, British man with high levels of technical expertise and a wide network of contacts. If he is working in a UK organisation, he will probably be perceived as having high power and privilege with respect to each of these elements. However, if this same person starts working for a company in France where the working language is French and his proficiency in French is weak, he will have low power and privilege in relation to this particular element.

Leaders not only need to be sensitive to their own sources of power, but also to the amount of power and privilege that their direct reports and team members have (or don't have). If one or more of the leader's direct reports has low power in many of the elements (e.g., because they are less fluent in the working language and are very young and inexperienced), it will be particularly important for the leader to ensure that their opinions are heard and that they are not disadvantaged by being overlooked or even discriminated against. In terms of handling such challenges in meetings and the need for strategies that promote inclusion, please see Chapter 5, where we deal with it in detail. Interestingly, it is also important not to neglect those with predominantly intermediate power characteristics, as may occur for the middle child in a family.

All this means that it is important for leaders to consider their own relative power and privilege, as well as that of their direct reports. We recommend that you work through Activity 8.3.

Part 2 – Relationship challenges at work

Activity 8.3: Reflecting on power and privilege
First map your own pattern of power by listing in the relevant column each of the features shown in Table 8.2. Then do the same for your key direct reports, or those you're particularly concerned about.

	High power characteristics	Intermediate power characteristics	Low power characteristics
Me – the leader			
Direct report 1			
Direct report 2			
Direct report 3			
Direct report …			

1. What does this reveal about your own power and privilege?
2. What does this reveal about the relative power and privilege of your various direct reports?
3. What are the implications for promoting psychological safety among your staff?

We also recommend that you look (back) at Table 7.1 on types of toxic culture behaviour in the workplace. Reflect, as honestly as possible, whether you have sometimes overstepped your power by engaging in any of those behaviours.

In this section we have encouraged you to reflect on various aspects of your personal self: your people management strengths, the values you hold for the workplace, and your power and privilege in relation to those you lead. The next step is to implement the insights you have drawn by connecting with your team in suitable ways.

Step 2: Engage and Connect
Leaders need collaborators – not just direct reports on an organisational chart, but people who are engaged and motivated to work constructively with them. This requires connection – the effective handling of the horizontal axis of the Interaction Compass (see Figure 1.1). Without this the leader counts as absent – physically absent, psychologically absent, and/or interpersonally absent – all of which are detrimental to staff wellbeing and their productiveness at work. In other words, the focus here is very much on the I: Interaction of the TRIPS framework. We draw attention to three facets of connecting through interaction, all of which need addressing.

Connect through informal interaction opportunities
Connecting with others requires some kind of interaction, whether face-to-face or online. This means thinking through both how frequently you need to allocate catch-ups with specific people or teams, as well as how often you need to be pres-

ent, available, and 'seen' by staff. In other words, it is often beneficial to have both spontaneous opportunities for contact, as well as scheduled ones.

In the previous chapter, we mentioned the problem of absent leaders (e.g., see Case Studies 7.1 and 7.2). Sometimes the leader can be very conscious of being absent, but sometimes it can be more inadvertent. For example, when Helen was a head of department, some people complained 'we never see her' – even though she arrived before 8am and stayed until at least 5:30pm. Although she had many scheduled meetings with individuals in her team, as well as with senior management, the problem was that there were few informal opportunities for others to see her or interact with her. She therefore decided to eat her lunch in the communal kitchen whenever possible, rather than in front of her computer, catching up on emails. She found there were numerous benefits to this. Some staff took the opportunity to discuss work-related matters, but often it was simply an excellent chance to socialise informally and to get to know people better. (See also Chapter 10, Situation Selection.)

This fits in with some of our research data. The following comments come from some leaders working internationally for a British third sector organisation.

> *You know if somebody new arrives in a team, perhaps not every day, but if they're not prepared to come down occasionally and sit down and have lunch, there's a real distancing put in place. [Male British leader, based in Chile]*

> *I told the director that it's better to have lunch with us, not at your desk. I told him immediately. And he follows it because he sits there and chats informally and he finds it very helpful as well. On the other hand, our teaching centre manager still prefers to eat at his desk, and that's how he separates, and people immediately feel that distance and difference. [Female Ukrainian leader, based in Ukraine]*

Some staff (especially those new or less experienced) may be unsure when or whether they can approach a leader about an issue, so these informal opportunities for contact can help overcome such uncertainties.

In contexts of diversity, though, care needs to be taken to interact as equally as possible with different groups – whether work-based groups (e.g., different project teams) or identity-based groups (e.g., different ethnic groups). This is something that one British leader, recently posted to Malaysia, realised she needed to be very conscious of:

> *I need to be mindful, checking up on myself, as to who and how I'm engaging with people across the office, so that without realising it, I'm not seen as talking unequally to, for example, Chinese or Malaysian staff (i.e., talking more to staff from one group than another].*

Part 2 – Relationship challenges at work

When people are working remotely, connecting informally is particularly challenging. Nevertheless, many managers have been very creative in findings effective ways of addressing the issue. One such manager interviewed early in the pandemic said the following:

> *I realised that what would happen organically when we were in the office, when I would meet people in the kitchen or in the corridor and I would ask them how they are, or stop and have a chat about whatever, had now disappeared. And I could not pop into someone's office and check on them and they could not do this with me if they wanted a chat. I recognised that I needed to redesign these moments back in and I had to be intentional in doing so….it would not happen by chance. So I started scheduling catching up meetings with my team, one to ones and team social get-togethers. I also made it clear that my team could do the same with me – no agenda needed.*

A manager of a dispersed IT team in a global company said:

> *I trust my team and I know they work very effectively remotely; we have been doing this for some time, using a range of collaborative tools. However, during the pandemic I felt that it was important that we came together not just to do our work, but also to play. I introduced quiz nights and computer game tournaments. I knew everyone was under a lot of stress, we all operated in an uncertain, scary environment and I felt it was important for us to have fun and laugh and be silly together – it helped create a sort of esprit de corps and help us support each other and get through the tough bits.*

Different strategies may suit different groups of people, but what is clear is that finding opportunities to connect through some form of informal meet-up – in a way that addresses the Attention GAAFFE Trigger – is vital.

Connect through caring
CEO Natalie Williams[50] writes:

> *I don't know what I imagined leadership would be like but … I now realise it has less to do with what my heart is burning with, and a lot more to do with what's on the hearts of others. One of the biggest challenges of leadership – what I am finding the most stretching – is playing my part in helping those around me to thrive.*

In other words, caring about staff is core to the leadership role. On the one hand, it means being empathetic to others' concerns, professional or personal. On the other, it means facilitating and supporting their development. Here we focus on the former.

Caring is not only beneficial for direct reports – it can have significant benefits for the leader too, as Case Study 8.1 illustrates. This case study was reported by

---

[50] Williams, 2023

a business consultant, Madeleine, reflecting on an experience with a leader early in her career.

> **Case Study 8.1: A caring boss**
> *Early in my career I worked for a boss who was extremely caring. She would go to huge lengths to look after her whole team in many ways. She invested time in getting to know us and making sure we were happy and fulfilled in our work. She gave us all a lot of support to develop as professionals, and I personally got to do some wonderful projects with her. Whenever a project had gone well, she made sure we celebrated our success and that we – not her – got the credit. We also had time as a team to relax and have fun together.*
>
> *Interestingly, she actually had a very disorganised manner of working – often re-writing reports and restructuring presentations at the very last minute, initially causing me great stress. But her care and concern for us created such goodwill that when it came to her chaotic style of working, we ended up giving her a lot of leeway. I knew I could trust her, even when she was abrupt in critiquing or even demolishing my work. I knew she 'had my back' and that she was doing the right thing for the team. It helped, of course, that her interventions time and again turned out to be genuine improvements!*
>
> **Reflect**
> 1. How did Madeleine's boss show care for her team?
> 2. What benefits did Madeleine gain from her caring boss?
> 3. What benefits did Madeleine's boss gain from showing her team care?
> 4. If you are a leader, how do you show care for your staff? How might you increase your care, in an appropriate way?

Clearly, Madeleine and her boss both benefited from these caring relationships, and it is important to remember this. However, it is also important to bear in mind that what counts as an appropriate amount and type of care can be interpreted differently by different people. This relates closely to the GAAFFE Trigger of Attention. Leaders have to balance the amount of attention they give to each member of staff (not too much and not too little), and also be sensitive to the extent to which each person wishes or does not wish to share anything about their personal lives. This requires appropriate flexing, in line with individual needs and preferences.

Connect through openness to feedback
We mentioned in Step 1: Think and Reflect, the value of considering how staff perceive their leader's management of rapport. Often 365-degree feedback mech-

Part 2 – Relationship challenges at work

anisms are used to obtain feedback, but a more interpersonal approach can (also) be very helpful. Leadership expert, Brené Brown refers to this as 'rumbling' – to discuss or talk through an issue with an open heart and mind even though it makes us feel uncertain and vulnerable.

Criticism or negative feedback is, of course, a face-threat and so can trigger a rapport reaction. However, if we can face up to it with courage, realising that the aim is to 'serve the work and each other, not our egos'[51], it can be extremely helpful for enhancing connection and building trust. Case Study 8.2 reports a published example.

Case Study 8.2: Reacting to critical feedback[52]
My team asked if we could meet for an hour. When I (Brené) realized there was no agenda, I got that sinking 'what now' feeling. Chaz cut right to the chase. "We keep setting unrealistic timelines, working frantically to meet them, failing, setting new timelines, and still not meeting them. It's keeping us in constant chaos and people are burning out. When you set a timeline and we push back because we know its unattainable, you get so insistent that we stop pushing. It's not working. You have a lot of strengths but you're not good at estimating time, and we need to find a new process that works for all of us."
I looked at my team and said, "Thank you for trusting me enough to tell me this. It's not the first or even hundredth time I've heard this feedback about my sucky time estimation skills. I'm going to work on it. I'm going to get better."
I could tell they were a little disappointed in my response. I took a deep breath and said "Tell me more about how this plays out for y'all. I want to understand." I'm glad I asked. I needed to hear what they had to say, and they needed to hear how frustrating, demoralizing, and unproductive [my behaviour was]. ...It was painful and uncomfortable. After listening, I thanked them for their courage and honesty and promised again that I would think about it. I asked if we could circle back the next day.

Reflect
1. How do you think Brené felt when hearing the feedback from her team?
2. How do you think you would feel in that situation?
3. Why do you think Brené's team were disappointed with her first response?
4. Why was her second response more fruitful?
5. Why did she ask to 'circle back' the next day?

---

[51] Brown, 2018, p. 10
[52] Brown, 2018, pp. 45-46

Brené goes on to explain that she went home to work through in her own mind the issue that her team had raised. She realised that a major factor influencing her unrealistic timelines was fear – fear that someone else would think of the idea, fear that they wouldn't keep up with the competition – and that she needed to face up to this. When they discussed the issue again the next day, they agreed that they'd work together on estimating timelines and due dates.

Several important points emerge from this example:

- Hearing critical feedback from people who work for you can be very painful;
- Encouraging people to explain how they are affected makes the need for adjustment clearer;
- Taking time to reflect is helpful, rather than trying to talk it through fully on the spot;
- All these steps help build connection and a more fruitful working relationship.

Brené, though, has this word of warning: "If we shield ourselves from all feedback, we stop growing. If we engage with all feedback, regardless of the quality and intention, it hurts too much, and we will ultimately armor up by pretending it doesn't hurt." Clearly, balance is needed.

The notion of balance is actually the third step of the Supportive Leadership Tool and we turn to that now.

Step 3: Engage and Balance
Much of life is about achieving an appropriate balance between too much and too little of something, and this applies as much to managing rapport in leadership as to other areas of life. Here we explore two continua that leaders particularly need to balance: autonomy–control and directness–indirectness. These are the same two continua that we noted in Chapter 6.

Balancing autonomy–control
As mentioned previously, the autonomy–control continuum is one of our GAAFFE Triggers, as well as one of the axes of the Interaction Compass. The question here is: How much autonomy or control do staff need in order to perform well? To form a judgement on this, and achieve a suitable balance, several of the TRIPS elements need considering, especially P: People, S: Setting, and E: Ethicality.

Amount of direction: People's roles and level of experience
When a subordinate is new and junior, they are likely to need quite a lot of direction. Consider the following feedback comment from a male undergraduate who spent a year as an intern:

Part 2 – Relationship challenges at work

You have to keep on going to see them to check your understanding. In terms of the feedback I received at the end of the year it was that I needed to take more responsibility or to act on my own initiative. I think to a large extent that was an unfair piece of feedback.

In this particular case, the intern felt he needed more explanation and guidance; his leader (or responsible contact), on the other hand, felt he needed to act with greater autonomy. It's a pity that neither party were able to address the issue during the year. For the intern, it led to a sense of unfairness (the Fairness GAAFFE Trigger was activated), and it's likely that the leader was dissatisfied with the intern, perhaps regarding him as too much of a burden to manage.

The opposite can occur when a staff member is promoted to manager. As we noted near the beginning of the chapter, delegation can be a common problem among newly promoted managers. Letting go of things that you have previously handled personally and passing over the responsibility to another person, can be very difficult, especially if that person has problems performing the task well. In these circumstances, and as we noted above, it can be very tempting simply to do the work yourself, for the sake of achieving the project goal. This is not good for two reasons. On the one hand, it will overburden the new manager with too much work. On the other, it overlooks another important goal for leaders – developing the skills of their direct reports and giving them the feedback and support to perform the job well themselves. This in itself raises another autonomy–control dilemma – how closely to monitor the subordinate's performance, to be able to give constructive feedback while avoiding micromanagement.

Amount of direction and cultural expectations
Moving to a very different leadership setting, such as a different organisation or different country, where the cultural norms and values are very different, can pose further challenges around the handling of autonomy–control. Case Study 8.3 illustrates this. It concerns a German manager, Jürgen, who took up a new leadership role in Istanbul, Turkey.

Case Study 8.3: Leading in unfamiliar cultural contexts[53]
Jürgen had a very good track record of operating in senior roles in different international organisations and he was delighted when he was sent to Istanbul to establish a start-up operation. He realised that managing a mainly young local workforce could present some cultural adjustments, but he was confident in his ability to succeed and felt the new job offered an excellent opportunity for his own professional development.

However, he soon ran into difficulties. He was used to delegating responsibility – to giving people a task and letting them to complete it

---
[53] Spencer-Oatey et al., 2022, p. 149

Part 2 – Relationship challenges at work

with minimal intervention. He explained it like this: *"I am naturally a very egalitarian leader. I believe in personal responsibility, giving people a task and trusting them to get on with it. But here I have found that I cannot do this. It is different; people are used to this 'father culture' where they expect you to know best. You give someone a task and then you have to follow up and check all the time or it won't get done"*. He tried to adjust, but says he felt uncomfortable, inauthentic as a leader, that he felt like an actor.

Reflect
1. Describe Jürgen's challenges and his reactions in your own words.
2. Why do you think Jürgen's experience of delegating was 'not working' in his new job context?
3. What advice would you give Jürgen?

This case study draws attention to the impact of S: Setting, in that there can be different cultural expectations (organisational and sometimes national) regarding the role responsibilities of a 'good leader'. In settings where great importance is attached to hierarchy, stronger direction and control is often expected, and failure to give it can be seen as a sign of weakness.

Having to change significantly and flex more easily on the autonomy–control continuum can affect people's sense of identity, and especially challenge their sense of authenticity, as Jürgen mentions. In such situations, it can be helpful to think of the Goals you are trying to achieve and realise that expanding your skill set to include flexing on the autonomy–control continuum can help you achieve them.

Amount of autonomy and remote or hybrid working

Achieving an appropriate amount of control can be particularly difficult when staff are working remotely or when decisions need to be made about levels of working from home. In terms of the autonomy–control continuum, how far managers accept and feel comfortable with a large amount of working from home may be linked (to a certain extent) to their attitudes towards this axis. Those with a stronger sense of personal power (see Chapter 12) may feel the need to retain greater control.

When staff are working fully remotely (e.g., when working in a different country), handling appropriate levels of both connection (see Step 2) and autonomy–control, can be particularly challenging. Consider Case Study 8.4, which was narrated by a young professional, Anna, who was sent on a secondment to a different country early in her career.

Part 2 – Relationship challenges at work

Case Study 8.4: Working remotely – connection and control
I liked my manager and respected him hugely. He had recruited me personally and we got on very well right from the word go. In many ways we had very similar ways of thinking and working and it was very enjoyable working in projects with him. He was approachable, fair, egalitarian, and extremely intelligent, so working with him was always stimulating and challenging and very rewarding. He was well organised and expected the same from us. I enjoyed being given responsibility and clarity. I responded well and it was all going very well while I was working in the same office as him. Then I got an oversees assignment and everything went downhill.

While we were used to having regular stimulating discussions around client requirements when working on a number of client projects, all that simply stopped. Our weekly phone calls ended up being little else than task reports and financial updates and became shorter and shorter. I felt I had been abandoned and I later found that he felt that I had lost interest in anything else and had become a native of the client team, for which somehow he blamed me.

This went on for months, until, towards the end of my secondment, I had an 'urgent' call from my boss. He sounded very stressed and said to me he needed to talk to me about my targets for next year. I said, "Can't we wait until I come back to discuss these? There is so much we need to touch base on first." He said "No, it can't wait. I have already agreed my targets with my boss, so I have to give you yours." So, there wasn't even going to be a discussion! I was going to be given my targets! That made me angry and put me on the defensive even before he told me what the target was. So, when he came up with a number that was double what my previous year's target, I almost put the phone down, I could not believe it!

"You can't possibly be serious – you can't impose this on me, surely we have to discuss it". "I'm sorry there is no room for discussion, I'm afraid. Everyone has to pull their socks up!".

There was very little that I could say after that. I don't remember how the conversation ended. I do remember that I was so terribly upset that I decided there and then to hand in my resignation, which I did upon my return.

The interesting thing is that I had the highest professional regard for my manager, and I had really enjoyed working with him in the past. Yet it took one (very) poorly managed remote conversation, preceded by increasing lack of connection, to destroy all that!

Part 2 – Relationship challenges at work

> **Reflect**
> 1. Why do you think the manager imposed the new target on Anna without discussion?
> 2. Why do you think this caused such a negative reaction in Anna?
> 3. How would you have reacted if you were in Anna's shoes?
> 4. How would you have handled the situation including the remote conversation about targets if you were Anna's manager?

In this case, Anna's manager did not feel (or realise) that he needed to invest in maintaining the relationship with his direct report while she was working remotely. At the same time he allowed her a relatively high level of autonomy in her work until the point where he very abruptly took all of that away by deciding to enforce new targets without time to listen and discuss.

Amount of control and unacceptable behaviour

Sometimes leaders need to address unacceptable behaviour in the workplace. This could be any of the serious behavioural problems identified in Table 7.1, including bullying and intimidation, sexual exploitation, and discriminatory remarks or behaviour. Here it is clear that the leader needs to operate at the control end of the continuum and deal robustly with the unacceptable behaviour.

Unfortunately, all too often no meaningful action is taken. For instance, one study[54] found that one third of their respondents reported being as distressed by the lack of support received from their organizations as they were by the behaviour to which they were subjected. In line with this, there have been several recent case studies involving well known organisations where problems of (sexual) harassment and abuse have continued for four years or more. In other words, there seems to be a major problem in (an unknown number of) workplaces of failure to deal with seriously problematic behaviour. In terms of autonomy–control and the Interaction Compass, leaders are functioning at the autonomy end, but inappropriately so. As we explain in Chapter 9, each end of the continuum can have positive and negative versions. Here, the lack of control constitutes negligence and a shunning of responsibility.

There are several ways in which leaders may avoid taking necessary action, including:

1. Avoid the issue completely
2. Partially and inadequately deal with the issue
3. Delay doing anything
4. Pass the responsibility to someone else

---

[54] Webster et al., 2016

In 2019 the Bakers, Food and Allied Workers Union in the UK reported that they had received more than 1000 complaints from MacDonald's staff about harassment.[55] Yet in 2023 further allegations revealed that little or nothing had been done. The top management had either avoided the issue completely or procrastinated for a very long time! In November 2023, Alistair Macrow, the chief executive of McDonald's UK & Ireland, was summoned to parliament to face questioning about the issue. Acknowledging that the cases were absolutely horrendous, he also admitted that previously they had simply moved misdemeaning managers to different stores, thereby allowing the problem to continue in another location (i.e., the second of the avoidance strategies listed above).

What then can be done to overcome avoidance? An important starting point is moral conviction: a deep ethical sense that can override the fear that naturally accompanies any realisation of the need to address the issue. This takes us back to the need for self-reflection and clarification of one's own values.

Balancing directness–indirectness in communication
A second important continuum that needs balancing is directness–indirectness in communication. This is used to manage the impact of a message: to minimise the risk of triggering a negative rapport reaction when the message is unwelcome for the other person (e.g., criticism), and to maximise the positive impact when the message is pleasing (e.g., praise).

For leaders, there are two types of situations when it is particularly important to manage directness–indirectness effectively:

- When giving instructions or directives, making requests, or giving advice;
- When giving evaluative and developmental feedback, especially when it is critical.

The former particularly affects the GAAFFE trigger of autonomy–control; the latter affects the GAAFFE trigger of Face.

Giving instructions/advice and making requests

The greater the directness of a message, the clearer it is for the hearer to understand it. Sometimes this is a good thing, such as if a direct report wants to know clearly what they should do. However, on other occasions, it interferes with their desire to decide things for themselves, and any imposition on their freedom of choice may annoy them. Indirectness is a widely used method for addressing this. Unfortunately, this means that there can be a trade-off between two of the GAAFFE Triggers – Goals and Autonomy. Direct wording helps ensure that the direct report understands what to do, yet risks damaging rapport through controlling them more than they want.

---

[55] Woolley, 2023

Part 2 - Relationship challenges at work

Case Study 6.8 illustrated the interpretation problems that can occur when one person's wording is more indirect than the hearer is used to. In that example, Anke genuinely did not realise when Shirley needed the work completed. On other occasions, recipients may not know whether something is an instruction or a piece of advice. For instance, a Chinese team member, working collaboratively on a project with some people in the UK, commented as follows:

> *Sometimes the UK project manager sent some suggestions to us. When we got the suggestions, we usually got nervous and wondered 'must we do it immediately'? or are they commanding us to do this?*[56]

The reverse problem can occur when a leader is more direct than the direct report expects or wants. In such cases, an explicit instruction may cause offence because it comes across as too blunt and controlling.

So, what factors influence people's decision-making on this? The following are all important and need to be born in mind when decided how direct or indirect to be to minimise activating any of the GAAFFE triggers:

- I: Interaction: the extent to which the content of the (leader's) message is potentially annoying or upsetting or objectionable to the other person;
- P: People: the links between people – how equal or unequal, close or distant, they are perceived to be;
- S: Setting: culturally-perceived role responsibilities of the individuals – whether they have the right or obligation to communicate the message;
- S: Setting: cultural norms and expectations (organisational and societal) associated with all the above.

In other words, the more potentially objectionable the message to the other person, the greater the perceived power differential, and the less role-related right they have to give that message, the greater the need for indirectness. Cultural factors can affect people's perceptions of all the above and need to be born in mind.

(For more information on directness–indirectness, see Chapter 11. For more information on each of the above TRIPS factors, see Chapters 11, 12, and 13 respectively.)

Giving critical feedback

Many of the same issues and principles apply to giving negative or critical feedback. Here the trade-off is between the GAAFFE triggers of Goals and Face: too much indirectness may hinder the goal of giving the feedback (i.e., that the person will understand what they need to work on), while too little indirectness may greatly upset them.

---

[56] Spencer-Oatey & Tang, 2007, p. 169

Part 2 – Relationship challenges at work

A middle-aged German manager, Klopfer, commented on this as follows:

In Germany, we typically use strong words when complaining or criticizing in order to make sure the message registers clearly and honestly. Of course, we assume others will do the same. My British boss during a one-on-one "suggested that I think about" doing something differently. So I took his suggestion: I thought about it and decided not to do it. Little did I know that his phrase was supposed to be interpreted as "change your behavior right away or else." And I can tell you I was pretty surprised when my boss called me into his office to chew me out for insubordination.

I learned then and there that I needed to ignore all of the soft words surrounding the message when listening to my British teammates and just analyze the message as if it were given to me raw.[57]

Indirectness can be conveyed in various ways, including through wording an instruction as gentle advice and through the use of hedging words – the 'soft words' that Klopfer refers to.

However, other ways are also possible. For instance, when handling feedback, sequencing and the relative amount of positive and critical feedback can also be really important. In Anglosphere countries, a widely used pattern is the traditional 'feedback sandwich' of positive comments ⟶ critical comments ⟶ positive comments. However, other patterns also exist, as illustrated in Table 8.3, and both cultural and individual factors can influence their acceptability to the recipient, as Case Study 8.5 illustrates.

Type of 'feedback sandwich'	Balance of positive and critical comments
Traditional feedback sandwich	Positive comments – critical comments – positive comments
Weak feedback sandwich	Lots of positive comments, a few critical comments which may be swamped and lost
The untraditional wrap	Positive and critical comments are intertwined
Open-faced feedback sandwich	Lots of critical comments, one or two positive comments either at the beginning or at the end
Paleo diet sandwich	Only critical comments

Table 8.3: Structuring options for giving feedback[58]

---

[57] Meyer, 2014, p. 68
[58] Based on Molinsky, 2016

Part 2 – Relationship challenges at work

Case Study 8.5: Adjusting feedback styles[59]
Anat Berger was an Israeli consultant working for a professional services firm in the United States. After only a few months on the job, Anat was surprised to learn that her cultural style of giving frank, demanding feedback was intimidating fellow workers and giving her a negative reputation in the firm. In Israel, Anat had always been taught to deliver straightforward feedback. However, in the United States, as Anat quickly learned, people were used to a much softer style – the traditional feedback sandwich, which cushioned the blow and protected a person's face when delivering potentially negative news.
Yet this approach felt disingenuous to Anat – when she used it, she felt evasive and as if she were obscuring the truth. She considered multiple ways to resolve this conflict, and in the end decided to use an 'open faced' sandwich style, giving only one dose of positive feedback at the beginning. Her colleagues felt that this was far less intimidating than before. It was clearly more direct than the typical American style but was still appropriate and effective.

Reflect
1. If you are a leader, what type of feedback style do you prefer using?
2. If you have a line manager, what type of feedback style do they use with you? How do you feel about their style?

Activity 8.4: Giving critical feedback
1. Which of the 'feedback sandwiches' do you use most often? How satisfied do you feel with it?
2. When giving critical feedback, how direct or indirect are you in your wording? What factors influence your choice of wording?
3. How satisfied do you think your staff are with your style of giving feedback? What adjustments or variations could you try?

[59] Molinsky, 2013, pp. 90-91, very slightly adjusted

8.4 Key takeaways

- This chapter has focused on providing supportive and brave leadership in managing colleagues.
- Leaders and managers face many different challenges, including the need for a wide range of skills, challenges to their identities as they take on new and different responsibilities, and the difficulties of managing remote and hybrid working.
- The Supportive Leadership Tool identifies three key steps for addressing these issues:
  o Step 1, Think and Reflect, explains the need to increase self-awareness, especially of the manager's people management strengths and weakness, their leadership values, and their personal power. Gaining insights from others on their perceptions of the manager can help with growth in the accuracy of self-awareness.
  o Step 2, Engage and Connect, explains the importance of building connections with colleagues, creating opportunities for informal contact, demonstrating care for staff, and being open to feedback from others.
  o Step 3, Engage and Balance, explains the need to balance key tensions, especially autonomy–control and directness–indirectness in giving instructions/making requests and in handling critical feedback.

A template for using the Supportive Leadership Tool, with steps and prompts, is given in Chapter 14.

Part 3

THE TRIPS RAPPORT MANAGEMENT FRAMEWORK

Part 3 – The TRIPS Rapport Management Framework

Introduction to Part 3

In Part 3 of the book, we provide more detail on each of the TRIPS elements – one chapter on each element.

The aim of this part is to:

- Provide a more detailed account of the component elements of the TRIPS framework;
- Include additional relevant information on topics and issues mentioned in Part 2;
- Explain links with existing academic research;
- Provide references for further study and follow-up reading, if desired.

Part 3 – The TRIPS Rapport Management Framework

Chapter 9: Triggers:
Understanding what undermines or enhances rapport

9.1 Introduction

This chapter provides a detailed explanation of the T: Triggers in the TRIPS Rapport Management framework for those who want to delve more deeply into the topic.

'T: Trigger' identifies six key issues that people are particularly sensitive to from a relational perspective and that therefore need to be handled carefully. Without this, there is a risk that rapport will be threatened or undermined. Conversely, if the Triggers are handled well, they can help establish and promote rapport. In other words, the Triggers function as risks and opportunities – risks to rapport if mishandled but opportunities for enhancing rapport if handled well.

We use the acronym GAAFFE to refer to these potential triggers. They are illustrated in Figure 9.1 and summarised in Table 9.1. In the sections below, we explain each Trigger in turn. It is important to remember, though, that although they are identified as six separate rapport triggers, in reality they are quite closely interconnected. In fact, it is common for concerns about rapport to be triggered by more than one type of sensitivity.

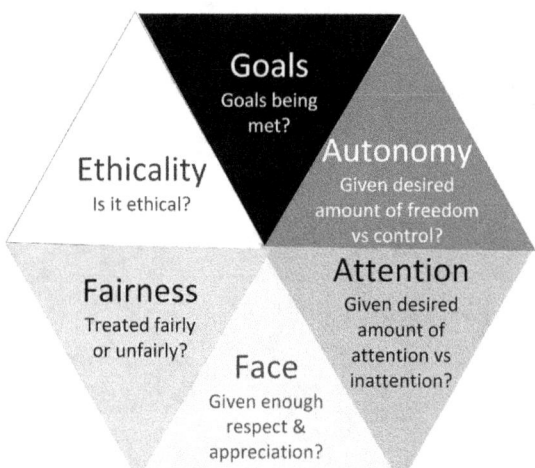

Figure 9.1: The dilemmas associated with the GAAFFE Triggers

Rapport Triggers	Rapport management dilemma
G: Goals	Are people's goals being met or thwarted, and which people's goals?
A: Autonomy	How much autonomy or direction/control should be given to which people?
A: Attention	How much attention or disregard/inattention should be given to which people?
F: Face	Are people being sufficiently and appropriately respected and appreciated for their skills and qualities?
F: Fairness	Are people being treated fairly, and which people's interpretations of fairness?
E: Ethicality	Are people's behaviour or directives ethical, and which people's interpretations of ethicality?

Table 9.1: The GAAFFE Rapport Triggers

9.2 G – Goals

Goals are an extremely important factor affecting rapport. This is because if someone hinders us or thwarts us in achieving a task-based goal, we typically feel annoyed with them and rapport between us is undermined. Conversely, if we understand another person's goals and take them into account in our dealings with them, they are likely to appreciate this and rapport can be strengthened.

This means that in managing rapport, taking everyone's goals into account is of vital importance. It is quite normal for people's goals to be different; for instance, senior managers may focus on company-related goals (e.g., profit and financial stability) while more junior staff may focus on their personal needs (e.g., getting a pay rise). Sometimes people's respective goals may be compatible, but sometimes not. Either way, to manage rapport well, these differing goals need to be understood and taken into account whenever possible. For instance, in Case Study 3.2, Becky, Paul and Jane each had slightly different goals regarding the installation of the solar panels. Becky was focusing on getting the panels up and running as soon as possible to help reduce the very high utility bills. Paul and Jane, on the other hand, wanted to maintain good community relations and didn't want to upset them by turning off the electrical supply at an inconvenient time. Becky accepted that their goal needed to be given priority and compromised on hers, realising that in the big scheme of things, the delay was actually quite brief.

Problems arise, of course, when neither party is willing to compromise, as is common in disagreement situations. This requires careful handling, as we explained in Chapter 5 on conflict.

Part 3 – The TRIPS Rapport Management Framework

In intercultural negotiations, understanding people's different goals is particularly crucial. This is because not only may there be differences in people's individual goals, but there may also be significant differences in the goals associated with a particular type of communicative event, such as an initial negotiation meeting (see also Chapter 14 on Settings). Case Study 9.1 illustrates this (Spencer-Oatey et al., 2022, pp. 79-80, derived from Marriott, 1990).

> **Case Study 9.1: Expectations of an initial business meeting**
> An Australian businessman, Jim, wanted to sell his cream cheese products to Japan and arranged a meeting with Mr Iguchi, a representative of a Japanese company based in Melbourne. At the meeting, Jim made it clear right from the start that he wanted either to export the cheese to Japan or manufacture it there. He brought samples with him and wanted Mr Iguchi to taste them. If Mr Iguchi was interested in the product, he would continue the discussions and provide more samples to be sent to Japan. On the other hand, if he wasn't interested, no more time need be wasted on the matter. By the end of the meeting, though, Jim wasn't sure whether Mr Iguchi was interested or not, and concluded that this probably meant he was not. He felt frustrated by this, maintaining that Mr Iguchi should have made his intentions clearer.
>
> For Mr Iguchi, on the other hand, the purpose of this first meeting was to learn more about Jim's company and its plans. He asked quite a lot of questions on this, since Jim was not forthcoming on them, and he negatively evaluated Jim afterwards for not pro-actively providing this kind of information. He declined to taste the samples but asked to visit Jim's cheese factory so he could gather more information. His plan was to send as much information as possible back to his head office in Japan and for them to decide whether to continue discussions. He regarded it as not part of his role to make an initial decision.
>
> In separate meetings afterwards with a researcher, they both expressed dissatisfaction with the meeting and each other's behaviour.
>
> **Reflect**
> 1. How did Jim and Mr Iguchi differ in their goals for their initial business meeting?
> 2. What impact did this have?
> 3. How could they have overcome the problem?

In this example, Jim and Mr Iguchi had different goals for their initial meeting, but neither was aware of the other's goals. As a result, when their expectations as to what they would achieve from the meeting were not met, they were each disappointed and dissatisfied with the other. Whenever possible, therefore, it is useful to learn as much as possible about the other person's goals. This is not always easy, because people may not have clarified their own goals and they only become consciously aware of them when they have been breached. Moreover, managers may not feel it appropriate or helpful to share their goals if they are going to be detrimental to their staff (e.g., in the case of restructuring and job losses). Nevertheless, it is always helpful to try and take the likely goals of the other person into account, whether they've been communicated explicitly, anticipated, or inferred from the communication and cultural setting.

Often a distinction is made between task-based goals and relationship-focused goals. Becky, for instance, was focusing on a task-based goal (installation of the solar panels) while Paul and Jane were prioritising relational goals (community relations). Here we can see that the distinction between the two is clear. However, in Case Study 9.1, the distinction is a little more blurred. Jim was very task-focused – he simply wanted to know whether Mr Iguchi was interested in buying his cheese. Mr Iguchi, on the other hand, wanted to learn more about Jim's company – a task-based goal in itself – but with the underlying goal of finding out whether Jim's company was one that they could build a good business relationship with. In other words, Mr Iguchi only wanted to do business (i.e., a task-based goal) with someone whom his company could work well with (i.e., a relationship-focused goal). So, from a rapport management perspective, it is important to take both task-based goals and relationship-focused goals into account. (See also our discussion of values in Chapter 1.)

9.3 A – Autonomy

Another potential threat to rapport is autonomy or freedom from inappropriate control. Generally speaking, we don't like to be controlled by others or imposed on by them; we don't like to be bombarded with instructions or micromanaged. We certainly don't like to be manipulated, coerced, or deceived.

This need for autonomy has been widely referred to in the academic literature. For instance, Brown and Levinson (1987), in their renowned model of politeness, identify freedom from imposition as of central importance for avoiding offence. They argue that every 'competent adult member' has a need for their actions to be 'unimpeded by others' and they identify the following speech functions as risking this to a greater or lesser extent: orders, requests, threats, warnings, dares, remindings, suggestions, and advice.

Alison and Alison (2020) also identify autonomy as one of the 'cornerstones of rapport', explaining it as follows:

Autonomy is an incredibly powerful feature of how we interact with other people. Whether or not we feel someone is trying to control us has a huge influence on our behaviour. Freedom to choose appeals to an instinctive drive within all of us to be in control of our own destiny. (p. 90)

On the other hand, others have questioned whether autonomy is always required and whether functions such as suggestions and advice or even direct instructions are necessarily always problematic. People may sometimes be grateful for the direction and – especially in the workplace – may actually want to be given clear instructions, for example in a crisis situation or when they do not know what to do.

We therefore prefer to treat the Autonomy trigger as a continuum that ranges from self-direction and autonomy at one end to direction and control at the other. This is in line with research in both pragmatics (e.g. Brown & Levinson, 1987) and interpersonal psychology (e.g. see Gurtman, 2020, for an overview) that identify power as one of two key factors influencing what people say and do and how people react to that.

As we briefly explained in Chapter 1, there are two fundamental dimensions of interpersonal interaction: a control dimension and a connection dimension. Psychologists represent these dimensions by two intersecting axes, one vertical and one horizontal, and in the form of a circle. The vertical axis is variously labelled as agency, dominance, or control, and the horizontal axis as affiliation, connection, or communion. In our work, we call the model the Interaction Compass.

In this section we focus on the power and control dimension because this is the one that relates to Autonomy. We consider the distance dimension in the next section when discussing the trigger, Attention.

Employees at all levels need to manage how much control they exhibit in their interactions. This is reflected in the vertical arrow, labelled high control and low control in Figure 9.2. In other words, there can be variation, on the one hand, in how much autonomy people give to others or expect from others, and on the other hand, how much direction they give to others or expect from others.

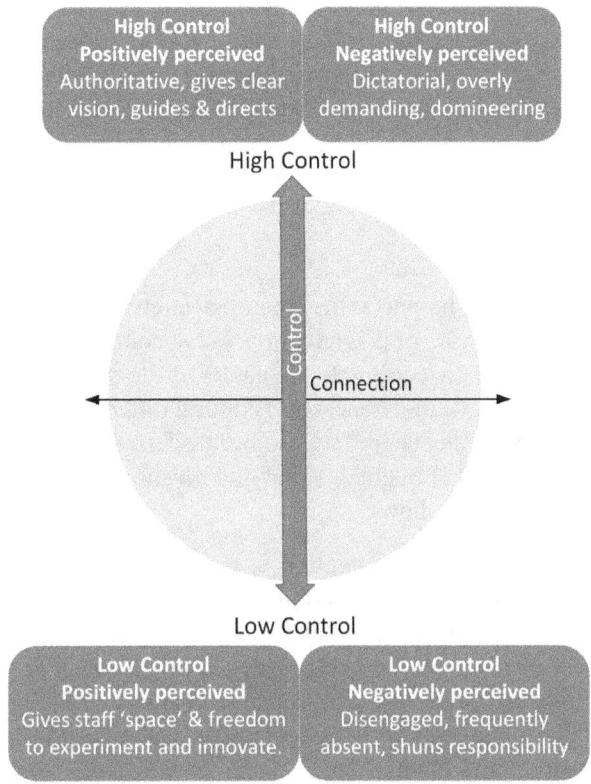

Figure. 9.2: The control dimension in the workplace

In the workplace, it is inevitable that we are subject to a certain amount of control. We are normally in hierarchical relationships of some sort (e.g., line manager–direct report) and those in authority are expected to implement a certain degree of control or direction. Nevertheless, two key issues should be taken into account:

- How much direction or autonomy is regarded as appropriate by the people involved;
- How the direction or autonomy is handled.

Cultural factors (organisational and societal), as well as personal preferences, influence both of these key issues (see Chapter 13, Settings). So, this means that people may perceive high control and low control with different degrees of positivity or negativity. This is shown in Figure 9.2 by the different boxes at each end of the control axis.

Of crucial importance here is that people's expectations and preferences may differ and so what counts as an appropriate amount and type of control can be judged differently by different people. There can be both personal and cultural reasons for this (for example, people's values and attitudes towards hierarchy and power differentials), and in both cases, handling this rapport trigger requires mindfulness and flexibility. This is reflected in the Engage and Balance steps in Chapters 6 and 8. See also Case Studies 7.2 and 7.3 where problems arose when the control axis was not managed in line with employee preferences.

9.4 A – Attention

A third potential threat to rapport is the amount of attention that people show each other and the form or nature of that attention. What counts as a suitable level and type of attention will vary according to the nature of the relationship and will also be influenced by individual preferences and cultural differences.

As with autonomy, this factor has also been referred to in the literature. For example, Fukushima (2015) maintains that attentiveness is a core component of politeness, explaining it as follows:

> Attentiveness means paying attention to the others by ... reading the atmosphere in a situation and anticipating or inferring the other party's feelings, needs and wants through ... verbal and nonverbal cues. ... Manifestation of attentiveness involves offering both material things (such as lending a pen) and non-material things, including actions, such as ... helping someone who is in trouble, ... before or without being asked, taking verbal/nonverbal cues and the situation into account. (p. 271)

Attentiveness also has some links with the pragmatic concept of distance (i.e., how close or distant a relationship is), yet it is not quite the same. It is closer to the second main axis identified in interpersonal psychology and that is variously labelled as proximity, affiliation, and nurturance. Here we call it connection. It refers to the extent to which people connect with and collaborate with others on the one hand and keep their distance on the other.

Once again, from a rapport perspective, there are two key issues to take into account:

- How much attention is needed or wanted by the people involved;
- How appropriately the attention is manifested or handled.

Figure 9.3 illustrates these two issues.

Firstly, employees at all levels need to manage how closely they build or maintain connections with their colleagues. This is reflected in the horizontal arrow, labelled high connection and low connection. In other words, there can be variation in the extent to which people connect with others or expect others to connect with them.

In addition, employees at all levels need to manage the manner in which they handle their connections with others. This is reflected in the two boxes at each of the ends of the connection axis. In other words, high connection can be perceived either positively or negatively, and low connection can similarly be perceived either positively or negatively.

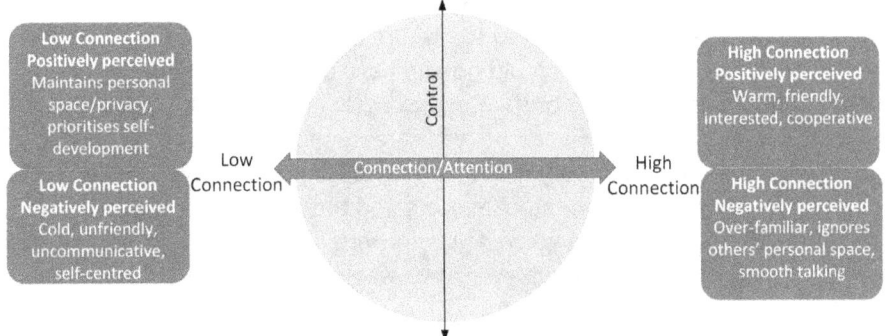

Figure. 9.3: The connection dimension in the workplace

As with autonomy, of crucial importance here is that people's expectations and preferences may differ and so what counts as an appropriate amount and type of connection can be judged differently by different people. There can be both personal and cultural reasons for this. For example, American anthropologist Edward T. Hall (1966) showed how different cultures have very different perceptions of what constitutes 'personal space' which in turn affects people's communicative behaviours with others such as how close they like to be when they talk and how tactile they are/how they use touch to show connection. Whatever the source, it requires mindfulness and flexibility in handling this rapport trigger.

When the attention trigger is handled well, it can enhance rapport, but when it is overlooked or handled badly, rapport can be seriously undermined. For instance, if the attention is too little and an individual is excluded or ignored when they want to be included, this will undermine rapport because it prevents the building of a connection and growth in mutual understanding that one of the parties desires. On the other hand, if an individual receives more attention than they want, and especially if it is of a nature that they dislike, this will undermine rapport. Unwanted sexual attention falls into this category. Case Study 9.2 illustrates differing perceptions around attention.

> **Case Study 9.2: What counts as 'good' attention?**
> Malcolm was a senior executive at a large company. He had a very outgoing personality and loved chatting to anyone he met. He liked to get to know staff personally as well as professionally, and often asked about their families, hobbies, and interests. After the Covid-19 pandemic, many employees worked from home more frequently, coming into the office just once or twice a week. He wanted to be sure his direct reports were OK, so whenever they came in, he would go and have a chat with them.
> Later, he was told that one of the female employees, who only rarely went into the office, had complained he was harassing her. She maintained that he always went to talk with her whenever she went into the office and that he didn't do this with other staff. Malcolm, on the other hand, argued that she didn't see all the times when he spoke with other staff, because she only came into the office once every two weeks.
>
> **Reflect**
> 1. What experiences do you have of 'good' or 'bad' attention at work?
> 2. What happened and how did it make you feel?

9.5 F – Face

Face is a concept that is somewhat difficult to pin down and yet is hugely important in relation to rapport. It is a core concept within pragmatics and communication theory and has been a central tenet of several key theories of relationship management, including Brown and Levinson's (1978) classic model of politeness, Ting-Toomey's (2005) Conflict face negotiation theory, and Spencer-Oatey's (2008) rapport management framework.

Face is concerned with people's sense of worth, dignity, and identity, and is associated with issues such as respect, honour, status, reputation, and competence. In English, a common expression is to 'lose face'; other languages have additional common phrases such as to 'save face', 'gain face', 'give face', or 'threaten face'. We lose face when we feel embarrassed, humiliated, or shamed by the negative comments that someone makes about us, or when they do something that undermines our sense of self-worth. This damages rapport and when it is said or done in public, the risk to rapport is even greater. In contrast, we may gain face if someone compliments us, praises us, or otherwise appreciates what we have said or done. Table 9.2 summarises these key phrases.

	Your face
Threaten face	Someone says or does something, typically publicly, that risks causing you to feel embarrassed, shamed, or humiliated.
Lose face	You feel embarrassed, shamed, or humiliated by something that someone has said about you or done to you, typically that others are aware of.
Gain face	You feel proud, honoured, and respected by something you have achieved or that someone has awarded you with, typically that others are aware of.
Save face	Steps taken, by someone else or yourself, to reduce or eliminate any loss of face.
Give face	Steps taken, by someone else or yourself, to enhance another person's face.

Table 9.2: The meaning of key phrases associated with 'face'

(For an overview of face, see Spencer-Oatey & Kádár, 2021, pp. 127–138.)

What then can threaten our face or cause us to lose face or gain face? It is always to do with our sense of identity – the qualities and affiliations that are important to us, such as the status or competence we feel we have.

So, when someone criticises us for not reaching the standard they want or expect, or simply explains how they want us to improve, this can undermine our sense of self-worth and threaten our face. This is why giving critical feedback to a colleague at work, even when intended to be constructive, can be so difficult – the person may easily feel offended and upset because their face has been threatened. (See, for instance, the discussion on leaders giving feedback in Chapter 8.)

While face is linked with our sense of personal qualities and characteristics, it is also associated with our group identities, such as our gender, ethnic background, or religious affiliation. When people make jokes about one or more of the groups we belong to, often calling it banter, this can be extremely hurtful and damaging. Likewise, when people make assumptions about us on the basis of our group identities, this can be insulting and excluding. For instance, if a British-born black person is asked by a white British person where they 'really come from', this can make them feel alienated. Similarly, if a female leader and male subordinate attend a business function, and the woman is assumed to be the man's secretary, this can be highly offensive. In all these cases, face is threatened and rapport undermined. Case Study 9.3 illustrates this. It was reported to us by a manager whom we interviewed. (See also the discussion of microinsults in Chapter 11.)

Part 3 – The TRIPS Rapport Management Framework

> **Case Study 9.3: Disagreement and face sensitivity**
> *I recently took part in a meeting where we reviewed a new ad that had been put together by our marketing department. Many colleagues praised the ad creators saying how refreshing they found it that the faces and voices on the screen were representative of the truly global nature of our organisation. The old ad was full of white faces, and it was great to see colleagues from across the world represented in the campaign. However, one of our colleagues, Maria, was critical. She said that it was still not good enough because the main protagonists in the film were still the white presenters, while people from other races seemed to be in secondary, supporting roles. Before she could finish her point, another colleague, Steve, interrupted to disagree and say that he still thought the new ad was a great improvement which sent out an inclusive message. Now, we always tend to have robust discussions in our team, so none of us thought much of this interaction at that point. After the event, however, Maria came to me visibly upset. She felt that Steve had seriously undermined her during the meeting and that his interruption was effectively challenging her right to have an opinion, trivialising her alternative, non-white, perspective. "How dare he tell me what and how to think about whether my race is represented fairly or not!". Clearly what for the rest of us was a small point of disagreement for her became a huge issue of face. What struck me in particular was how the way Maria talked; this was not just about her; it became somehow about disrespecting a whole group of people she felt she belonged to.*
>
> **Reflect**
> 1. Why was Maria dissatisfied with the ad? How does that relate to face?
> 2. Why did Maria feel disrespected by the discussion within the team? How does this relate to face?
> 3. Why did Maria refer to disrespecting the group of people she belongs to? How does this relate to face?

Individuals can vary in their sensitivity to face-threats, and hence how easily rapport reactions are triggered. Some people may be more sensitive to one type of face threat than another type. In this case, Maria was particularly sensitive to racial representation issues; somebody else (even with the same racial background) may be less sensitive. In addition, people's level of self-confidence and self-worth can also affect how much face threat they feel. This means that it is not always easy to judge how far another person will feel offended (or not) by a particular comment or action. Nevertheless, it is extremely important to always take it into account.

When we take steps to address and manage people's face sensitivities this is known as facework. Ting-Toomey and Chung (2005) explain it as follows:

> 'Facework' is about the verbal and nonverbal strategies that we use to maintain, defend, or upgrade our own social self-image and attack or defend (or 'save') the social images of others. (p. 268)

In other words, in Table 9.2, 'threaten face' and 'save face' count as facework, in that they refer to actions that can affect face. 'Lose face' and 'gain face' refer to the outcome or consequence of facework or the failure to engage in it.

Many of the tool strategies explained in the chapters in Part 2 of the book, including Engage and Connect, Engage and Empower, and Engage and Balance, are all ways of conducting facework to enhance, manage or save others' face.

9.6 F – Fairness

A fifth rapport Trigger is fairness or equity. Children from an early age are very conscious of this, frequently complaining 'it's not fair'. We all have a strong sense of fairness – that we should not be unduly disadvantaged or mistreated. Any undermining of fairness can damage rapport with the person responsible.

Psychologists have drawn a distinction between 'distributive justice' and 'procedural justice'. Distributive justice refers to the fair sharing of rewards and often entails one person comparing their situation with someone else's. Case Study 9.4a illustrates this. The Kenyan interviewee compares the pay of Chinese and Kenyans and regards it as unfair that a Kenyan in a more senior role (i.e., himself) should be paid less than a lower-ranked Chinese employee. (See also the example of Christoph in Activity 2.1.)

Procedural justice refers to the fairness of the procedures for deciding how the rewards are allocated. Here, any comparative judgement is linked with 'typical practice' which comes to be regarded as 'the right way of doing things'. Case Study 9.4b illustrates this. The Chinese manager is not used to paying staff for overtime work – he maintains that Chinese employees regard it as normal to work overtime without extra pay, and so objects to Kenyan employees expecting it.

Both these case studies come from a study of Chinese-Kenyan workplace relationships and were reported by the interviewees as issues that undermined rapport between them (Tian, 2023).

> **Case Study 9.4: Perceptions of fairness in Chinese companies in Kenya**
> These two case studies come from interview data collected in Chinese companies located in Kenya and with Kenyan employees:

a: Differential salaries

This Kenyan interviewee mentioned that his company operates different pay scales for Kenyans & Chinese, such that a low skilled junior Chinese is paid more than a senior Kenyan. He questioned it as follows:

"If someone is learning from me, if I'm passing my experience to a Chinese person, why is he earning more than me. It doesn't make sense." Kenyan interviewee

b: Overtime pay

This Chinese manager

"Chinese people think that it is normal to work overtime, and it is normal not to get paid overtime, but the local people definitely won't think like this. [They maintain] overtime must be paid for, but the Chinese don't think that way. For example, if a Kenyan driver was supposed to get off work at 6 o'clock, but actually worked till 9 o'clock, they would ask you for overtime pay. But we don't want to pay them." Chinese interviewee

Reflect

1. How fair or unfair would you regard the issues reported in these two case studies? Give reasons for your viewpoints.
2. What issues of unfairness have you experienced at work? How did they make you feel?

Somewhat surprisingly, fairness has rarely been included within pragmatic theorising. An exception is in Spencer-Oatey's (2008) notion of 'equity rights' but few others have included it. In fact, fairness is also closely linked with the notion of reciprocity, which is concerned with maintaining a balance of 'payments'. This aspect has recently been explored and commented on by the pragmatics researchers, Culpeper and Tantucci (2021):

> Reciprocity is fundamental to the way (im)politeness works in interaction yet has not been accorded the attention it deserves. ... we defined it as: a constraint on human interaction such that there is pressure to match the perceived or anticipated (im)politeness of other participants, thereby maintaining a balance of payments. Maintaining reciprocity through politeness matching is what people normally do, ... [it] is the stuff of everyday, routine politeness. ... deviating from reciprocity through mismatching (im)politeness is abnormal and triggers further inferencing. (pp. 161–162)

In other words, if someone speaks to us in a friendly manner, the principle yields some social pressure to respond in a similarly positive way. If someone fails to do this, we are likely to question why. This can apply to the use of language (as was the focus of Culpeper and Tantucci's work), but also to behaviour. For instance, if someone does us a favour or performs some kind of act of kindness towards us, there is an implicit social obligation that we should repay it at some point – usually in the not-too-distant future. If we do not do that, our rapport with the other person may be undermined. (See Chapter 6 for a discussion of this as it relates to the workplace.)

The psychologist, Robert Cialdini (2021), identifies reciprocity as one of seven ways to influence other people. He argues as follows:

> The rule [of reciprocity] requires that one person try to repay, in form, what another person has provided. By obligating the recipient of an act to repayment in the future, the rule allows one individual to give something to another with confidence that it is not being lost. This sense of future obligation within the rule makes possible the development of various kinds of continuing relationships, transactions, and exchanges that are beneficial to society. Consequently, all members of all societies are trained from childhood to abide by the rule or suffer serious social disapproval. (p. 71)

In other words, adhering to the principle of reciprocity is a form of fairness, and if it is breached, it will disturb rapport. On the other hand, the principle of reciprocity also applies to negative behaviour. If someone insults us, there is a natural tendency to insult them back. It is not easy, therefore, to reject the natural tendency towards reciprocity when we've been treated negatively. This may be 'fair', but it doesn't usually help promote rapport with the other person. In these cases, we need to resist the natural tendency.

Fairness, therefore, is another potential threat to rapport that always needs to be managed effectively.

9.7 E – Ethicality

The sixth potential threat to rapport is triggered when other elements are mishandled to a high degree – especially autonomy, attention, face, and/or fairness. In these cases, the breach becomes an ethical matter when it is regarded as serious enough to be legally or morally 'wrong'. In these cases, values also play a critical role.

Consider Case Study 9.5 on an ethical challenge at work.

> **Case Study 9.5: An ethical challenge**
> Charlotte was recruited at mid-management level to a PR agency. Shortly after starting work for the company, she was asked to work on a client account that is very important for the agency (the account is a high income generator), but one that concerns a country with well-known human

rights issues. Her line manager asked her if she had any ethical objections to this work. As a brand new employee, Charlotte didn't feel able to refuse the work – she was afraid that if she declined, this could affect her manager's impression of her. So, she agreed, but since then has been trying to justify to herself why it is OK for her to do this work. She has not told friends about it, lest they criticise her and it affects their relationship.

Reflect
1. How would you feel if you were in Charlotte's position?
2. Have you ever experienced an ethical challenge at work?

In this case, the ethical values at stake were not human rights issues per se (both Charlotte and her boss were agreed about the human rights issues in the country concerned), but rather whether it is right to engage with people or regimes that you disapprove of. Some believe that talking and engaging is the only feasible way of bringing about change; others believe that sanctions and increasing isolation will bring pressure to change. Employees such as Charlotte can be caught in the middle of such debates.

Ethical challenges are particularly difficult to handle when management don't acknowledge the issue or simply ignore it. It can require imagination and tact to find routes that are acceptable to all. Case Study 9.6 illustrates one successful solution. It is reported by Sifa, a female leader in the finance sector in Kenya, who found an amicable resolution to an abuse by people above her in their use of company vehicles (Mutooni et al., 2020).

Case Study 9.6: Managing ethical abuse among seniors at work
Once when I was in charge of administration, people who were senior to me were misusing vehicles, they were abusing their position. It was tricky, because I did not want to confront them, but at the end of the day – during an audit – I would be responsible and held accountable for it. Ultimately, I proposed to senior management the introduction of procedures that would make staff accountable. This was accepted and became the new policy and managed to stop the misuse. I thus managed to solve the situation amicably and without personal confrontation. (p. 245)

When employees are in a more senior role and/or are highly regarded by those in power, it may be easier to take a clear stand. Case Study 9.7 is reported by a Hong Kong bank official who faced quite a lot of opposition from colleagues when he made an ethical decision that could have a negative impact on profit (Spencer-Oatey et al., 2022, p. 182).

> **Case Study 9.7: Clients and money laundering**
> *Some months ago, a client of ours was involved in money laundering. It was a very important client, and the bank wanted us to hush the matter up because we made a lot of money from him. However, I decided to exit the client. The people in China were very upset with me; when my colleagues met me, they literally turned their backs on me. But I knew I had done the right thing; it comes from my faith, I am a committed Christian. I spoke to my boss, and I explained why I did it; my boss was happy. I brought these Chinese bankers together and explained why I had made that decision. They understood; they still disagreed with me, but I never doubted that I did the right thing.*

In this case, it is clear that the bank official held strong values – especially honesty and legality – and he was determined to uphold them. His actions caused relationship problems, but he was able to explain his position clearly, and while his colleagues still disagreed with him, his boss was supportive.

The main responsibility for dealing with ethical dilemmas rests on the leaders. They need to promote integrity at all levels, along with strong ethical values. In addition, they need to foster an atmosphere of psychological safety, so that if problems do occur, people feel able to report the issue and not fear victimisation. Without this, perceived breaches of ethical standards can trigger rapport reactions.

9.8 GAAFFE Priority clashes

So far, we have considered each of the GAAFFE Triggers in turn and implied that rapport issues can be triggered if people's perceptions of them are different; for instance, if people hold different goals or prefer different levels of autonomy or control.

An additional challenge arises when people differ in how much they prioritise one of the GAAFFE triggers over another.

Consider the following two case studies, Case Study 9.8 (a) and (b). They both come from Tian's (2023) project on Chinese–Kenyan relationships in Chinese companies in Kenya. In the first case study the Kenyan manager is insisting on paying all taxes while the Chinese manager wants him to pay only some of the taxes since they are a start-up company. In other words, the Kenyan manager gives priority to Ethicality, while the Chinese manager gives priority to Goals – company success in this case. As a result of their different priorities, the Chinese manager is dissatisfied with the Kenyan manager.

In the second case, the Kenyan company driver experienced a conflict of obedience. His Chinese boss was ordering him to drive on and in normal circumstances he would obey his boss. Yet he did not want to break the law and risk getting a fine or penalty. In other words, there was a clash between ethicality (obeying the law) and autonomy–control (obeying his boss).

> **Case Study 9.8: Priority clashes**
> **a. Should we pay taxes or prioritise company profit?**
> *"He [Kenyan manager] wants everything done according to the laws and regulations of this country. I said, let's take it slowly. We're a small, start-up company – if we pay all the taxes we won't survive. Just pay some of them. But he said we need to pay all the taxes."* Chinese manager.
> **b. Should I obey traffic laws or my boss?**
> *"I was driving my Chinese boss for work purposes when our car was hit by another driver. We both stopped and the other driver admitted he was at fault. We began waiting for the police to come to investigate, as is legally required. However, my manager started shouting at me, insisting that I drive on. The other driver also tried to persuade me to move on. However, I refused to do so, because this is against the law, and I didn't want to get a record for a driving offence. I also couldn't be sure that the other driver would report the incident accurately to the police."* Kenyan company driver

9.9 Summary and follow-up reading

Triggers are issues that have the potential to undermine or enhance rapport. The TRIPS rapport management framework identifies six key triggers, known as the GAAFFE Triggers. This chapter has explained each of the six in turn.

A summary template of the TRIPS T-Triggers is given in Chapter 15, giving questions that are useful for checking and reflection purposes.

For further information, refer to the references mentioned within the chapter. The following are particularly useful.

Spencer-Oatey, H., & Kádár, D. Z. (2021). *Intercultural politeness: Managing relations across cultures.* Cambridge University Press. Chapters 7 and 8 explore several of the key concepts associated with the GAAFFE Triggers, including Face and Ethicality.

Spencer-Oatey, H., Franklin, P., & Lazidou, D. (2022). *Global fitness for global people: How to manage and leverage cultural diversity at work.* Castledown. This book focuses on dealing with cultural diversity at work, and includes several chapters that interface with concepts in this chapter, including Chapter 5 on managing rapport and Chapter 10 on managing ethical challenges.

Part 3 – The TRIPS Rapport Management Framework

Chapter 10: Reactions

Understanding emotional reactions, thinking and evaluative judgements

10.1 Introduction

This chapter provides a detailed explanation of the R: Reactions in the TRIPS Rapport Management framework.

'R' stands for Reactions – the impact that rapport-related triggers can have on those involved in an interaction and ways of managing those reactions. There are two types of reaction: emotional and cognitive.

Emotional reactions concern how we feel (e.g., anger or fear) and any accompanying physiological and nonverbal changes (e.g., sweating, frowning). Cognitive reactions concern our associated thinking and the judgements we may make of the person(s) involved.

Both of these types of reactions – emotional and cognitive – can occur not only during an interaction or immediately after it; it may also occur in advance. This is particularly the case if we anticipate a forthcoming interaction is likely to be difficult and/or if we have previous experience (positive or negative) of interacting with the individuals involved.

In this chapter we explore both types of reaction and start by considering what we mean by emotions and emotional reactions.

10.2 Understanding emotions

Subjectively, we all have a sense of what emotions are and yet the psychologist Brian Parkinson (2019, p. 1) points out that there is still no definitive answer to the question 'what are emotions?' One of the reasons for this is that they can be studied from many different angles, including:

- How emotions are manifested
- How emotional feelings can be classified
- What functions emotions play
- How emotions can be controlled

In terms of the first point, the psychologist James Gross (2015) identifies three key facets to emotions. He explains that they are manifested through the following:

- People's subjective experience of feelings, such as anger or fear
- Physiological changes, such as increased heart rate or sweating
- Non-verbal changes, such as in facial expression and posture

Much attention has been paid to the first facet – how to classify the range of emotions that people experience. In Chapter 3, we presented one way of doing this. Building on classic work by Shaver and his colleagues (1987), we identified two core clusters:

- Positive versus negative feelings
- Groupings of 'basic' or core emotions: love, joy, peace, hate, sadness, fear, anger

We added to this emotional intensity – how strongly or weakly we experience the emotion.

Gaining insights into the ways in which emotions are manifested, as well as how emotional feelings can be conceptualised, is very important for controlling our emotions. Research (e.g. Barrett et al., 2001) has shown that this affects the extent to which individuals can handle negative emotions.

Barrett and her colleagues (2001) found that people differ considerably in the extent to which they differentiate their emotions. Some view them just in terms of degree of pleasantness or unpleasantness; in other words, using just one dimension of variation. Others differentiate their feelings in a much more nuanced way, distinguishing among a variety of negative and positive emotions, as well as their levels of intensity. The researchers found that these latter types of individuals – in other words, those who drew distinctions between different types of emotions and how intensely they experienced them – were able to manage their negative emotions more effectively than those who made less nuanced distinctions. This was especially the case as emotional intensity increased.

This suggests – in line with theorising in emotional intelligence – that people need to build greater 'emotional granularity' if they are to manage their emotions more effectively and thereby manage rapport. One way of doing this is to encourage greater reflection on emotional experiences by regularly using the framework presented in Chapter 3 (Table 3.1). Barrett (2017) suggests another rather surprising one – learning new words!

> You've probably never thought about learning words as a path to greater emotional health, but it follows directly from the neuroscience of construction. Words seed your concepts … people who exhibit higher emotional granularity go to the doctor less frequently, use medication less frequently. … it's what happens when you leverage the porous boundary between the social and the physical.
>
> So, learn as many new words as possible. … Don't be satisfied with 'happy': seek out and use more specific words like 'ecstatic', 'blissful', and 'inspired'. Learn the difference between 'discouraged' and 'dejected' versus generally 'sad'. As you build up the associated concepts, you'll become able to construct your experiences more finely. (p. 181)

Turning now to the functions that emotions play in our lives, early research focused on the role of emotions within the individual, pointing out, for example, that they help us act quickly with minimal conscious awareness. This could include rapid decisions such as whether to flee from danger or whether to attack. More recently, though, greater attention has been paid to the interpersonal function of emotions. For instance, Parkinson (2019) maintains that emotions are particularly important for managing relationships:

> Emotion's special ingredient is its capacity to align and realign people's relations with each other and with objects and events in the shared environment. (p. 2)

This points to the need for all parties in an interaction to manage their own emotional reactions to what is said, done or overlooked, and to be sensitive to the reactions of others. Normally the aim from a rapport perspective is to manage or minimise any negative emotions (ours and/or that of the other person) and to enhance positive ones. This does not necessarily mean, though, that negative emotions should always be avoided; sometimes they need to be faced up to and worked through.

The chapters in Part 2 of the book deal with some of the challenges of handling this well. In this chapter, we consider strategies for managing emotion – known technically by psychologists as 'emotion regulation'. First, though, we consider the issue of displaying emotions.

10.3 Displaying emotional reactions

When one or more of the GAAFFE triggers have been activated and at least one of the people involved has experienced an emotional reaction, this raises the issue as to how far the emotional reaction should be revealed if rapport is to be managed effectively.

Consider Case Study 10.1. The incident is reported by an early career professional, Delia, about a recruitment interview she experienced.

Case Study 10.1 A 'failed' recruitment interview

I was interviewed by the boss of a small business consultancy for a role within her company. She did quite a bit of the talking and did not appear to be interested in what I had to say. She was clearly annoyed if I disagreed with her and at no time did she make any effort to put me at ease or seem curious about the reasons for my disagreements. The whole conversation felt like a battle or a test. She seemed very sure of herself, almost arrogant. She definitely did not warm to me and the feeling was mutual. About 20 minutes into the interview, she brought out a piece of paper and started drawing shapes and colours on it, asking me to say which one I preferred. When I started asking why, and expressed scepticism about the validity of such tests (saying something like "I don't really believe that this will tell you anything very useful about me"), she got visibly angry. She suddenly got up and without saying anything at all walked out of the room. After ten minutes or so she sent someone else in to tell me that the interview had finished and that I had not got the job! No surprise there!

Reflect
1. Which of the GAAFFE triggers gave rise to the reactions that Delia and her interviewer experienced?
2. What emotions does Delia refer to, thinking of both her own emotions and those she attributed to her interviewer?
3. Delia refers to her interviewer as being 'clearly annoyed' and 'visibly angry'. What evidence do you think she might be drawing on to make those inferences?
4. In your view, how acceptable or unacceptable was it for the interviewer to leave the room in the way she did?
5. What evaluative judgements does Delia make of the interviewer?
6. What advice would you give to Delia and her interviewer to help them manage rapport in interviews more effectively?

One of the key emotions reported by Delia is her interviewer's anger. She refers to her as being 'clearly annoyed' and later as being 'visibly angry'. So, this raises two issues:

- How openly should people display their emotions?
- How can we perceive other people's emotions? What signals do we need to pay attention to?

The extent to which people show their emotions can vary across individuals (see Chapter 11 on communication style) but it can also be influenced by the setting (see Chapter 13). For instance, if we're told some bad news at work (e.g., that we didn't get the promotion we were looking for), we may cover up the level of disappointment we show at the time but let it come out in a different situation.

Part of the reason for this is that 'display rules' influence how openly we reveal our emotions. These are behavioural norms that affect whether we modify (or not) the extent to which we show our emotional reactions (Matsumoto, 2009). We may therefore reveal exactly how we feel, or we may:

- Show less than we feel (Deamplification);
- Show more than we feel (Amplification);
- Show nothing (Neutralisation);
- Show another emotion, concealing the real emotion (Masking).

Display rules (like all norms and conventions) can be subject to both personal and cultural variation. The consultancy boss in Case Study 10.1 did not seem to have any reservations about revealing her annoyance – perhaps she felt able to allow that in her own company. However, such overt display would not normally be expected in most similar interview situations and from that perspective, she breached widely accepted professional display rules. By revealing her anger so blatantly, she almost certainly affected the level of rapport between her and Delia.

With the help of the reflection questions in Activity 10.1, think about your own attitude towards revealing emotions, and the extent to which there are display rules in your workplace.

> **Activity 10.1: Reflecting on emotional display**
> Thinking about your workplace:
> 1. How acceptable is it to shout at a colleague in anger? Might you do it? Why/why not?
> 2. How acceptable is it to shout at a subordinate in anger? Might you do it? Why/why not?
> 3. How acceptable is it to cry in a departmental meeting? Might you do it? Why/why not?
> 4. How acceptable is it to cry in front of your boss? Might you do it? Why/why not?
> 5. How acceptable is it to laugh at a colleague when something unexpected happens to them in a meeting? Might you do it? Why/why not?
> 6. How acceptable is it to laugh at your boss when something unexpected happens to them in a meeting? Might you do it? Why/why not?
> 7. If feasible, compare your viewpoints with a colleague. How could you characterise them in terms of display rules?

10.4 Regulating emotional reactions

When the emotions we are experiencing – or that we anticipate experiencing – differ from the ones we want to have or that conflict with the display rules we feel subject to, we usually engage in some kind of 'emotion regulation'. In other words, we try to change our emotional reactions in some way. We may seek to reduce their intensity, reduce their duration, or alter their nature.

This can be particularly important in the workplace when experiencing negative emotions, partly because of the display rules that may apply and partly because of the potential consequences for collaborative working. Two key negative emotions are anger and fear. These often permeate the relationship challenges we experience in the workplace and that we explored in Part 2.

Part 3 - The TRIPS Rapport Management Framework

For instance, in Chapter 4 we considered the challenge of handling disagreement well and noted the importance of managing emotions in order to enhance mutual understanding and achieve creative, synergistic solutions. This is what the consultancy boss in Case Study 10.1 failed to do. She let her feelings become so intense that she left the room – presumably to avoid shouting at Delia. As a result, she not only damaged the relationship with Delia, but also lost an opportunity to learn something from her.

There are five main strategies of emotional regulation (Gross, 2015) and we explain them in turn below.

10.4.1 Situation selection

Situation selection entails "taking actions that make it more (or less) likely that one will be in a situation that one expects will give rise to the desirable (or undesirable) emotions" (Gross, 2015, p. 7). Gross mentions going to see a film or avoiding a disliked colleague as examples.

In the workplace, though, avoiding problematic people or conversations are not always effective strategies, either from a business perspective or for managing rapport. As we considered in Chapter 4, if disagreement is approached positively, it can lead to new insights and synergistic solutions. Avoidance precludes that possibility.

Consultant psychologists, Alison and Alison (2020), comment on this as follows:

> Much of our work currently is tackling what we call 'avoidant practice' within organisations. Avoidant practice is where, by design or circumstance, an organisation attempts to passively or indirectly deal with a situation rather than confront and resolve it directly. You only have to look at recent large-scale organisational scandals to see the problems that avoidant practice can cause. … We don't want to cause upset, so we hesitate and keep quiet, only to regret it later. Part of this is down to avoiding confrontation or conflict and part of it is not feeling confident to deliver what we want to say without it coming out as aggressive or demanding. (p. 73 & p. 74)

So, when managing rapport in the workplace, situation selection needs to be handled purposefully and thoughtfully – not for unhealthy avoidance, but rather for positive reasons. For example, as mentioned in Chapter 8, when Helen was head of department, she consciously chose to eat her lunch in the departmental kitchen (rather than at her desk in front of the computer), so that she could socialise with staff and build a sense of greater connection with them. For line managers, it could mean seeking to ensure that people are allocated to the type of work that suits them best and thus minimises their levels of anxiety.

10.4.2 Situation modification

Situation modification involves "taking actions that directly alter a situation in order to change its emotional impact" (Gross, 2015, p. 8). As examples, Gross mentions filing away a rejection letter so that it's out of view, or (for teachers) introducing a group activity to increase students' interest.

Case Study 10.1 provides another example. When the interviewer left the room, she modified the situation and avoided the danger of shouting at or even abusing the candidate. From that perspective, her strategy was effective, yet it did not leave a positive impression on Delia. Ideally, she should have used a different emotion regulation strategy to cope with her anger (e.g., see Cognitive change below). On the other hand, there may be occasions when it can be helpful to take a break or 'time out', when emotions start running too high in a meeting or conversation.

We can infer from this that neither situation selection nor situation modification are necessarily always effective – they may be, but not in all circumstances. Judgements need to be made as to their suitability.

10.4.3 Attentional deployment

Another type of emotional regulation strategy is 'attentional deployment'. This entails people changing the focus of their attention in a way that influences their emotional reactions. Gross (1998) refers to three possibilities, and we add a fourth, Preparation:

- Distraction – focusing on a non-emotional aspect of the situation;
- Concentration – engaging in an absorbing task that leaves little spare attention for the emotional issue;
- Rumination – focusing on one's feelings and consequences;
- Preparation – focusing on the things under your control.

When emotions are negative, rumination usually makes them worse – intensifying them and extending their duration. Business psychologist and executive coach, Helen Frewin (2021), has some helpful advice here. She points out that if someone lacks confidence, instead of focusing on their fears and uncertainties and all the negatives that might occur (e.g., what will others think? Will I come across as incompetent?), it is important to be outcome-focused and others-focused. This means moving your thinking (i.e., what you're attending to) away from how you are feeling towards what you know and what you want to achieve. She gives the following personal example about an occasion when she was asked to lead a development workshop for senior sales leaders in a business. She was concerned because she had no background in sales. She reports:

> Instead of focusing on all the things I didn't know, or imagined the sales team knew better than I did, I focused on what I did know. I started listing on paper all the knowledge, skills and experience I had that could in any way be relevant to this piece of work. And that meant going beyond sales expertise, because it's my skill in helping people change their behaviour, try new things and discover better ways of working that could be most useful of all. (Frewin, 2021, p. 57)

Her workshop went well but she admits that managing her emotions beforehand was an ongoing battle. Each time she started fearing she didn't know enough or would be asked for her track record in sales, she deliberately turned her attention to non-emotional aspects of the situation – what she wanted to achieve and what value she could bring.

A fourth strategy is preparation – finding out as much information as possible in advance, including preparing for the worst. Michelle Obama (2022, p. 248) argues that "Preparedness becomes a hedge against panic." Helen recently experienced the value of this when she was due to travel from Birmingham UK to Hamburg Germany for an important business meeting. She had a tight connecting flight in Copenhagen and started worrying what would happen if she missed her connection. So, she explored her options. She checked whether there were later flights and whether it would be feasible to go by train if those were full. As it turned out, her connecting flight in Copenhagen was cancelled at the last minute when she was already in Copenhagen and there was no other suitable flight the same day. So, she took the train instead. Her preparation enabled her to switch plans easily and without too much stress.

10.4.4   Cognitive change

A fourth type of strategy for managing emotions is cognitive change. This entails adjusting one's interpretation of a situation or viewpoint in order to alter its emotional impact. This can help prevent ruminating, which as we noted above is usually unhelpful. One of the main ways of changing one's thinking is through reframing (also known as reappraisal) of the issue.

Michelle Obama (2022, pp. 110-111) writes movingly of how she used reframing to try and deal with the racial discrimination she was experiencing – a sense that she was different and was being judged and didn't belong. She writes:

> In my own head, in real time, and for my own benefit, I could rewrite the story of not-mattering:
>
> I'm tall and that's a good thing.
> I'm a woman and that's a good thing.
> I'm Black and that's a good thing.
> I am myself and that's a very good thing.

When you start to rewrite the story of not-mattering, you start to find a new centre. You remove yourself from other people's mirrors and begin speaking more fully from your own experience, your own knowing place.

In this way, she was reframing her sense of identity.

Reframing can be very valuable in a wide variety of situations. Suppose, for example, your line manager points out some areas where you need to improve. That can be face-threatening and may therefore trigger a reaction in you, making you feel upset and worried. However, if you genuinely want to progress in your career, it will be helpful to use reframing to manage your emotions. You can try to see it as an opportunity for learning and growth. Then, instead of becoming defensive, you can gain a better understanding of how you can improve your performance.

In Case Study 10.1, the consultancy boss failed to do this. She reacted dismissively when Delia disagreed with her, failing to take advantage of an opportunity to learn about a different point of view. If she had reframed the disagreement from an attack or face threat, or recognised an opportunity to learn about a different perspective that could bring learning opportunities for them both, she could have engaged constructively with Delia and avoided becoming so angry.

10.4.5 Response modulation

A fifth type of strategy for managing emotion is what Gross (2015) labels 'response modulation'. This refers to controlling the physiological manifestations of emotion. Our bodies are built to help us respond to danger, and so when we experience a threat of some kind, our sympathetic nervous system puts our body into alert mode. This leads to features such as a pounding heart, faster and shallower breathing, sweating, tense muscles, a dry mouth, and feeling hot and flushed.

It's important not to suppress these feelings, but rather to find effective ways of managing them. Michelle Obama (2022, pp. 74-75) puts it like this: "Your fearful mind is basically a life partner you didn't choose. ... Rather than pretending she doesn't exist or constantly trying to defeat her, I've gotten to know my fearful mind as well as she knows me. And this alone has loosened her hold and lessened her stealth. I'm not so easily ambushed when the jolts arrive."

In other words, the first step is to notice our physical sensations and to accept them. This provides the foundation for managing them through techniques known as grounding; in other words, strategies for managing strong emotions. Grounding techniques can be physical or mental, and include things like the following:

Physical grounding techniques:
- Breathing slowly and deeply;
- Tensing and relaxing your shoulders.

Mental grounding techniques:
- Imagine yourself with a person or in a place that means a lot to you;
- Visualise yourself blowing your worries away one by one.

10.5   Perceiving emotions in others

Regulating emotions is clearly important for managing rapport. However, the irony is that the higher the level of masking or neutralisation, the more difficult it may be for people to perceive each other's emotions. Yet effective perception of others' emotions has been found to be linked with positive performance in a range of workplaces, including in health, business, and education (Blanch-Hartigan et al., 2016).

Emotions are revealed in a wide variety of ways (in addition to any explicit comments), including the following:

- Pitch, tone and volume of voice
- Paralinguistic sounds, such as exhaled breath
- Shape of mouth (e.g., smiling)
- Eye modification (e.g., narrowing)
- Direction of gaze (e.g., looking down or away)
- Body movement (e.g., posture, head nodding, forward lean)
- Physical actions (e.g., banging on table)

Unfortunately there is no clear link between behaviours such as these and the emotions they signal. Tickle-Degnen and Rosenthal (1990) explain this as follows:

> Nonverbal behaviour is a continuous stream of action with movements and expressions occurring simultaneously and in fluid temporal succession to one another. ... Out of this continuous stream of action, the human observer perceives socially meaningful discrete events ... for example, 'she smiled' or 'he nodded'. ... [Yet] the same types of nonverbal behavior may occur in negative or positive interactions, and their interpretation depends on the roles that participants are playing in an interaction, the history of the relationship of the individuals, and the perceived function of the interaction for the participants. ... Under conditions of cooperative tasks among peers, for example, eye contact is indicative of positive feelings, yet under conditions in which the interactants feel personal threat or competitiveness toward one another, it may indicate aggressiveness. Likewise, smiling may be a positive expression of warmth or a negative expression of anxiety. (p. 288)

In other words, in line with our TRIPS Rapport Management framework, factors associated with People (Chapter 12) and Setting (Chapter 13) are both important for interpreting nonverbal signals.

What does this mean in practice, then? It clearly means being highly attentive to all types of signals, especially nonverbal signals, and gradually learning to interpret them more effectively. How far, though, can such skill be acquired?

Blanch-Hartigan and her colleagues (2012) carried out a meta-analysis of studies on improving person-perception effectiveness through training and found that the approach was more important than length of training. They report that practice and feedback were more effective than instruction alone, although a combination of approaches was the most effective. In another study which used audio-visual clips of patients (rather than photos, as used in many studies), some of the same researchers examined different training conditions (practice, practice with feedback, practice with discussion and feedback). They found that the most effective condition was when trainees worked in pairs, were given the opportunity to evaluate a clip, discuss it with their partner, decide on an emotion, receive feedback, and then discuss it again (Rubin et al., 2014). Discussion with feedback was particularly valuable.

10.6 Cognitive reactions – sensemaking & evaluating

So far in this chapter we have focused on people's emotional reactions. However, a second very important aspect – typically closely intertwined with emotional reactions – is people's cognitive reactions. We mentioned cognitive changes above in relation to the regulation of emotion and noted that our thinking can affect our emotions. Here we go a step further and argue that we need thinking to interpret effectively and fairly what happened. Technically known as cognitive sensemaking reactions, this refers to the appraisals and evaluations we make of an interaction or incident – the likely causes, levels of accountability of those involved, and the evaluations we make of the person(s). All of this can affect rapport, strengthening or weakening it.

10.6.1 Cognitive sensemaking

When something happens to activate one of the GAAFFE Triggers and we react emotionally in a negative way, it is easy to jump to conclusions and simply blame the other person. We explored above how and why we need to manage our emotional reactions, but this is not sufficient for effectively managing rapport. We also need to manage our cognitive reactions.

Unfortunately, it is all too easy simply to blame the other person rather than to think things through. However, this is unlikely to help the situation. Figure 10.1, which draws on work by Tomlinson and Mayer (2009), identifies the key issues that people can helpfully consider when trying to interpret problematic incidents and when trying to work out how far the other person is responsible or to blame for what happened.

Part 3 – The TRIPS Rapport Management Framework

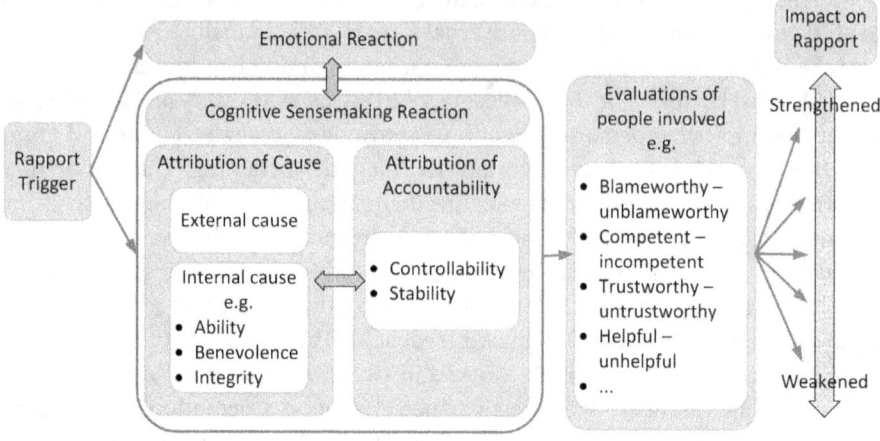

Explanatory notes
External cause: Is the cause of the problematic event external to the person involved; e.g., late for a meeting because of a car breakdown
Internal cause: Does the cause of the problematic event lie with the person, such as in one of the following ways:
o Ability: Does the person have the required skill, aptitude, or knowledge?
o Benevolence: Is the person positively oriented towards those involved?
o Integrity: Does the person act in accordance with accepted principles?
Controllability: How much control could the person have over the outcome?
Stability: How constant or occasional is the issue?

Figure 10.1: The process of cognitive sensemaking and evaluative judgements

Since the process is a bit complex, we use Case Study 10.2 to help explain it. So please read that first.

Case Study 10.2: Failing to meet a deadline
Sophie works for a PR agency and leads a project for a Middle Eastern client. Yasmin is on the project team and one of her roles is to provide translation support. The agency supports hybrid working.
　　One week, Sophie informed Yasmin about some upcoming deadlines and explained how Yasmin should prioritise her various tasks. It turned out that Yasmin was due to take two days' leave just before

a key deadline, but they both agreed that Yasmin would be able to complete the work before it. Sophie emailed her to check progress a few days later but didn't receive a response. Time passed, Yasmin was about to start her leave, and yet Sophie still couldn't get in contact with her. Eventually she was left with no choice but to try and resolve the issue herself. She checked the online folder to see if Yasmin might have simply uploaded the work and forgotten to inform her. Sure enough, there were two documents relating to the project – one in English and one in Arabic – and so Sophie decided to send both of them to the client. The client was very happy with the English version, but highly critical of the Arabic version. Needless to say, Sophie was very unhappy about the whole affair, especially as Yasmin had a track record of not responding to emails and of failing to meet deadlines.

The next week, Sophie asked Yasmin to explain what had happened. Yasmin said that other staff in the agency had given her some work, and she had focused on that. She couldn't get through everything before her leave and had just done as much as she could, completing a first draft of the Arabic document. Sophie was not willing to accept this, pointing out that Yasmin (a) needed to learn to prioritise her work in line with agreed deadlines, and (b) she should have maintained contact with Sophie, letting her know the situation. Yasmin seemed unconvinced and this was particularly difficult for Sophie to understand.

The first step in our sensemaking is to try and understand the cause or the source of the problem: Was it an external cause or an internal one? In Case Study 10.2, Yasmin maintained that she had been given too much work and that this was why she hadn't completed the work for Sophie on time. In other words, she maintained it was an external cause – the 'fault' of others through the amount of work she had been given.

When there is an external cause, it may well be the case that the individual is not to blame. For instance, if Yasmin had experienced some kind of family emergency, that would usually be considered as a genuine external cause and in such circumstances little or no blame would be attributed to her. However, we also make judgements as to whether the individual could have done anything to handle the external cause. In Figure 10.1, this is shown as controllability.

Sophie felt that Yasmin could have handled the issue of too much work more effectively – prioritising her work so she could keep to the deadline that the two of them had agreed, keeping in touch with her, and letting her know about any issues. For that reason, she didn't fully accept Yasmin's denial of personal responsibility; in other words, she doubted Yasmin's claim that the cause was truly external.

Part of the reason for this was that Sophie was also conscious of Yasmin's poor performance record in communicating. This was not the first time that Yasmin had failed to respond to emails and had missed a deadline. In other words, in terms of the framework, Sophie considered stability – whether the issue was recurrent or rare. Noting that it was recurrent caused Sophie concerns. She then wondered what the root of the problem was. For example, did Yasmin feel negative towards the agency and/or towards Sophie (a benevolence issue) or was her sense of work ethics and work responsibilities particularly low (an integrity issue)? Sophie wasn't sure. However, the whole incident (which followed other similar failures to engage with the work as required) led Sophie to regard Yasmin as an untrustworthy and unreliable member of the team.

The internal causes of ability, benevolence and integrity come from Tomlinson and Mayer's (2009) work. However, other aspects of a person's internal qualities and characteristics could well be added, including those explained in Chapter 12.

It is important to remember when engaging in cognitive sensemaking that we may not have all the necessary information to make a 'fair' judgement; for example:

- Might there be any personal or external circumstances that we are not aware of?
- Might there be any cultural differences? For instance, could there be different understandings around responsibilities for keeping in touch with project managers (but not line managers)?

Chapters 12 and 13 provide information on the kinds of issues to look out for and that need considering.

10.6.2 Evaluative judgements

Cognitive sensemaking is an extremely important component of rapport management because it leads to evaluative judgements. As a result of our interpretations, we make judgements about others, such as that they are polite or rude, trustworthy or untrustworthy, competent or incompetent. As we noted in Chapter 3, it is actually common for people to immediately jump to such judgements, merging them with their descriptions or complaints of what happened. Several of our case studies have shown that – see Case Studies 3.1 and 3.2, for example.

However, we risk making unfair and unhelpful judgements if we don't take the time to pro-actively engage in cognitive sensemaking, drawing on and seeking out as much information as possible.

This is important because, as Figure 10.1 illustrates, the judgements we make of others usually inform our longer-term opinions about them. They then almost inevitably colour (for better for worse) our future interactions with the individual(s) concerned, forming part of the contextual background that underlies how we interact with them.

> **Activity 10.2 Thinking through problematic incidents**
> Think of an incident, involving someone else, when you were annoyed or upset about what they did or didn't do.
> 1. Recall what happened.
> 2. Did you make any evaluative judgements – consciously or subconsciously – about the person? If so, what were they?
> 3. Was the cause of the problem external or internal?
> 4. How far could the person have controlled what happened?
> 5. How often had the problem occurred previously?
> 6. What characteristics of the person might have played a role?
> 7. Having re-thought the incident, would you now make any different evaluative judgements?
> 8. If possible, discuss the above with someone else who knows the person and consider how far your interpretations are similar or different.

10.7 Summary and follow-up reading

When one or more of the GAAFFE Triggers have been activated, we have some kind of Reaction. Our Reactions are usually a combination of emotional and cognitive responses, both of which need to be managed effectively. This chapter has considered ways of doing this.

A summary template of the TRIPS R-Reaction Concept is given in Chapter 15. It gives questions that are useful for checking and reflection purposes.

For further information on Reactions, refer to the references mentioned within the chapter. The following are also particularly useful.

Frewin, H. (2021). Better than confidence. *The thinking tools you need to get the results you want:* Butterfly House Publishing. This book offers practical solutions for those who doubt their ability or credibility.

Peters, S. (2012). *The chimp paradox. The mind management programme for confidence, success and happiness.* Ebury Publishing. This book, by a consultant psychiatrist, is a highly accessible, detailed guide to understanding and managing our emotions and thoughts.

Part 3 - The TRIPS Rapport Management Framework

Chapter 11: Interactions

Understanding how communication can trigger rapport reactions

11.1   Introduction

This chapter provides a focused explanation of I: Interactions in the TRIPS Rapport Management framework.

'I' stands for Interactions or encounters. These sit at the core of the model because it is through interactions that rapport is managed or mismanaged. This means that we always need to pay close attention to what is said and done – both prior to any planned/expected communication and during it. We need to do this to help us manage what reactions are triggered, and to reflect during and afterwards on what aspects of the communication give rise to the triggers and reactions. In other words, we need to be mindful of how we communicate, bearing in mind the people we're communicating with (P: People – see Chapter 12) and the context in which we're communicating (S: Setting – see Chapter 13). In this chapter, we explore the aspects of communication that we need to pay particular attention to:

- Communication style: How to word and deliver the message
- Communication dynamics: How the dynamics of communication are co-ordinated

To understand each of these aspects, it is important to consider how communication works and so we start with that. At the end, we link these features of communication with an important issue for diverse workplaces – the problem of microinsults (also known as microaggression).

11.2   How communication works

It is relatively common to read in books on communication about 'decoding' a message. This assumes that speakers encode their thoughts into words and phrases, and hearers then decode those words and phrases into meanings, with the decoded message typically being identical to the original encoded message. It further assumes that any mismatch between the message sent, and the message received is either due to different levels of familiarity with the language code or due to some kind of 'noise' that interferes with the encoding/decoding process. Unfortunately, the communication process is more complicated than this.

Human communication to a large extent exploits a language code (e.g., English, Chinese, German, British sign language); however, it is not always feasible or desirable for everything to be conveyed explicitly in the code. Much has to be left for the participants to work out, and they do this by drawing on their background knowledge of the topic, their knowledge of the people involved (see Chapter 12 on P: People), and their knowledge of the communication setting (see Chapter 13 on S: Setting). In other words, meaning is negotiated and constructed rather than simply exchanged via a code. This has several consequences for relationship management:

- If people's proficiency and familiarity with the working language, its regional version, and/or its nonverbal patterns are different, they may misunderstand each other and upset or annoy each other.
- If the participants' background knowledge of the topic being discussed is different, they may have difficulty understanding each other and become frustrated or annoyed.
- If the participants differ in their expectations as to the content and manner of ideas communicated, they may react negatively if their expectations are breached.
- If the participants lack a shared understanding of the cultural norms of language use, including the type of interaction they are engaging in (see Chapter 13 on communication setting and communicative event), they may misinterpret various communication cues such as the tone of voice or body language that the other person is using, and end up assigning the wrong meaning and intent to them.

In all these cases, one or more of the GAAFFE triggers may be activated and a rapport reaction occur. To minimise negative reactions, a 'recipient design' approach is required, combined with mindfulness. In other words, the form, content and manner of the communication needs to be synchronised in some way with the needs and preferences of the other participants, with the extent to which this is being achieved being continuously monitored.

When one or more participants is less fluent than others in the working language or has less background knowledge of the topic under discussion, following the flow of the argument can be particularly difficult. That's why in Table 5.8 we illustrated some practical steps that can be used to promote mutual understanding.

In this chapter we consider other facets of communication that can lead to interpretation challenges and that can also impact on rapport in the workplace.

11.3 Disclosure – non-disclosure of information

One important aspect of communication that affects rapport is deciding whether or not to disclose certain information and whether or not to respond (immediately) to a message.

Disclosure refers to the sharing of information with others, personal and/or work-related. In terms of personal information, a certain amount of self-disclosure

Part 3 – The TRIPS Rapport Management Framework

is helpful for building new relationships (see Chapter 6) and for enhancing collegiality among peers. However, what counts as an 'appropriate amount' and its effect on rapport can vary across individuals and social groups, as well as across contexts. For instance, Spencer-Oatey and Wang (2020) report the following incident. An American host, when welcoming a Chinese delegation in a formal meeting, referred to his grandchildren. This really surprised the Chinese visitors and they commented afterwards that they would never mention such personal information in a formal speech. However, they did not seem offended by it, and actually seemed to appreciate it.

When the personal information is confidential and it is shared (without permission) with another party, this can trigger serious rapport issues as Case Study 11.1 illustrates. Gerald was a British expatriate working in an office in China and related the following incident to Helen.

> **Case Study 11.1: Informing someone's line manager**
> *I had developed a good relationship with one of the people in my office, Dawei, and regularly chatted with him at the end of the working day. Others often commented on his strengths and weaknesses, but nobody had talked explicitly with him about them. His line manager was based in a different office. So, one day I decided to give him some feedback and we had a real meeting of minds. He was genuinely grateful for what I'd shared with him and thanked me profusely. Afterwards, his line manager asked me for feedback on his performance and I wrote up exactly what I had said to Dawei in our one-to-one. The line manager was hugely impressed and emailed me to say so. However, the colleague came to me in tears the next day and was really angry, in fact he was furious with me. It was three days before he would speak to me again.*
>
> **Reflect**
> 1. Why was Dawei so angry and upset? What GAAFFE trigger(s) had been activated?
> 2. In your view, should Gerald have shared the details of their conversation with Dawei's line manager? Why/why not?
> 3. In your view, how should Gerald have responded to the line manager's request for feedback on Dawei's performance?
> 4. Have you experienced any occasion when information that you felt was personal and confidential was shared with someone else? How did you feel and why?

In terms of work-related information (e.g., on projects, new initiatives), it is important to remember that control of information is a form of power. If people want or need the information that someone else has, resisting access to it or providing misleading information can be highly detrimental to rapport. Of course, sometimes there are security or welfare-related reasons for not disclosing information; for example, when a company is facing financial difficulties, decisions as to how much to share (and when) are crucial. Too much sharing too soon can worry people unnecessarily and may also worsen the financial situation by increasing external parties' concerns. Nevertheless, keeping people in the dark, while rumours or speculation simultaneously abound, can seriously undermine trust in senior management. In these cases, it is usually best to share as much information as is feasible and likely to be helpful.

Case Study 11.1 (when Dawei's line manager asked Gerald for feedback on Dawei's performance) raises the issue of how to respond to an awkward question. In Chapter 10 we mentioned reactive responses; here we just touch on the notion of response more generally. In linguistic terms, a response is often the second part of what is known as an adjacency pair; for example, greeting – greeting, invitation – acceptance/refusal, request for information – provision of information. When the second part of an adjacency pair (i.e., the response) is missing, this breach of expectation often triggers a reaction, such as annoyance or confusion. In other words, in these cases it is not what people have said or done that triggers a reaction, but rather the failure itself to respond.

11.4 Communication style: deciding how to frame the message

Rapport is affected not only by what is communicated but also by how it is communicated. A key aspect of this is communication style – the manner in which a message is conveyed. Linguists have identified a number of different styles, but unfortunately there is no current consensus over the exact number and their labelling. However, they all involve some kind of contrast as the list below indicates:

- Direct–indirect
- Expressive–restrained
- Self-enhancement – self-effacement
- Person-oriented – status-oriented

People's preferred communication style in a given context is partly influenced by their personality, values and working style characteristics (see Chapter 12 on P: People) and partly by the patterns of use within their social/cultural group into which they have been socialised (see Chapter 13 on S: Settings). People often find it quite difficult to change their core communication styles and as a result, relationships can become strained because of different preferences and expectations.

11.4.1 Directness–indirectness

In terms of relationship management and rapport, directness–indirectness is probably the most important communication style that needs attending to. It not only affects how easily others can interpret the message, but also how controlled and/or respected others feel by what is said. It can activate several of the GAAFFE triggers if mishandled, including Goals (if the message is not understood), Autonomy (if the wording sounds like an order), and Face (if the person feels disrespected). So, care needs to be taken to use an appropriate level of directness. How, though, can different levels of directness or indirectness be conveyed?

Several elements affect the level of directness–indirectness that people perceive. One of these is degree of explicitness: whether a message is conveyed explicitly or just hinted at. Suppose you'd like a colleague, Tom, to make a cup of tea for the team. Theoretically, you could communicate this to him with varying degrees of explicitness, as the following example illustrates.

- Tom, get the tea for us.
- Tom, get the tea for us, will you?
- Tom, could you get the tea?
- Tom, I think it may be your turn to get the tea
- Gosh, I'm feeling really thirsty.
- It's 10 o'clock I think.

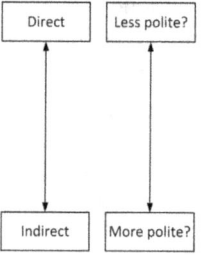

Figure 11.1: Degrees of directness and politeness

Traditionally in linguistics, politeness is linked with indirectness or hinting, as the example above shows. More specifically, it is argued that the more imposing or challenging a message is, the greater the need for indirectness. This is because greater indirectness typically gives greater optionality, thereby addressing the GAAFFE trigger of Autonomy. However, the situation is often more complex than this.

Consider Case Study 11.2. It reports an authentic interaction between three people working together in a bank (Weeks, 2004, p. 76). The employees normally take it in turns to make tea/coffee for the others.

Case Study 11.2: A reminder to make tea

Helen: [apparently speaking to no one in particular]: What time is it? I'm thirsty. [She smacked her lips for effect]
Helen: Kathy, are you thirsty? [Kathy smiled and nodded]
Helen: Oi, Tom, we're thirsty.
Tom: You're thirsty, are you?
Helen: Mmm, parched.

Tom: I guess it's my turn to make the tea, then, is it?
Helen: Oh that would be nice, yes please. Coffee for me.

Reflect
1. How explicit at first was Helen in reminding Tom that it was his turn to make tea?
2. Why do you think she handled the situation in this way?
3. Would you have handled the situation in this way? Why/why not?

Several factors affect what counts as a suitable level of directness–indirectness. Key ones are:

- The content of the message itself – whether it is likely to be face-threatening;
- The degree of effort required by the other person to carry out any response to the message;
- The nature of the relationship between the participants (e.g., equal/unequal, close/distant) – a P: People issue;
- Role responsibilities (e.g., informal/formal arrangements for who does what) – a P: People issue;
- The context in which the communication takes place – an S: Setting issue.

We suggest that you consider these issues as you reflect on questions 2 and 3 in Case Study 11.2. Chapters 12 and 13 explain more about People and Settings and how to take them into account.

A second way in which directness–indirectness is managed is through 'hedging' or 'mitigation'. This involves the use of small words or phrases (e.g., just, sometimes, a bit, I mean), tags (e.g., will you, isn't it), or hesitations that weaken the impact of what is said, thereby making it more indirect and less forceful. The following example from Janet Holmes illustrates this (Holmes, 2023, p. 36). A workplace advisor in New Zealand was giving some feedback to an intern who had been speaking in her native language at lunchtime to a friend. The advisor was recommending (rightly or wrongly) that the intern be careful when doing this. As the quote below illustrates, she used a lot of hedges (underlined) to soften the blow of what she was saying:

Advisor: <u>Sometimes</u> people, especially New Zealanders, they feel <u>a bit</u> uncomfortable 'cos they don't know what's going on, <u>you know,</u> but <u>I mean</u> if you're aware <u>maybe</u> keep your voice down <u>a bit</u>.

For a further example of mitigation, see Case Study 2.2.

Part 3 – The TRIPS Rapport Management Framework

Clearly, directness–indirectness needs to be handled well in order to manage relationships effectively. Table 11.1 identifies some of the problems that may occur when people with different style preferences interact. For instance, high levels of indirectness can lead to problems interpreting what is really meant; hints may be missed, especially when working in contexts of diversity (see, for example, Case Study 6.8) and hedging can be very confusing for less fluent speakers of the working language.

Changing one's style can also be difficult. For instance, one British manager, working in a situation where high levels of indirectness were valued, commented as follows on his difficulty adjusting to greater indirectness: *"How do I demonstrate that, although I'm not openly addressing this issue, that I'm not a fool, that I'm aware of the issue?"* In other words, he wasn't sure whether his hint comments on the issue at stake had been picked up by the others. He was used to being more explicit and was uncertain how to ascertain awareness in others of his indirect messaging. There are no easy answers to this, except seeking regular feedback and developing one's mindfulness skills.

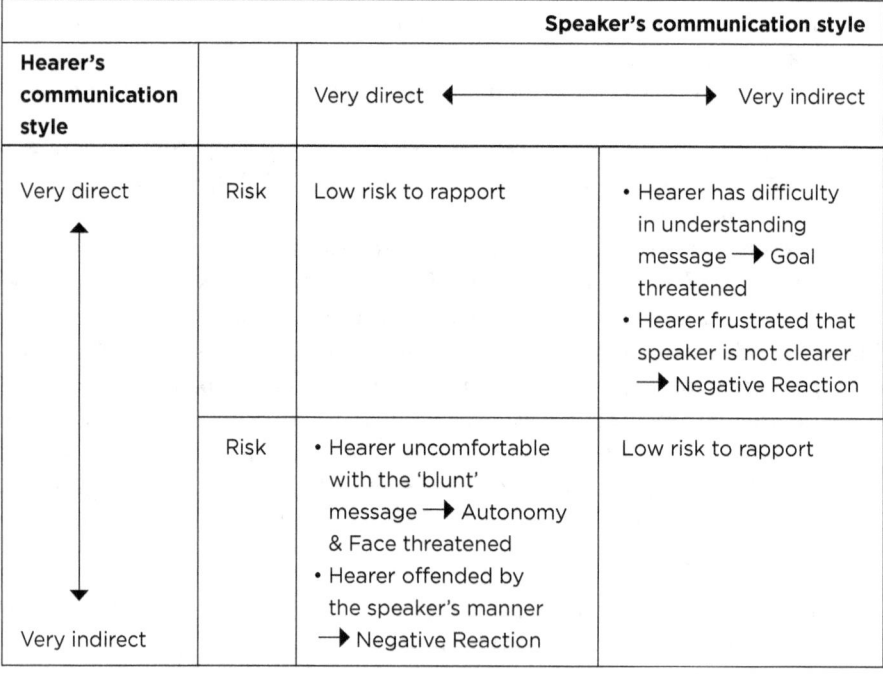

		Speaker's communication style	
Hearer's communication style		Very direct ⟵⟶ Very indirect	
Very direct ↑↓ Very indirect	Risk	Low risk to rapport	• Hearer has difficulty in understanding message → Goal threatened • Hearer frustrated that speaker is not clearer → Negative Reaction
	Risk	• Hearer uncomfortable with the 'blunt' message → Autonomy & Face threatened • Hearer offended by the speaker's manner → Negative Reaction	Low risk to rapport

Table 11.1: Potential impact of differences between Speaker and Hearer in directness–indirectness in communication style

11.4.2 Other communication styles

Given the scope of this book, it is not feasible to explore each type of communication style in detail (but see the follow-up references given at the end of the chapter), so here we just touch on some that can be particularly important for relationship management.

Expressive–restrained: People with an expressive communication style tend to convey their feelings and thoughts openly and enthusiastically, while those with a restrained communication style tend to convey their feelings and thoughts in a controlled and unemotional manner. A restrained style can be regarded by some as 'more professional' but this may be an unfair judgement on those who are more expressive. Consider Case Study 11.3. The comments come from a Greek manager, Vasiliki, about her interactions with her British boss.

Case Study 11.3: Showing passion at work

My boss kept giving me feedback that I needed to be more self-aware. At first I didn't understand what he meant. Later I found out that he didn't like the emotional passion I showed when we were discussing things. For me, it is a way of showing my commitment to the work and the issue, but he didn't like it and judged me negatively. He expected me to be more detached.

Reflect
1. What assumption did the boss make when he simply told Vasiliki to be more self-aware?
2. What GAAFFE trigger(s) might his feedback activate?

Conversely, those with an expressive communication style may feel those with a restrained style are cold, boring, and uninvolved, which may also be an unfair judgement.

Self-enhancing – self-effacing: People with a self-enhancing communication style are very comfortable and confident talking about their strengths and achievements, while those with a self-effacing communication style feel uncomfortable doing that and are more modest about their strengths, playing down their achievements. In contexts such as job interviews or performance reviews, employees may be taken at face value, and if self-enhancement is expected, those with a self-effacing style may be disadvantaged; in other words, the F: Fairness trigger would be activated. Among colleagues, those with a self-effacing style may regard someone with a self-enhancing style as arrogant and pushy, and dislike them for it.

Person-oriented – status-oriented: People with a status-oriented communication style are very conscious of hierarchy and are deferential in what they say and do, while people with a person-oriented style pay more attention to the individual rather than their role or position and tend to be more informal in their interactions with others. This communication style is typically closely linked with people's values and beliefs about hierarchy. Some languages are more status-oriented in their form than others (e.g., Japanese has many honorific forms and 'politeness levels'), thereby promoting a status-oriented style. Nevertheless, decisions over things like terms of address (e.g., deciding whether to use Title+surname or given name) apply in all languages. Whatever the circumstance, failure to use the level of deference or informality that the other person is expecting, can annoy or upset them. Case Study 11.4 illustrates this. It happened to Helen when she was managing an international collaboration project involving British and Chinese personnel. Over 50 people were involved and when Helen needed to send a message that was relevant to everyone, she would email the whole team in one email. However, after a while she received email feedback from one of the Chinese managers as shown in Case Study 11.4.

> **Case Study 11.4: Mass emails and seniority**
> "Sending mass emails is a good way. But when we send such emails, it will infringe Chinese principles. If I send such an email to a person in a higher position, s/he will feel offended. Nowadays we send various materials by email, but ... superiors will feel particularly insulted. ... Sending emails to superiors is not a good way, because it shows no regard for status differences between people." [Chinese project manager]
>
> **Reflect**
> 1. Why did the Chinese manager make a positive comment initially and then proceed to say something different?
> 2. How far is acknowledgement of status important in your workplace? What evidence supports your view?

To become more mindful over communication styles, we suggest you engage with Activity 11.2.

> **Activity 11.2: Becoming mindful of communication style**
> In the coming week, pay attention to the communication styles that people use.

1. If anyone speaks or acts in a way that you feel is inappropriate in some way, try to note down as soon as possible what they said and the context in which they said it.
2. Consider whether your sense of inappropriateness was linked to any of the communication styles explored in this section.
3. What can you learn from this about your own communication style preferences?

11.5 Communication dynamics: handling the dynamics of interactions

Effective communication is not just a matter of deciding what messages to convey and how to word them; issues such as who speaks when, overlaps (interruptions), and silence can also be crucially important. In Chapter 5 we explored the impact that this can have on people's sense of inclusion–exclusion. Here we explain a little more of the conceptual background to this.

11.5.1 Participation and turn-taking

When two or more people are interacting, the issue of turns and turn-taking inevitably arises. Questions that need considering and addressing include:

- Can more than one person talk at the same time? Does this count as interest and enthusiasm or rude interruption?
- Can a speaker decide who speaks next? What circumstances allow or disallow that?
- If someone wants to take a turn and contribute to the discussion, what difficulties may they face?
- How long can silence last before it becomes uncomfortable?

These are all issues that linguists have studied in detail, and unfortunately the straightforward answer to all of them is 'it depends'. It particularly depends on the nature of the communicative event, such as whether it's a formal meeting or an informal discussion, as well as cultural norms associated with the event/activity (see Chapter 13).

In Chapter 5, we considered the sense of exclusion someone may feel when they can't find the 'space' to join in a discussion and the need to slow down the turn-taking to accommodate this. Related to this is inadvertent domination. Holmes (2023) gives an interesting example of this. It concerns some mentors (Jess and Gina) in a New Zealand workplace who advise an intern, Mary, that she should speak more loudly. They start by asking Mary how loudly she speaks at home. She tells them that she also speaks quietly at home but will try to speak louder at work.

After this, Jess and Gina get into a prolonged discussion between themselves over who they prioritise when people want their attention. At one point, Jess says she wouldn't want to ignore Mary, and yet that is exactly what they are both doing. Jess and Gina have a close, friendly relationship and they allowed this to override what they were meant to be doing – supporting Mary. Rather than involving her, they engaged in an extended discussion between themselves on their own working practices. Holmes argues that by doing this, they reinforced their own rapport but simultaneously marginalised Mary.

This type of exclusion can easily occur when some staff know each other very well and others are new or less familiar to them. For those who have a close and friendly relationship, it is easy for them to get carried away following up on their own interests and ignoring others. Mindfulness is needed in order to avoid it.

11.5.2   Code-switching

When teams or collaborating partners comprise people who speak different languages (and who may also have different levels of proficiency in the working language), it is common for code-switching to occur – that is, switching from one language to another during the course of an interaction. This can become particularly problematic for relationship management because it can easily generate a sense of exclusion.

Case Study 11.5 illustrates this. The case concerns interactions between Israeli and American employees following a merger between a successful Israeli high-tech company, Isrocom, and an American competitor, Amerotech (Ailon, 2007).

> **Case Study 11.5: Code-switching during international business visits**
> Following a visit to New York by Isrocom staff, the Israeli COO sent the following email to 'all Isrocom management':
> "I have received some negative feedback from New York employees related to behavior of Isrocom people visiting New York. On several occasions at New York's office, Isrocom employees have been heard conversing in Hebrew in the presence of Amerotech employees. While it is perfectly understandable that it is easier and more efficient to converse in one's native tongue, be aware that it can create feelings of exclusion, estrangement and paranoia among the Amerotech people. Please give your people appropriate instructions so as to avoid similar instances in the future."
> During a visit to Tel Aviv by Amerotech staff, the following happened: One of the Amerotech staff, Tim, was giving a presentation on pricing to Isrocom staff which they disagreed with. Then a senior Isrocom manager, Nadav, started making negative comments about Tim in Hebrew, speaking

loudly so everyone in the room could hear. Others starting whispering to each other and this continued for a while, confusing Tim and his colleague. Later, when another Isrocom staff member, Gur, asked his colleague a question in Hebrew, Tim somehow figured out what he had said and answered it appropriately. This startled the Isrocom staff, making them wonder how much Tim had understood of their earlier comments.

Reflect
1. Why do you think the Isrocom staff spoke in Hebrew in the presence of Amerotech employees while in New York?
2. Why did the New York employees in New York react negatively to the Isrocom employees speaking in Hebrew?
3. Why do you think the Isrocom staff spoke in Hebrew during Tim's session?
4. Tim could not speak Hebrew. How do you think he understood the question Gur had asked in Hebrew?

For those who engage in code-switching, they may do it for a number of different reasons, including:

- To aid linguistic understanding, especially when one person's level of proficiency is lower;
- To aid conceptual understanding, such as when one person has less background knowledge of the topic;
- To test out thoughts with colleagues before sharing them with everyone;
- For comfort and convenience; e.g., because they can't find the right words in one language, or are more used speaking about a topic (e.g., business) in another;
- To convey messages that one party does not want the other to understand (e.g., in business negotiations).

Each of these reasons can be beneficial, depending on the circumstances. Monolinguals (or those unfamiliar with the code-switched language) need to understand and accept that others may code-switch for justifiable reasons. Conversely, those who engage in code-switching need to be aware that others may feel excluded because they don't know what is being said. In fact, how far people feel excluded by code-switching is often strongly influenced by the level of trust between all concerned. In the case of the Amerotech and Isrocom employees, they were all unfamiliar with each other, and the merger had caused a lot of uncertainty and change that everyone was needing to adjust to. In such circumstances, it is particularly important to be highly mindful over language choices and the challenges to rapport that it can trigger. It is also wise never to assume that others will be unable to understand what you are saying!

It's worth noting that monolinguals could also be said to code-switch if, for example, they change from a standard form of their language to a local dialect, or from everyday usage to very technical language. This too can exclude those who are unfamiliar with the different variety/form.

To become more mindful over communication dynamics, we suggest you engage with Activity 11.3.

> **Activity 11.3: Becoming mindful of communication dynamics**
> In the coming week, choose a communicative event (e.g., formal meeting, team discussion) and note down how participation and turn-taking occurred.
> a. How evenly were turns distributed between participants? Did some people speak more than others?
> b. How fast or slow was the changeover of turns? Were there any noticeable gaps or overlaps (i.e., two or more people speaking simultaneously)?
> c. Did everyone seem to have the opportunity to contribute?
> d. What was the impact on the interaction?
> After you've paid attention to your chosen setting, choose another to focus on.
> e. What insights are you beginning to gain?

All the aspects of communication that we've covered in the chapter so far have the potential to affect rapport, positively or negatively. In the final section of this chapter, we focus on an issue that is particularly problematic for positive rapport: microinsults.

11.6 Microinsults

Microinsults – also known as micro-incivilities and microaggression – are increasingly recognised as potential problems in the workplace. Drawing on the definition given by Sue and colleagues (2007), we define it as follows:

> Microinsults are brief and commonplace verbal and behavioural indignities, whether intentional or unintentional, that communicate hostility, disrespect, outsider-status, or other message of negativity.

Kandola (2018, p. 102) lists a number of examples, including being ignored, being talked over, having assumptions made about you, and being repeatedly criticised for seemingly small issues. He points out that it can also include omissions, such as not giving eye contact, not giving someone your attention, and persistently not saying someone's name correctly.

In the workplace, incorrect perception of a person's status, based on their visible personal characteristics, such as their gender or ethnicity, can be particularly common and problematic. For example, a white male middle-aged British manager, responsible for projects across sixteen countries, commented to us as shown in Case Study 11.6.

Case Study 11.6: Who is the manager?
I don't manage anybody but I sit with the team in Turkey and the Head in Turkey is a young woman, but people always assume that I'm the head. She said as soon as there's somebody male middle aged and British in the room the meeting will become about them and not about her, she's the one with the budget, she's the one with the programme, she's the one with the authority. [Unpublished interview data]

Reflect
1. In what way is this a micro-insult?
2. How do you think this problem could be overcome?
3. Have you experienced any incorrect perception of your status/position? What happened and how did you feel?

Another particularly common (potential) microinsult, as mentioned in Chapter 6, is asking where someone is from. This does not necessarily have to be problematic – the person could be genuinely curious and interested. For example, when Helen was working in China in the 1980s, she was very regularly asked where she was from. At the time, there were few foreigners in the country and people were genuinely curious about her nationality. Helen was not offended by this, as she was clearly not ethnically Chinese, and she had no expectation that people would regard her as a local. However, in more multicultural societies it can be much more problematic. This is where recipient design and mindfulness are so important – the need to pay attention to how such a question might be perceived by the individual concerned. The key is not to stop asking people about their background, but rather to word your questions in a way that shows genuine interest, instead of conveying the impression that you regard them as an outsider.

In our definition above of microinsults, we noted that they may be intentional or unintentional. Holmes (2023) goes a step further and points out not only that the speaker may or may not consciously or deliberately want to cause offence, but that the perception and interpretation of the recipient can also vary. This is shown in Table 11.2. In other words, when an insult is intended, the recipient may or may not interpret it as offensive. Conversely, when the intent is positive, the hearer/recipient may either perceive it as such or else may regard it as an insult.

Speaker/Doer Intention	Recipient Perception/interpretation
Cause offence/challenge rapport	Insult/challenge perceived
	Insult/challenge not perceived
Maintain or build rapport	Positive rapport perceived
	Insult/challenge perceived

Table 11.2: Interconnections between intention and perception in microinsults

Sue and his colleagues (2007) point to a dilemma that recipients often face: uncertainty whether or not a microinsult has occurred. They go on to ask how one can prove that a microinsult has actually occurred. In fact, uncertainty is a normal part of the communication process and proof is often elusive. As explained at the beginning of this chapter, this is because meaning always needs to be interpreted rather than decoded. Since interpretation is carried out by the recipient, this is why the recipient's perception is of crucial importance. The linguists Miriam Locher and Richard Watts (2008, p. 80) explain it like this:

> … it is the interactants' perceptions of communicators' intentions rather than the intentions themselves that determine whether a communicative act is taken to be impolite or not. In other words, the uptake of a message is as important if not more important than the utterer's original intention.

This underlines the need for speakers to be very mindful of how the other party may interpret what they say.

11.7 Summary and follow-up reading

Interaction is at the heart of rapport management. This chapter has explained the interpretive nature of communication and two key features that need to be attended to and managed: different styles of communication and the dynamics of handling interaction.

A summary template identifying the key features of the TRIPS I-Interaction Concept is given in Chapter 15. It also gives questions that are useful for checking and reflection purposes.

For further information on interaction issues, refer to the references mentioned within the chapter. In addition, the following are particularly useful.

Gaynor, Z., & Alevizos, K. (2019). *Is that clear? Effective communication in a multilingual world:* Self-published. This is a superb little book for native/highly fluent speakers of English, providing easy-to-follow tips for adjusting their English.

Holmes, J. (2023). Rapport management and microaggression in workplace interaction. In T. McConachy & P. Hinton (Eds.), *Negotiating intercultural relations. Insights from linguistics, psychology, and intercultural education* (pp. 35–53). Bloomsbury. This chapter explores microinsults and rapport from a sociolinguistic perspective, illustrating some of the complexities associated with the issue.

Spencer-Oatey, H., Franklin, P., & Lazidou, D. (2022). *Global fitness for global people: How to manage and leverage cultural diversity at work.* Castledown. Chapter 4 explains how communication works and how to enhance mutual understanding, providing lots of authentic case examples.

Ting-Toomey, S., & Dorjee, T. (2019). *Communicating across cultures.* 2nd edition. The Guildford Press. Chapter 7 describes a number of different communication styles.

Vigier, M., & Spencer-Oatey, H. (2017). Code-switching in newly-formed multinational project teams: Challenges, strategies and effects. *International Journal of Cross-Cultural Management,* 17(1), 23–37. This journal article reports a research study into the ways in which teams comprising French and English speakers experienced code-switching and found (or failed to find) ways of handling it.

Part 3 – The TRIPS Rapport Management Framework

Chapter 12: People

Understanding the impact of the people involved

12.1 Introduction

This chapter provides a focused explanation of P: People in the TRIPS Rapport Management framework.

'P' stands for People – the individuals involved in an interaction or those who are particularly relevant to it. They are typically referred to by linguists as participants. Several features are important to pay attention to for rapport management purposes:

- The number of people involved – those who are present or, in the case of email or asynchronous online communication, those who are copied in or have access to an exchange;
- The characteristics of the people involved;
- The links or connections between the people involved.

These features affect how an interaction is carried out (e.g., the way in which a message is conveyed) and the likelihood of a rapport reaction being triggered (e.g., a sense of face threat or a feeling of exclusion).

12.2 Number of participants

The greater the number of people present in a face-to-face interaction, or included in a digital exchange, the greater the potential impact on rapport. If someone is criticised in front of others, this is likely to be much more face-threatening than if it took place in private. In contrast, when an individual's performance or achievement is praised publicly, this can be face-enhancing for the individual. On the other hand, it may also be embarrassing for that person and others may feel resentful that they themselves have not been praised. Number of people is thus particularly connected with the Trigger 'Face' and when giving critical feedback, the presence of other people always needs to be taken into account and normally avoided.

When negative evaluative remarks need to be given, the chosen setting is often (and correctly) pre-planned, such as in a one-to-one meeting between line manager and direct report. This is as it should be. At other times, however, people may easily be provoked into making spontaneous critical remarks when something in a meeting annoys them. Particular care needs to be taken in these situations. The linguist Janet Holmes (2018) provides an interesting example, which we report in Case Study 12.1.

Part 3 – The TRIPS Rapport Management Framework

> **Case Study 12.1: Negative comments on individuals in a meeting**
> This incident took place at a regular staff meeting in a Māori workplace in New Zealand. There were 16 people present, including the CEO (Daniel), a very senior manager (Frank), and a more junior manager (Steve). Steve was speaking at length on a particular topic, and while he was talking, Frank was unclear about something Steve had said, so he whispered a question to Daniel, asking for clarification. Daniel whispered a reply, after which Steve said the following to everyone: "One of the important things in communication is not to talk when others are talking."
>
> **Reflect**
> 1. If you had been Steve, would you have made this comment? Why/why not?
> 2. If not, what would you have done instead?
> 3. How would you have reacted if you had been Daniel or Frank, and why? Explain your thoughts on this.

In this incident, Steve made a critical comment of two people in front of 13 others – something that could easily offend Daniel and Frank and might also lead the others present to make an evaluative judgement of Steve and his behaviour. The incident also raises a number of issues relevant to People and also to Settings, which also need to be taken into account. These include:

- The hierarchical connections between Daniel, Frank, and Steve;
- The level of closeness/trust between Daniel, Frank, and Steve;
- The norms for whispering comments in meetings when others are talking;
- The norms of criticising people openly in meetings in front of others.

We explore the first two points in Section 12.4 and the third point in Chapter 13. In fact, on this particular occasion, Daniel and Frank were not offended because their relationship with Steve was good and there were also some cultural norm issues that they knew Steve was unfamiliar with. However, if this had not been the case, Steve's critical comment towards his superiors – and in front of so many others – could have led to serious rapport issues.

The impact of the number of people present can also be linked with the Trigger 'Attention'. When several people are present at a meeting or holding a team discussion, the issue of participation inevitably arises; in other words, whether each person has the opportunity to contribute their ideas when they want to. Inappropriate turn-taking patterns are of particular importance here. If some members dominate the conversation, so that one or more others finds it difficult to share their ideas, this can activate the 'Attention' trigger, whereby they can feel neglected or ignored. This can have other knock-on trigger consequences, such as on Goals (unable to achieve their goals), and Fairness (sense that their treatment is unfair). Chapter 5 explored such a situation in detail; see also the discussion of turn-taking in Chapter 11.

Number of participants is thus an important factor to take into consideration in order to avoid triggering undesired rapport reactions.

12.3 People's identity characteristics

People's identity characteristics are another extremely important facet of rapport management – they affect numerous aspects, including people's attitudes towards each other, how comfortable they feel with each other, and their styles of working together.

Many psychologists distinguish between individual identities and group identities. Individual identities refer to the features that are specific to us as individuals, such as our appearance (e.g., height, colour of hair), our abilities (e.g., poor dancer, good tennis player), and our hobbies (e.g., enjoys bird watching and hiking). Group identities refer to the social groups that we belong to or are members of (e.g., sports group, musical ensemble, faith community). Some of our identities (whether individual or group) tend to be more central or core to our sense of 'who we are' than others. As a result, we are likely to be more sensitive to any critical comments on our core aspects than on other identity features.

Figure 12.1 illustrates some common features of individual and group identities. There is actually not a watertight distinction between the two. For instance, one of our hobbies may lead us to join or feel an affinity with a group with similar interests, in which case it becomes both an individual characteristic and a group characteristic (with the setting often influencing which is more prominent). Nevertheless, as we unpack the impact of personal characteristics on rapport, it can be helpful to treat them separately.

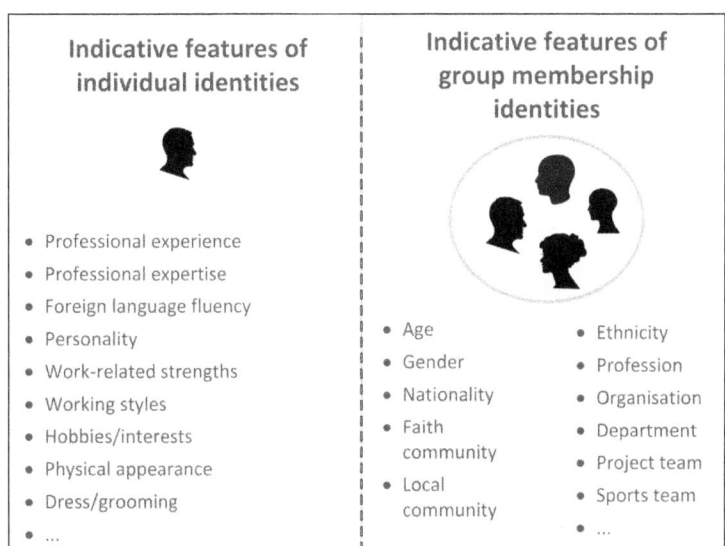

Fig. 12.1: Indicative features of people's individual and group identities

12.3.1 Individual identity characteristics

Our individual identities and associated characteristics are very numerous and wide-ranging. Some, such as professional experience and professional expertise, are clearly of crucial importance for the workplace, and inform procedures such as recruitment, job allocation and so on. Others, such as hobbies are less so and yet can be important for building connections when people are seeking areas of shared interest and common ground.

Some characteristics should not normally be important (such as accent or physical appearance) and yet people may judge others – or even discriminate against them – on that basis. For instance, it emerged in April 2023 that the grooming policy of the Ritz Hotel in London stated that staff cannot have "unusual hairstyles such as spiky or Afro-style" (Warren, 2023). This meant that an applicant with an Afro hairstyle, who had reached the final stage of the interview process, was unable to continue with his application. The Ritz denied it was being racist, perhaps because they regarded hairstyle as an individual characteristic not a group one. Yet the applicant (and many others) felt he was definitely being discriminated against.

Yet other individual characteristics are particularly important for getting on well with others. These include language, values, personality, working styles, and work-related strengths. In terms of language, in today's globalised organisations, employees may have different levels of proficiency in the working language, especially when they are located in different parts of the world. Even when everyone is equally proficient, one may use vocabulary or phrases differently from others because of dialectal or regional differences. Such language issues can easily affect rapport (see Chapter 11 for more on communication).

Personality and working styles can often lead to 'clashes' among employees, as we often want (and may expect) others to work and interact in a manner that is compatible with our own. From a positive perspective, we feel comfortable and energised when we can work in a way that is in line with our own working style preferences. From a negative perspective, we can feel stressed and irritated when we need to work in a way that is quite different from our own preferences. For instance, people who work quickly and expect others to handle tasks in a similar manner can get very frustrated if they work with someone who pays great attention to detail, checking a report time and again before submitting it. The reverse also applies. Similarly, people who care deeply about what others think of them may be good at building rapport with others but get too stressed from overwork because they feel unable to say 'no' to requests.

Working style relates to issues such as those shown in Activity 12.1. As you read through them, think of your own tendency in relation to each of them. Note down your thoughts in columns 3 and 4.

Activity 12.1: Reflecting on working style tendencies

Working Style issue	Reflection questions	Your own tendencies	Alignment with your manager
Management of time	• Do you keep to deadlines? • Are you a last-minute person?		
Speed of working	• How quickly do you work? • How quickly do you expect others to work?		
Management of workload	• Do you take on too much? • Do you complete what you take on?		
Sharing of ideas	• Is your manager very fussy about detailed things? And you?		
Attention to detail	• Is the quality of your work compromised because of insufficient attention to detail? • Do you get bogged down from paying too much attention to detail?		
Level of self-motivation	• How self-motivated are you to keep persevering with (unappealing) tasks? • How easily do you give up on (unappealing) tasks?		

| Relating to others | • How much empathy do you feel for others?
• How much do you worry what others think of you? | | |

Gaining insights into the notion of working style preferences – our own and those of others – can help us become more aware of our own foibles as well as those of others.

Another approach to appreciating and accepting difference concerns work-related strengths. Some theorists (e.g. Belbin & Brown, 2023) have linked them closely with team roles. Others have simply focused on strengths. In both cases, the approach seeks to identify employees' stronger and weaker work-related characteristics, with the aim of helping develop more productive working relationships. Belbin and Brown (2023) refer to 'allowable weaknesses' and maintain that, unless they veer towards unacceptability, they should be allowed to remain as weaknesses so that they do not undermine the person's strengths. Other frameworks recommend that people build on their stronger characteristics and develop their somewhat less strong ones.

In some cases, teams and colleagues may naturally gravitate towards working in ways that match their strengths. For example, someone who is strong in supporting others may naturally come to play a nurturing role for less experienced colleagues. However, it can also be useful for people to explore their relative strengths more explicitly and a range of tools is available in the market to help with this. Most tools group a long(ish) list of items (e.g., 35 or more) into three or four categories. Figure 12.2 illustrates an indicative approach.

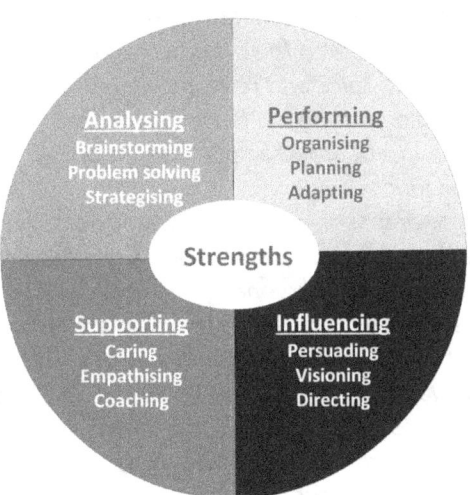

Figure 12.2: An indicative framework for conceptualising work-related strengths

Part 3 – The TRIPS Rapport Management Framework

Test reports present the results in rank order, usually listing the top 5 – the things that an employee is especially good at. The next five are sometimes identified as strengths that can be leveraged more, while the bottom five are labelled as ones for delegation.

Understanding work-related strengths can have several positive benefits for people management:

- Leaders or managers can focus on utilising each employee's top 5 skills and leveraging the next set of 5 skills. This can help people feel appreciated (thereby addressing their face needs), which in turn can increase their sense of satisfaction, motivation, and wellbeing.
- Team members can see themselves as complementing each other and be less competitive.
- Individual employees need not feel disappointed or dissatisfied with themselves over skills they feel weak at. Importantly, they get the opportunity and support to develop these skills.

Case Study 12.2 illustrates how useful one team leader, Isabella, found a strengths approach to be.

> **Case Study 12.2: The value of a strengths approach**
> *The one thing that has helped us function so well as a team goes back to something I started 5, 6 or 7 years ago. We follow a strengths approach, which says everyone has their own top set of talents. Knowing what they are across the team, helps us understand people's different strengths and how we should develop them to the maximum effect.*
>
> *We ensure people's roles and responsibilities are matched to their strengths. For example, if someone is strong on analytics and problem solving, they're going to be good as our lead on policy, process, work flow design, and product design.*
>
> *When we came across this strengths framework, we became a self-organising team, where people naturally gravitated towards what they like to do and do best. Everyone knows what everyone else's top talents are, so this gives us permission to celebrate what people do well and recognise that people don't need to have the same strengths to be successful and productive. That has really helped us. People talk to each other in terms of their strengths. Everyone knows who is good at what.*
>
> *That was also a big revelation for me. I have struggled with the numbers aspect of my job – budget matters and projects that require a lot of number crunching. That's not my strength. For a long time I felt*

Part 3 – The TRIPS Rapport Management Framework

bad that that was missing from skillset as a leader. When I came upon the strengths approach, I realised I don't need to beat myself up about it, I can let someone who is good at this handle those tasks. My focus should be on being a better leader, not a better budgeter."

Reflect
1. Thinking of your colleagues at work, how aware are you of their main strengths?
2. How could that awareness help you work together better?
3. What might be a drawback of a strengths approach?

At the same time, it is important for staff at all levels not to use their awareness of working strengths as an excuse to stereotype individuals or restrict their ability to learn and grow.

12.3.2 Group membership identity characteristics

We are all members of multiple groups; for example, of a profession, of a particular organisation, of a religious group, of an ethnic group, of a sports group, of an age group. Our memberships of those groups give us a sense of belonging and form a key part of our identity. However, they can also be a source of exclusion and discrimination, because there is a strong psychological tendency for members of one group to favour fellow members of their own group (known as the ingroup) and to give them preferential treatment over members of other groups (known as the outgroup). This relates to the issue of Attention and can also give rise to concerns about Fairness or equity (i.e., two of the GAAFFE Triggers), thereby affecting rapport.

Since group characteristics/identities are closely associated with links and attitudes between people, we explore this in more detail in Section 12.4.2. Here, we recommend that you think through your own senses of identity.

Activity 12.2: Reflecting on identities
1. Think about your own sense of who you are. Consider aspects such as your roles in life (professional and personal), your geographical or regional affiliations, your beliefs, hobbies and interests, your achievements, your working style, and similar. Now write down 5 -10 things that you feel reflect important aspects of your identity (your sense of who you are), particularly in relation to work. Start each one with "I ..."; e.g., I am an academic; I've worked in many different countries; I dislike doing things at the last minute.
2. If possible, ask a trusted colleague to do the same as #1 above. Then, if you are comfortable, share and compare your lists. How do your senses

> of identity affect your working relationship?
> Note: Our identities can change and develop over time, and the centrality of certain aspects of our identity can vary according to circumstances and setting. So, if you were to repeat this activity on another occasion, you might find you produce different lists. This is normal. In fact, it can be useful to reflect on those changes!

12.4 People's links with each other

People are linked with each other in various ways, and these also need to be taken into account in managing rapport because they have a major impact on people's behaviour and attitudes towards each other.

12.4.1 Association links: Role responsibilities, power, and familiarity

In the workplace, we are linked with other employees and with clients, suppliers, and other stakeholders in terms of the following:

- Our role responsibilities towards each other
- Our relative power over each other
- Our relative familiarity with each other

All three of these factors are integrally linked with rapport management because they have a major impact on people's use of language and interpretation of what is said and done. They are central to politeness theories within pragmatics.

Role responsibilities

In terms of role responsibilities, line managers, for example, have responsibilities towards their direct reports, and direct reports have responsibilities towards their manager(s). Similarly, university lecturers have responsibilities towards their students and students have responsibilities towards their lecturers. These are known as complementary rights and obligations. Key issues from a rapport management perspective are:

- whether both parties have shared understandings of what their mutual responsibilities are;
- how similar or different their expectations are of each other (see also Section 13.3);
- whether each party fulfils the expectations of the other party.

Very often responsibilities are not identified explicitly and/or in detail – in fact, it is no doubt impractical to cover all elements – and so people naturally make implicit, subconscious assumptions as to what the other person 'should' or 'should not' do. These beliefs and assumptions can be significantly different if their respective experiences and cultural backgrounds are different. As a result, each role member may hold different expectations regarding the other person's behaviour and if those expectations are not met, a reaction will be triggered. For example, if a direct report expects his/her line manager to give explicit instructions for a particular task, while the line manager expects the direct report to use his/her own initiative, each may easily become annoyed with the other.

People's (varying) conceptions of their respective role responsibilities thus affect rapport by potentially activating one or more of the GAAFFE triggers, especially that of autonomy–control, fairness, and attention–inattention.

Relative power
Relative power is another crucially important people factor that affects workplace relationships; in other words, who can impose on whom, and on what basis. Power is normally asymmetrical, which means that the person 'with power' is able to impose on the person with less power, while the reverse is not true. However, people's sources of power can be various, so an individual might have power in one respect and not in another.

Power often resides in a person's formal hierarchical position, and this is of key importance in the workplace. However, it is broader than this and a classic social psychological framework (French & Raven, 1959) identifies five main bases of power:

1. Reward power: when a person has control over positive outcomes for others (i.e., things that others want, such as bonus payments or a recommendation for promotion), that person has reward power over the others.
2. Coercive power: when a person has control over negative outcomes for others (i.e., things that others don't want, such as demotion or the allocation of undesirable tasks), that person has coercive power over the others.
3. Expert power: when a person has some special knowledge or expertise that others want or need, that person has expert power over the others.
4. Legitimate power: when a person has the right (because of their role, status, or situational circumstances) to prescribe or expect certain things of others, that person has legitimate power over the others.
5. Referent power: when a person is admired and looked up to by others, with others keen to emulate them, that person has referent power over the others.

Lack of psychological safety (see Chapter 13) is particularly associated with coercive power and reward power. Often coercive power and reward power are linked with legitimate power, insofar as a line manager typically holds the right to reward or punish others. But it can also occur in other situations, as Case Study 12.3 illustrates. This incident was reported by a consultant paediatrician in a radio interview in the summer of 2023 (BBC Radio 4, 2023) and it demonstrates the detrimental impact that coercive power can have, even when the original motivation for setting up a system was positive.

Part 3 – The TRIPS Rapport Management Framework

> **Case Study 12.3: The challenge for doctors of 'speaking up'**
> A community doctor in the UK was convicted for surreptitiously murdering 200 of his patients, and so after this a new system was introduced which required doctors to renew their licence to practise every five years. Revalidation of hospital doctors is carried out by a non-medical senior hospital executive, who has the power not to put a doctor forward for licence renewal if they choose not to do so. The consultant paediatrician commented that she knows from experience that a lot of doctors, even those normally willing and brave enough to speak up when their concern is high enough, don't want to raise any issues when the time for their revalidation is getting close. *"They are scared",* she said. She acknowledged that not all hospital executives would act like that but maintained that doctors are aware that those executives have the threat of non-revalidation available in their 'toolbox of intimidation' and are frightened.
>
> **Reflect**
> 1. What experiences have you had (if any) of coercive power in the workplace?
> 2. What impact did it have on you?
> 3. What other types of power have you witnessed in the workplace?

In other words, in this case, non-medical senior executives hold coercive power over doctors, even senior consultants, causing doctors to experience a serious lack of psychological safety.

In actual fact, it is very difficult to achieve full psychological safety, because the impact of coercive and reward power can rarely be completely eliminated. Often there is a clash of GAAFFE triggers. In the cases where doctors' concerns have been ignored by hospital executives, it seems the latter were prioritising their goal of reputation protection, while the doctors were concerned about their ethical duty of care for their patients. However, the risk of being treated unfairly by hospital executives (as in Case Study 12.3) or simply ignored (as reported around some other cases) meant that the medical risks were not addressed. This demonstrates how all of the GAAFFE triggers can affect psychological safety and need to be handled as effectively and mindfully as possible.

As Case Study 12.3 also illustrates, people may hold coercive power over others even when they do not have any hierarchical authority over them (i.e., when they do not have any legitimate power over them). And, as we discussed in Chapter 6, withholding key information is also an exertion of power. When it is withheld for reasons of personal gain and to obstruct others, this is a display of expert power. Language plays a key role in managing hierarchical relations. In (organisational and societal) settings where hierarchy is an important value, people in more senior roles are likely to require greater deference towards them.

Familiarity links
The third important type of association link between people is that of degree of familiarity, or distance–closeness.

In terms of level of familiarity between boss and direct reports, the key issue here is one of fairness. If senior staff are much closer to some more junior employees than others, does this mean that the people they are closer to will gain a work-related advantage, such as quicker promotion? Even if not, do others perceive it this way? This can affect employee morale as well as rapport between individuals.

Hobbies and social habits can play a role here. For instance, if some employees at different levels of seniority play together in a work sports team, some bonding will inevitably occur. Senior staff will become more familiar with those they socialise with, and this familiarity may easily influence their decision-making. Some ambitious junior employees may build strategically on such opportunities, leaving others feeling sidelined and overlooked.

This sense of exclusion can also apply among colleagues. If some team members like socialising together by going for a drink after work, they will no doubt get to know each other well and form a strong bond. Others may not be able to join for various reasons (e.g., family responsibilities) and this can easily lead to them feeling somewhat alienated; in other words, it can activate the attention–inattention GAAFFE trigger.

Another potential problem associated with familiarity is the level of closeness that is appropriate for the context (see also Chapter 9 on the A: Attention GAAFFE trigger). When one person is more senior than the other and wishes to develop a close relationship with the more junior person, the power differential – including the more senior person's reward and coercive power – can put unacceptable pressure on the more junior person. The latter may fear that if they don't accept the advances, it could threaten their career prospects. This means that it is always important to be mindful about familiarity, especially for those in more senior positions.

12.4.2 Attitude links: Relationship history, bias, and stereotyping

In addition to association links among people (role responsibilities, power relations, and level of familiarity), another very important facet is attitude links. Attitude links refer to the feelings, beliefs, and assumptions we hold towards others, including whether we like or dislike them and the qualities (positive or negative) we assume them to have.

Some attitude links stem from individuals' relationship history; for instance, whether a manager has previously been considerate or inconsiderate towards a direct report, or whether two individuals have had a major disagreement. Often, though, it relates to people's group identities and their senses of 'them' and 'us'. This differentiation can be based on people's perceptions of any group membership differences, such as demographics (e.g., nationality, ethnicity) or roles (e.g., 'divisions' between academics and administrators in universities, and doctors and administrators in hospitals).

Psychologists (e.g. Simon, 2004, pp. 66–68) have pointed out that identities serve several functions, two of which are belonging and distinctiveness. This is closely linked with our group identities. On the one hand, our membership of a group, and our associated identification with that group, provides us with a sense of belonging and rootedness. This is important for our wellbeing. On the other hand, it also provides us with a sense of distinctiveness, helping us realise not only where we belong, but also where we do not belong. In other words, our identities reflect both who we are and who we are not.

Social identity theory (e.g., Tajfel, 1982) further points out that there is a natural tendency to regard one's own group and its members (one's ingroup) more favourably than other groups and its members (one's outgroups). There is both a cognitive aspect to this as well as an emotional aspect. The former involves beliefs about outgroup members' characteristics, such as their competence, honesty, and trustworthiness. The latter involves attitudinal feelings towards outgroup members, such as fear, condescension, and distrust. In other words, our need to belong somewhere (and not somewhere else) results in a natural tendency to be biased or prejudiced towards people whom we regard as 'one of them' rather than 'one of us'.

In recent years, the notion of 'unconscious bias' has come to the fore – the notion that everyone in a society, even seemingly tolerant individuals, has implicit negative stereotypes embedded deeply and unconsciously within them, and that these need to be 'rooted out'. Blame is thus attached to individuals. Yet, as Fanshawe (2022) points out, on the one hand, people's biases are frequently very conscious, not unconscious; moreover, while bias is damaging, it's not a character flaw but a product of history. This is in line with recent theorising on stereotypes by the psychologist Perry Hinton (2023). He argues that unconscious bias is in fact implicit cultural knowledge, and explains stereotypes as follows:

> Stereotypes are cultural constructions known by the members of a culture (regardless of whether they agree with them or not). Hence, it is the normative structure of a culture and the underlying dominant ideologies within it that should be examined to reveal the source of stereotypical generalizations about a social group. (p. 108)

So, what does all this mean for rapport and relationship management? We note several points here.

- Everyone needs to be aware that people's prejudices may come out in interaction – through microinsults or even explicit discriminatory comments (see Chapter 11).
- If this happens, we need to avoid blaming the individual, either publicly or privately, because that will close down communication and the prejudice will never be faced up to. Blaming and shaming people with rules and re-education will alienate people rather than encourage reflection and change.
- Instead, we need to acknowledge that everyone (including ourselves!) has biases of some kind, and we need to encourage people to talk through their own biases, without fear of criticism. This will help raise people's awareness of the scope of bias and how it is manifested. (See Activity 12.3.)
- Beyond that, we need to enhance everyone's understanding of how prejudice can damage other people's wellbeing and seek to promote genuine empathy for others. This needs to be accompanied by mindfulness and sensitivity in all our interactions.

Activity 12.3: Reflecting on potential personal biases

1. When you meet a new colleague or client for the first time, what spontaneous reaction do you usually have if they ...

	Negative spontaneous reaction		No particular reaction		Positive spontaneous reaction
...are dressed in a way you regard as unfashionable	1	2	3	4	5
...speak with a strong accent that you find difficult to understand	1	2	3	4	5
...are significantly overweight	1	2	3	4	5
...are from a different ethnic group	1	2	3	4	5
...are extremely talkative and dominant	1	2	3	4	5
[other characteristic that is noticeable for you]	1	2	3	4	5
[other characteristic that is noticeable for you]	1	2	3	4	5

2. If possible, talk through your biases with a trusted colleague or friend?
3. How have you seen your biases (or those of any of your colleagues) show themselves at work?

12.5 Summary and follow-up reading

People are the individuals who experience rapport (or lack of it) and who also influence it. This chapter has explained how this variable – the number of people involved in an interaction, their identity characteristics, and the links and connections between them, all play a role in affecting rapport management.

A summary template identifying the key features of the TRIPS P-People Concept is given in Chapter 15. It includes questions that are useful for checking and reflection purposes.

For further information on interaction issues, refer to the references mentioned within the chapter. In addition, the following are particularly useful.

Spencer-Oatey, H., & Kádár, D. Z. (2021). *Intercultural politeness: Managing relations across cultures.* Cambridge University Press. Much of Chapter 5 provides a thorough discussion of the influence of people (called participants) on interaction.

Hinton, P. (2023). Rethinking stereotypes and norms in intercultural relations. In T. McConachy & P. Hinton (Eds.), *Negotiating intercultural relations. Insights from linguistics, psychology, and intercultural education* (pp. 95–112). Bloomsbury. This chapter explains and critiques classical models of stereotypes and of unconscious bias and then presents an alternative – stereotypes as cultural constructions.

Fanshawe, S. (2022). *The power of difference.* Kogan Page. Chapter 4 deals with unconscious bias, explaining the problems associated with it and arguing for a different approach.

Hay, J. (2009). Working it out at work. *Understanding attitudes and building relationships.* 2nd ed. Sherwood Publishing. Chapter 6 focuses on working styles and presents a particular framework for considering them and is available open access here: https://juliehay.org/wp-content/uploads/2020/01/wow_chapter_6_web.pdf

Chapter 13: Settings:
Understanding the impact of contexts

13.1 Introduction

This chapter provides a focused explanation of S: Settings in the TRIPS Rapport Management framework.

'S' stands for Settings – the contexts in which interactions take place. In order to handle rapport risks well, it is necessary to take the settings into account. This is because they affect people's expectations and interpretations of what is said and done, and thus in turn affect their perceptions of rapport, as well as the ways in which they choose to manage it.

In this chapter, we explain:

- The multilayered nature of settings
- The impact of settings on ways of doing things (i.e., norms, regulations, and values)
- The impact of the settings on psychological atmosphere (i.e., healthy versus unhealthy cultural climate)

13.2 An overview of settings

13.2.1 The multiple layers of setting

There are multiple layers to settings, nested within each other. All of them affect (to a greater or lesser extent) what is said and done and how people interpret the interaction. This in turn affects rapport.

Figures 2.5 and 13.1 identify four important settings layers:

- Interaction Setting
- Organisational Setting
- Societal Setting
- World Setting

The Interaction Setting: This is the context in which an interaction takes place. It covers things such as where it takes place (e.g., online or face-to-face; if the latter, its physical location), when it takes place (e.g., time of day, on what kind of occasion, whether it is synchronous or asynchronous), and its purpose (e.g., to make strategic plans or negotiate a sale). All of these influence the ways in which communication takes place and people's associated expectations and interpretations.

The Organisational Setting: The organisational setting zooms out a little from the interaction setting and considers the culture of the organisation and the workplace, including any local subcultures/ team microcultures. It can include branding requirements and any procedural specifications, such as norms, channels, and styles of communication. Of particular relevance for rapport, though, are the organisation's values (espoused and actual) and the workplace atmosphere associated with those values.

The Societal and World Settings: All organisations function within a broader context – within their societal (national), regional and world settings. These wider contexts can influence organisational and interaction settings in both direct and indirect ways, such as the following:

- National rules, regulations and laws that organisations need to adhere to;
- Cultural values and principles that influence the practices of organisations;
- Societal and world issues, such as the Covid-19 pandemic, natural disasters, and wars, and their impact on the functioning of organisations.

Other potential layers also exist; for instance, there could be a Departmental Setting that fits within an Organisational Setting. Similarly, there could be professional membership associations and societies (e.g., British Association for Applied Linguistics; Society for Intercultural Education, Training and Research) that could function within a Societal Setting, or if it is an international association, it would fit within a World Setting, probably with branches within different Societal Settings.

13.2.2 The impact of multilevel settings on interaction

These multilayered settings each have three types of cultural patterning embedded within them: norms, rules and regulations, and values and beliefs (see Figure 13.1).

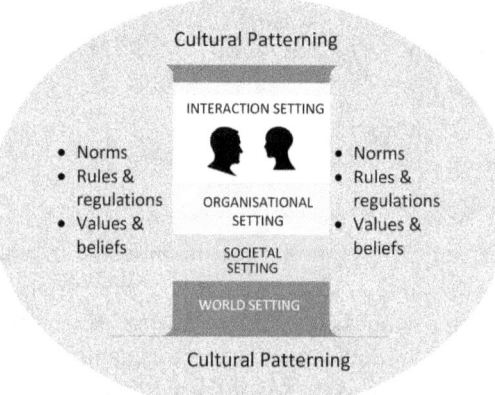

Fig.13.1: The infusion of cultural patterning into contextual settings

13.3 Settings and norms: the 'way we do things round here'

Norms are particularly important for rapport management because they set up expectations, and any breach of those expectations can trigger a rapport reaction. They cover organisational processes and procedures and are often referred to as 'the way we do things around here' (Bower, 1966). This interprets norms in a descriptive sense – what usually happens and what others expect will happen (see below for another interpretation). Breaches, however, are not always – or even often – carried out deliberately, but rather stem from different assumptions as to what will happen or needs to happen. Different organisations and different societies often develop different shared ways for carrying out their various activities, and 'newcomers' acquire them through a period of socialisation. So, if someone moves from one organisation or society to another, their respective expectations over what will happen could easily differ and they will need time and/or support to become familiar with the norms in their current situation.

13.3.1 Communicative events: norms and procedures

Norms are particularly important to types of interactions that linguists call 'communicative events' (also known as 'communicative activities') – interactions such as meetings, performance reviews, press conference, annual appraisal. These all have patterns – or norms – associated with them. The norms reflect common and typical ways of handling the communicative events and they give rise to expectations as to what will or won't happen. Problems may arise when people's norms and associated expectations are different.

Consider Case Study 13.1, about workshops. It concerns the setting for an international workshop that was part of a Sino-British collaborative education project, and was reported by the programme manager (Spencer-Oatey, 2007).

> **Case Study 13.1: The setting for a workshop**
> In the second year of the programme, we arranged a workshop in Beijing for the British and Chinese teams. The purpose was for the team members to share with each other what they had achieved so far, give each other feedback on what had been done, and to plan next steps. A similar workshop had been held very successfully in the first year of the programme in the UK.
> When we arrived at the location in Beijing where the workshop would take place, the British team members were shocked. The room was formally laid out with a very large U-shape of mahogany tables that could not be moved, with a podium at the front with a microphone, and with a massive number of flowering plants in large pots that surrounded the podium and

Part 3 – The TRIPS Rapport Management Framework

filled much of the gap in the U-shape.
One of the British project managers exclaimed: *"How can we discuss our projects in a room like this? We need to have small, moveable tables."* Our Chinese hosts responded that this would not be possible and that this was the best arrangement for a workshop in China.

Reflect
1. In your understanding, what is a workshop? What is its purpose?
2. What activities do you associate with a workshop?
3. What kind of physical setting do you associate with a workshop?
4. What kind of 'equipment' or facilities would you need for a workshop?
5. If feasible, discuss your answers with a colleague from a different country/part of the organisation or who has only recently joined from another organisation. How similar or different are your views?

Understanding the cultural patterns or norms associated with a communicative event is crucial for gaining insights into collaboration challenges such as this, as well as in all situations where there is any kind of diversity in background and experience.

Linguists point out that communicative events have recognisable components. We explain four key ones below (Allwood, 2007).

a. **The purpose of the communicative event**
Firstly, all communicative events have a purpose associated with them. However, it is important to be aware that while this is the case, not everyone will necessarily agree on what those purposes are. In Case Study 13.1, there were societal (i.e., national) cultural differences within the field of education. The British team members regarded the primary purpose of the workshop was to gain feedback on progress so far via small group discussion, so that the project goals could be achieved more effectively. The Chinese team members, on the other hand, reported later that they wanted to demonstrate to their leaders the importance of the collaborative project and how successful it had been so far.
  If people have different understandings of the purpose of a communicative event, they may easily hold different goals for it. Then, if one or more person's goals are not achieved, this will tend to lead to a Trigger reaction.

b. **Procedures for carrying out the communicative event**
The purpose of communicative activities is often (but not always) closely linked with the procedures for carrying it out. These are often known as scripts. In Case Study 13.1, the British team's goals for the event required small group discussion, while for the Chinese it meant formal presentations.

In fact, it is very common for there to be differences in the expected procedures for carrying out a communicative event, especially across different organisations. So, when an employee is new to an organisation (or an activity within it), it is important to bear this in mind and, where the procedures have been formalised, to provide appropriate induction. Often, however, people are not consciously aware of their procedures – they take them for granted and only notice them when they have been breached. So, it is also important for new employees to be very observant and to notice the way things are done.

c. **Role responsibilities for carrying out a communicative event**
Closely linked with the procedures for carrying out a communicative event are participants' role responsibilities for doing so.

Consider Case Study 13.2. It reports the negative comments of a Chinese head of delegation on a welcome meeting at a British engineering company in the UK (Spencer-Oatey & Xing, 2008).

Case Study 13.2: Introductions at meetings
Just as I was going to give my speech, on behalf of the whole delegation, I was rudely interrupted by the interpreter. The British chairman had given his speech, so it was my turn to say something in response. But I was stopped from making my return speech and instead we were asked to each introduce ourselves. According to our customs, it's my job to give a return speech and it's also my job to introduce each member of the delegation. The British were so condescending by preventing me from doing that. It just proves how the British look down on us Chinese!

Reflect
1. How are introductions during meetings handled in your organisation?
2. What variation occurs and what factors influence that variation

---

The head of delegation was expecting (a) to give a formal speech, and (b) introduce each member of the delegation on their behalf. He identifies this as 'according to our customs' and evaluated the British negatively for not allowing him to do so. The British hosts, however, assumed that each delegation member would introduce themselves, and they thought giving a formal return speech might put the head under too much pressure. Each party had different expectations around their respective role responsibilities.

It is important, therefore, to consider whether everyone has a shared understanding of each other's role responsibilities. Without this, a Trigger reaction is likely to occur.

Part 3 – The TRIPS Rapport Management Framework

d. The physical environment for carrying out a communicative event
Also closely intertwined with purpose, procedures, and role responsibilities, is the environment or surroundings in which the communicative event takes place. This can include a number of things, such as:

- Where the activity takes place; e.g.
  o In which country / countries
  o In what type of building (e.g., shop, open plan office, company boardroom)
  o What size and layout of room including a virtual room
- What tools and artifacts (e.g., furniture & seating arrangements, computers) are present and /or required.
- Whether the activity is face-to-face or online
- Physical aspects such as noise and light that may interfere with the message transmission and reception

We noted in Case Study 13.1 above that the furniture in the room was integrally connected with the purpose of the event. It affected the way it supported (or hindered) the procedures and whether the purpose could easily be achieved.

Environment is always an important element of a communicative event but can be greatly influenced by cultural patterning at organisational and societal levels.

Application

Given the possible variation in the norms and procedures of communicative activities, and the risk of different assumptions, it is very important to check on your and others' expectations and understandings of the various elements. We recommend that you use Activity 13.1 to think through these issues as they apply to your workplace.

Activity 13.1: Reflecting on the norms associated with communicative events

Think of a communicative event (e.g., appraisal meeting, recruitment interview, departmental meeting) that you are involved in. Use the questions below to reflect on its key features and where individuals may have varying conceptions.

Key features of the communicative event	Explanation	Questions to consider in order to avoid potential problems
Purpose	What the purpose of the event is / what is meant to be achieved.	Does everyone have a shared understanding of what they are all trying to achieve?

Role responsibilities	What the participants are expected to do or not do.	Does everyone have a shared understanding of what their role involves (i.e., what they should or should not do)?
Physical environment	The tools, media, instruments, and their required set-up needed to best support the event.	Does everyone have a shared understanding of the required set-up and which tools are best used for which purpose?

Norms, of course, can change when other features change. Take, for example, the Covid-19 pandemic, when many people needed to work from home. It rather quickly changed the environmental norm – people's location of work and the different ways of communicating with co-workers that this necessitated. In fact, prior to the pandemic, it was not unusual for people in some professions (e.g., university academics) to work from home one day a week. However, the pandemic normalised it for a large proportion of the population, with many people finding it highly attractive. Now that the pandemic is over, it is proving difficult to return to the pre-pandemic norms of office working. This demonstrates the power that norms can have on the world of work.

13.4 Settings, rules, and regulations

Interestingly, and perhaps related to the new norm of working from home, there is a tendency for norms to change from 'this is what we usually do' to 'this is what we/you must (allow or be allowed to) do'. In other words, common ways of doing things can turn into prescriptive and proscriptive rules. The psychologist, Robert Cialdini (2012), uses the terms 'descriptive norms' and 'injunctive norms' to refer to this. Descriptive norms are patterns of behaviour that are frequently or typically performed, while injunctive norms are prescribed or required behaviour.

Both give rise to expectations, and both can have negative consequences for rapport if they are not upheld. However, when required behaviour is not performed, or forbidden behaviour is carried out, the consequences are usually more serious. Yet for people who are new to a workplace, not only do they have to learn about the descriptive norms and procedures such as those associated with communicative events, they also need to be able to distinguish them from prescribed and proscribed behaviour. This may be difficult, as Case Study 13.3 illustrates.

> **Case Study 13.3: Settings, regulations, and probation**
> Shanlu had recently started work as a recruitment agent for an educational institution in the UK and was on probation. Her role was

Part 3 – The TRIPS Rapport Management Framework

to make contact with potential applicants, encourage them to apply for a particular course, and then support them through the application process. To do this successfully, she needed to learn many details about the organisation's recruitment procedures, rules, and regulations and how to handle them through the organisation's computer systems. She was given some training, but it was brief and she found it difficult to follow and remember all the details.

The first two months In post were very stressful, but she worked extremely hard in trying to achieve the recruitment targets set for her. She received regular positive feedback from her line manager, which encouraged her. Then one day, completely unexpectedly, she was told that her probation was being terminated with immediate effect because of a 'data breach'. She had allowed an applicant to complete one of the tasks online, when this was apparently not allowed – it should have been done on campus. Her line manager was aware that this had happened but had not criticised her over it.

She was upset with both the organisation and her line manager, especially as she'd received high feedback scores on all occasions up to then and her line manager had told her she was doing well. She felt extremely unfairly treated.

Reflect
1. In your opinion, was Shanlu unfairly treated? Give reasons for your viewpoint.

In this case, Shanlu was not clear on one aspect of the prescriptive and proscriptive regulations – that a particular task must always be completed on campus (the prescription) and must never be completed online or at home (the proscription). As a result, she was dismissed for a data breach.

Of course, all organisations need to have sets of rules and regulations that all employees are required to adhere to. Such requirements can cover a wide range of issues, including the following:

- Health and safety
- Equal opportunities
- Cyber security
- Data protection
- Financial compliance
- Recruitment and dismissal
- Promotion

Some of these derive from societal-level legislation, such as around data protection and financial compliance. Others may be more organisational (or even departmental) specific, and perhaps more negotiable. Yet whenever they are regarded as obligatory, they need to be explicitly and officially communicated to avoid the problem seen in Case Study 13.3 where the GAAFFE trigger of unfairness can be activated. They are often inculcated to staff via compulsory training, so when this is poor, problems can arise.

To think through the issues of norms, rules, and regulations in your workplace, consider the questions in Activity 13.2.

> **Activity 13.2: Common behaviour and required behaviour**
> 1. What 'common ways of doing things' (i.e., descriptive norms) exist in your department/team/organisation?
> 2. How do people react if someone doesn't keep to them?
> 3. What rules and regulations are you required to adhere to in your work?
> 4. How far are they organisation-specific or legal requirements?
> 5. How does the line manager or the organisation react if someone doesn't keep to them?

An important point to keep in mind when working in contexts of cultural diversity is differing attitudes towards 'rule rigour'. Rule rigour refers to three potential areas of difference:

- How precisely rules are specified; for instance, how clearly role responsibilities are identified, or operational procedures are formalised.
- How strictly people are expected to uphold the rules – whether the rules can be negotiated or treated as guidelines, or whether they need to be strictly adhered to.
- How people react when the rules are broken – whether a certain amount of infringement is regarded as normal and natural, whether it is treated as a learning opportunity for the employee concerned, or whether sanctions are immediately imposed (as for Shanlu, in Case Study 13.3).

Rule rigour is not just a practice, it often stems from underlying attitudes or beliefs. We consider these 'deeper' issues next.

13.5 Settings and Values/Beliefs

So far, we have focused on the impact of settings on ways of doing things from a procedural point of view. Often, however, the procedures stem from more deep-seated values and beliefs. So, to understand the impact of settings on interaction and rapport, it is also important to gain more insight into these.

13.5.1 Values: Research within psychology and anthropology

There has been a very large amount of research into values carried out by specialists in cross-cultural and organisational psychology and in anthropology, and quite a plethora of different types of value dimensions have been identified. In other words, these are issues where people may vary across a continuum in the values or principles they hold and believe in. They broadly fall into the following main areas:

- Group–Individual: how far individuals' needs are prioritised in comparison with those of the group. This dimension is typically referred to as Individualism–Collectivism.
- Hierarchy–equality: How far people accept differences in status and power as normal or prefer them to be minimal. This is typically referred to as High–Low Power Distance.
- Uncertainty–certainty: How far people seek to minimise uncertainty (e.g., through rules) or welcome it and embrace it. This is typically referred to as High–Low Uncertainty Avoidance.
- Task–relationship prioritisation: How far people prioritise in a project or seek first to build and strengthen relationships. This is typically referred to as Task–Relationship Orientation.
- Attitudes to time: How far people focus on the past (e.g., respect for traditions), on the future (e.g., long-term planning), or on the present (e.g., current realities and needs). This is typically referred to as Time Orientation. Also, how people manage their time, regarding it as a limited or unlimited resource, and whether they multitask or do things sequentially, referred to as Polychronic or Monochronic time management.
- Beliefs about human nature: How far people think others can normally be trusted or not. This is typically referred to as Basic Human Nature.
- Attitude to the environment: How far people try to master nature, accept subjugation to it, or seek to be in harmony with it. This is typically referred to as Man–Nature Relationship.

All of these values have implications for working relationships, and some examples are shown in Table 13.1. It's important to bear in mind that these are dimensions or continua, not discrete categories, and should be interpreted in that way. People may also hold different positions, depending on the particular interaction setting they are in.

Part 3 – The TRIPS Rapport Management Framework

Value	Indicative implications for the workplace
Group-Individual	How far are individual preferences taken into account when distributing tasks?
Hierarchy-equality	How controlling or collaborative is the leadership style?
Uncertainty - certainty	How uncomfortable do employees feel about change?
Task-relationship prioritisation	How far are tasks prioritised to such an extent that employee wellbeing is affected?
Attitudes to time	How much emphasis is there on current deadlines? How far is multitasking expected?
Beliefs about human nature	How far are employees trusted, e.g., to work efficiently from home?
Attitude to the environment	How far is the organisation upholding an ethical stance towards the environment?

Table 13.1: Examples of how values can potentially influence interaction and rapport at work

13.5.2 Organisational values

Most organisations place importance on identifying their own values. These are the guiding principles that underpin their work, including the goals they set and the key behaviours and actions for achieving those goals. The guiding principles are referred to variously as company values or principles, corporate values, and core values. They are typically publicly identified, such as on company websites and publicity materials, and in such contexts are known by academics as 'espoused values'.

There is a potentially massive number of different values that organisations can identify as core to their business. They can often be grouped according to foci and Figure 13.2 shows one possible configuration.

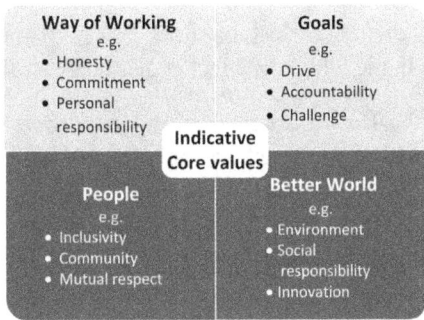

Figure 13.2: An indicative configuration of organisational values[60]

---
[60] Derived from various sites, including https://www.betterup.com/blog/core-values

Part 3 – The TRIPS Rapport Management Framework

From a rapport management perspective, two issues are particularly important:
- Is there an alignment between the organisation's espoused values and what happens in practice? If not, it is likely to provoke cynicism and disillusionment among staff.
- Is there an alignment between the organisation's espoused values and those of individual employees? If not, those employees are likely to experience a sense of personal discomfort, internal conflict, and lack of sense of belonging and commitment to the organisation. If there is a good alignment, it can enhance an employee's sense of belonging and sense of fulfilment.

> **Activity 13.3: Core values in your workplace**
> 1. What are your organisation's espoused core values?
> 2. How do they relate to the values identified in Table 13.2 and Figure 13.2?
> 3. How comfortable are you with their espoused values?
> 4. How far do the leaders of the organisation and your manager put the espoused values into practice and in what ways?
> 5. What impact (if any) do the espoused values have on your experiences of working relationships?

13.6 The dynamic interplay between Settings, norms, and values

The different levels of settings have a simultaneous, dynamic, and interactive effect on the way that employees experience their impact. A recent study by Taser-Erdogan (2022) illustrates this in quite a novel way. She was interested in the career experiences of senior women in three different types of organisations in Turkey and carried out in-depth interviews with 49 female managers working at three different types of bank:

- A Western private bank that had been operating in Turkey for more than 10 years;
- A large privately owned Turkish bank;
- A 'participation bank' which in effect is primarily an Islamic bank.

She points out that at the Turkish societal setting level, there is a mixture of secular, patriarchal and religious norms, with the role of women seen mainly as wives and mothers in some regions. In her study, she found that at the organisational setting level, there were differences across the three banks in the impact of societal culture on the female managers' career prospects. Table 13.2 summarises her findings, based on the experiences reported by her interviewees.

Western Bank	Turkish Bank	Participation Bank
Implicit bias against female managers	Implicit and explicit bias against female managers	Implicit and explicit bias against female managers
• Required to display masculine & aggressive characteristics • Competitive & ' long hours' culture	• Lack of transparent criteria for promotion & the importance of networking • Sidelined from certain (challenging) roles needed for career progression • Promotion opportunities advertised separately to men & women	• Lack of transparent criteria for promotion & the importance of networking • Not given any challenging tasks • Deliberate policy not to place women in important roles

Table 13.2: Career prospects reported by Turkish women working in three different types of bank

As can be seen from Table 13.2, the exact ways in which women's career prospects were affected by cultural patterning varied across the three banks. In other words, the organizational context influenced how women's career progression opportunities were experienced.

The organizational context in turn interacted with the beliefs and preferences of the individuals working in each of these settings. Table 13.3 illustrates this.

Western Bank Female Employees	Turkish Bank Female Employees	Participation Bank Female Employees
The employees:	The employees:	The employees:
• Believed that masculine characteristics were needed to be a successful manager • Believed that an attractive work opportunity is incompatible with functioning as a good mother, so the latter must be sacrificed for career success	• Doubted that women were suitable for managerial positions of networking • Commented that the bank's family-friendly policy enabled them to combine the two roles	• Believed that women are too emotional to be managers and too lacking in self-confidence • Prioritised their family responsibilities, linking this with their religious beliefs. Knew this would influence their career success and accepted this.

Table 13.3: Interaction between personal values and organizational values, as experienced by Turkish women working in three different types of bank

We can see clearly from this study how closely interconnected the multiple settings levels are and how they interact to influence workplace experiences.

> **Activity 13.4: Core values in your workplace**
> Consider a workplace issue (e.g., achieving promotion, meeting sales targets) that is relevant to you:
> 1. What are your own personal desires/goals in relation to it?
> 2. How does your organisation's procedures and values support or hinder you in achieving them?
> 3. How do regulations/attitudes/values in society more broadly support or hinder you in achieving them?
> 4. What interconnections can you perceive between these different Settings layers?

13.7 Settings and psychological atmosphere

So far in this chapter we have focused on the interconnections between multi-level settings and the behavioural requirements and expectations associated with norms, regulations, and values. We now turn to another very important aspect of settings – the psychological atmosphere of settings.

Values are of crucial importance here. For instance, if goal achievement is a top priority for an organisation or an individual line manager, employees are likely to experience a considerable amount of pressure and stress over the achievement of those goals. If the setting of targets and feedback on performance towards them are not handled appropriately, employee wellbeing may easily suffer. The example of Erica, given at the beginning of Chapter 1, illustrates this.

Sometimes the source of the stress is external. For instance, societal and world issues can have a huge and ongoing impact on the viability of organisations, as happened during the Covid-19 pandemic, following the invasion of Ukraine and the steep subsequent rise in utility prices. As a result, many businesses (especially small ones) have become vulnerable, leading to uncertainty and wellbeing issues for staff.

13.7.1 Psychological safety

A key concept associated with psychological atmosphere is that of psychological safety. In an influential article William Kahn (1990, p. 705) defined it as a "sense of being able to show and employ self without fear of negative consequences to self-image, status, or career." In his research, he found that employees experienced psychological safety (or lack of it) in interactions with peers, groups/teams, and managers, as well as in relation to organisational norms.

Relationships that he found linked with psychological safety were characterised by support and trust, so that individuals:

- could fail without fearing consequences;
- received constructive rather than destructive criticism;
- had no need to worry about others' reactions;
- experienced minimal control from others;
- experienced others to be consistent, predictable and sincere.

At the organisational level, he found that people felt safer if they kept to organisational norms and did not question them. Deviation from the norms resulted in anxiety and frustration.

The opposite of psychological safety is fear and dissatisfaction:

- fear of being excluded or marginalised (a face threat);
- fear of being laughed at or looked down on for our ideas (a face threat);
- fear of being criticised if we make a mistake (a face threat);
- fear of disapproval if we upset the harmony of the group/team by expressing disagreement (a face threat);
- dissatisfaction that our ideas will be repressed if we cannot share them openly (an autonomy threat);
- fear and dissatisfaction that if we disagree with our line manager, we may be overlooked for attractive opportunities and others may progress more quickly (a fairness threat and a goal threat);
- fear that our careers may be negatively affected if our line manager comes to regard us as a troublemaker (goal threat).

Since the publication of Kahn's research in 1990, the importance of psychological safety has been increasingly recognised as core to employee wellbeing, creativity, and initiative taking. The work of Amy Edmondson (2019), Professor of Leadership and Management at Harvard Business School, has played a significant role in this promotion. Another leadership consultant, Timothy Clark (2020), has also contributed significantly to the issue. He helpfully identifies four different stages of psychological safety in his definition:

> Psychological safety is a condition in which you feel (1) included, (2) safe to learn, (3) safe to contribute, and (4) safe to challenge the status quo – all without fear of being embarrassed, marginalized, or punished in some way. (p. 2)

Whether the four stages are necessarily sequential, or simply different facets to psychological safety, could be debated. However, the explicit identification of 'inclusion' and 'safety to learn' fits well with Kahn's research findings and helps clarify that psychological safety is not just about 'speaking truth to power', as some people have interpreted it to be.

With regard to 'safety to learn', Clark argues that people should not feel embarrassed or ashamed about making a mistake or failing in some way. This is because mistakes can offer excellent opportunities for learning; they can encourage us to reflect on what went wrong and help sow the seeds for future success through the insights gained.

So, an important facet of psychological safety is therefore to support people who make mistakes or fail in a project – not to blame them or criticise them, but rather to encourage them to reflect on what they can learn from the episode, while also giving them feedback on what went well and what they need to work on.

The degree of psychological safety in a workplace is closely linked with the workplace culture on the one hand, and with the behaviour and attitudes of line managers on the other. So, Schein (2017) points out that "The burden [to create psychological safety] ultimately falls on the higher level person to create an environment in which subordinates will feel encouraged to speak up and will be rewarded for doing so, but the manner in which this may work still depends on the prevailing norms in the macro culture." (p. 172)

Nevertheless, colleagues and team members can also play a significant role, especially regarding the first two stages. The table below shows some questions that all leaders – and also all employees particularly when they work in teams – need to ask themselves.

Types of Psychological Safety	Questions to reflect on	Key responsibilities
Culture of inclusion	• How well are newcomers inducted into the group? • How easy is it for everyone to contribute comfortably to discussions or meetings? • To what extent does everyone contribute equally? • How carefully are you monitoring this? What signs are you looking out for?	• Everyone who is part of the team or group • Leaders

Part 3 – The TRIPS Rapport Management Framework

Culture of learning	• How accepting are you when someone else makes a mistake? • How do you demonstrate a 'no blame culture'? • How often do you ask for help/admit mistakes/say you don't know? • What support do you offer those who lack confidence or experience? • How do you plan for yours and others' learning and growth?	• Everyone who is part of the team or group • Leaders
Culture of innovation	• How much freedom or autonomy do you give to your team to try new initiatives? • How do you encourage this? • How do you respond if the initiative doesn't go well?	• Leaders
Culture of debate	• How often do your direct reports disagree with you or propose alternative strategies? • How comfortable do you feel when they do? • How far do you monitor your reaction, verbal and nonverbal?	• Leaders

If there are unhealthy levels of competition and distrust among senior management, the working environment is likely to be toxic and stressful for employees, particularly new employees who have been previously socialised in less competitive cultures. If employees are to achieve their best, especially (but not exclusively) when they take on new responsibilities and start to grow into their new roles, they need to feel:

- comfortable in their working environment;
- a sense of belonging, acceptance and inclusion by others;
- supported when they make mistakes and encouraged to keep on improving;
- able to share their thoughts without fear of retribution, when they notice a problem or have new ideas.

In other words, they need to work in an atmosphere of psychological safety.

In actual fact, full psychological safety is very difficult to achieve, because the impact of differentials in power can rarely be completely overcome. When psychological safety is low, the GAAFFE risks to rapport will be much higher, and careful attention will need to be paid to them in order to minimise risks to rapport. Conversely, the more rapport can be built among colleagues, the more it can promote and enhance psychological safety.

Part 3 – The TRIPS Rapport Management Framework

13.8 Summary and follow-up reading

All interaction and the management of rapport takes place in a setting. This setting has multiple layers, and influences both what people do and say, and what they expect others to do and say. Breaches will typically affect rapport.

A summary template of the TRIPS S-Setting Concept is given in Chapter 15. It includes questions that are useful for checking and reflection purposes.

For further information on Settings, refer to the references mentioned within the chapter. The following are also particularly useful.

Spencer-Oatey, H., & Kádár, D. Z. (2021). Intercultural politeness: Managing relations across cultures. Cambridge University Press. The following chapters are particularly useful: Chapter 3 on cultural patterning; Chapter 5 on the notion of context; Chapter 6 on norms and expectations

Spencer-Oatey, H., Franklin, P., & Lazidou, D. (2022). *Global fitness for global people: How to manage and leverage cultural diversity at work.* Castledown. Chapter 3 provides a clear account of cultural practices.

Gelfand, M. J. (2018). *Rule makers, rule breakers.* Robinson. This book explores the tightness or looseness of rules – whether people devise and abide by them or push against them.

Clark, T. R. (2020). *The 4 stages of psychological safety. Defining the path to inclusion and innovation.* Berrett-Koehler Publishers. This book explores the notion of psychological safety and how to achieve it at work.

Part 4

YOUR TRIPS TOOLKIT: TEMPLATES FOR APPLYING THE TOOLS

Part 4 – Your TRIPS Toolkit

Introduction to Part 4

Part 4 of the book provides you with some resources and ideas for following up on the concepts and tools in the book, so that you are better equipped for applying the TRIPS Toolkit in your own context.

The aim of this part is to:

- Provide you with an easy reference point for all the components of the TRIPS toolkit;
- Provide you with a summary of the key elements and issues that are useful to pay attention to and reflect on;
- Help you apply your learning from the book to challenges and issues in your own workplace;
- Provide a useful set of resources for consultants, HR practitioners, and trainers.

Chapter 14 gives templates for each of the challenge tools presented in Part 2 of the book:

- The Reaction Management Tool
- The Discord Management Tool
- The Participation Management Tool
- The Cooperative Colleague Tool
- The Upward Management Tool
- The Supportive Leadership Tool

Chapter 15 gives templates for each of the TRIPS concept tools presented in Part 3 of the book:

- Triggers: Reflection questions
- Reactions: Reflection questions
- Interactions: Reflection questions
- People: Reflection questions
- Settings: Reflection questions

Chapter 16 summarises the RelATE family of strategies that need to be used on combination with all of the templates. It also gives some suggestions for further follow-up.

Chapter 14: The TRIPS Challenge Tool Templates

This chapter provides templates for using the six challenge tools in the TRIPS Toolkit.

Reaction Management Tool: Steps and Prompts

This tool will help you gain insights into annoying or upsetting incidents and to overcome the negative emotions associated with them. It will do this by helping you understand your reactions and those of others and thereby make fairer judgements.

Step 1: Attend and Record Attend (i.e., pay attention) and record key facts and features associated with the incident	
What happened	• Note down exactly what was said or done. Avoid any interpretation of evaluation - simply state the 'facts'
Your reaction	• Note down how you felt emotionally about what happened
Any evaluative judgements you made	• Note down any evaluative judgements you made about the other participant(s)
The People who were present	Note key information about the People: • How many • Their roles and role responsibilities • Their links in terms of equality-inequality and distance-closeness • Any other People that you think could be relevant
The Setting for the incident	Note key features of the Setting: • The physical setting • The purpose of the communicative event • The organisational and societal setting
Step 2: Think and Reflect Think through possible reasons for what happened and your reactions. Do it first from your perspective, then from the other person's perspective.	

Part 4 – Your TRIPS Toolkit

	Reflections from your perspective
T: Triggers	Consider whether any GAAFFE Triggers might have been involved: G: Goals A: Autonomy A: Attention F: Face F: Fairness E: Ethicality
R: Reaction	• Consider how your reactions were influenced by any of the Triggers
I, P, S	Look back at your answers in Step 1 to what was said or done I), and the People (P) and Settings (S) involved Consider which could have contributed to your reactions. e.g., • Might the age or ethnicity of one of the participants played a role? • Did someone dominate the conversation?

Reflections from the other person's perspective

Now try to think of the situation from the other person's point of view. It can often be helpful to talk confidentially with a suitable colleague or friend. You could try talking through the questions with them.

T: Triggers	Consider whether the other person might have been affected by any of the GAAFFE Triggers: G: Goals A: Autonomy A: Attention F: Face F: Fairness E: Ethicality
R: Reaction	Recall how the other person reacted: • What emotions did they seem to feel and what judgements might they have made?
I: Interaction	Consider what might have led the other person to say or do what they did • Might they have been having a bad day or under some kind of other pressure?
P: People	Think over how the characteristics of the other person(s) might have played a role
S: Settings	Consider how the setting might have played a role.

Step 3: Think and Reassess	
Use your Step 2 reflections to reconsider your interpretations and reactions.	
Reassess the situation and your reactions	Reconsider the upsetting /annoying incident. In the light of your reflections: • How do you feel about what happened now? • What have you learned about yourself, your ways of doing things, your expectations, preferences etc.? • What have you learned about possible factors affecting the other person's behaviour or the situation more generally? • How far is it fair to 'blame' the other person? • How do you evaluate the other person now?

The Discord Management Tool: Steps and Prompts

This tool will help you deal with disagreement at work. Note: These stages may need to be – and often are – cyclical, because disagreement can take time to resolve.

Step 1: Think and Prepare	
This stage applies to situations where a disagreement is known about in advance or where differences could be expected to arise.	
Think about the disagreement	• Gather relevant information relating to the issue of disagreement • Clarify what conflict-related changes you want to achieve
Think about the GAAFFE Triggers	Consider the role of the GAAFFE Triggers – as a source and as issues to be careful about: • Goal • Autonomy • Attention • Face • Fairness • Ethicality
Think about the People and Setting	• Consider the characteristics of the People involved and how to take them into account • Consider the features of the likely Setting and how to plan for them
Take stock	• Manage your anticipatory emotions • Take stock and plan how best to proceed (if at all)

Part 4 – Your TRIPS Toolkit

Step 2: Engage and Connect This stage refers to the interaction between the people concerned. The mode in which this is conducted is key.	
Get started	• Establish a cooperative atmosphere
Explore	• Explore each other's ideas and viewpoints with curiosity and openness • Avoid dogmatic arguing and listen attentively to others • Manage your 'in-the-moment' emotions .
Connect	• Generate connectedness by tuning in to different perspectives and seeking synergy. • Adjust your resolution/negotiation goals if needed • Continue to manage your 'in-the-moment' emotions
Step 3: Think and Accept This is the stage after the interaction has ended, at least for now. It is important to remember that disagreements are not necessarily fully resolved after one period of connecting.	
Accept	• Acknowledge any limitations to resolution progress. • Accept that more preparation and connecting work may be needed

The Participation Management Tool: Steps and Prompts

This tool will help you discern whether anyone is having difficulties participating in a meeting or group discussion, identify the sources of the problem, and take steps to address the issue.

Step 1: Attend and Discern Pay attention to features of the I: Interaction that reveal any participation difficulties	
Discern any difficulties in understanding	Pay attention to features such as the following: • Speed of speech, accent, use of slang, unfamiliar abbreviations, or idiomatic expressions • Use of comprehension or clarification checking • Clarity of communication (e.g., level of directness/indirectness) • Nonverbal signals (e.g., frowning, puzzled expression)

Part 4 – Your TRIPS Toolkit

Discern any difficulties in taking a turn	Look out for signs such as the following: • Balance among the members in amount of talking time • How the turn-taking is occurring (e.g., very quickly, with overlaps) • Whether anyone is controlling the turn-taking and if so, how 'fairly' it is being handled • Nonverbal signals (e.g., moving forward in seat, hand raising)
Step 2: Think and Analyse Explore the possible sources and likely consequences of any participation difficulties	
Consider whether any GAAFFE Triggers might have been activated	G: Goals A: Autonomy A: Attention F: Face F: Fairness E: Ethicality
Consider whether any People factors could be having an influence	Think about People factors such as the following: • Individual identity characteristics, such as language fluency, working style • Group identity characteristics, such as national identity, professional affiliation • Links between participants, such as role responsibilities, distance-closeness, attitudes towards each other
Consider whether any Setting factors could be having an influence	Think about Setting factors such as the following: • The physical setting • The psychological atmosphere • Norms for turn-taking (e.g., organisational)
Step 3: Engage and Tackle	
Actions for leaders and managers	• Try out different procedures for chairing meetings • Promote psychological safety • Arrange suitable training
Actions for everyone	• Monitor your own behaviour in terms of inclusion/exclusion • Take positive actions to promote inclusion • Pro-actively decide how to respond to excluding behaviour by others.

Part 4 – Your TRIPS Toolkit

The Cooperative Colleague Tool: Steps and Prompts

This tool will help you build cooperative relations with your colleagues. Note that the steps are interconnected; they may occur in any order and almost simultaneously.

Step 1: Engage and Connect Use this stage is to establish and/or maintain professional bonds, i.e., focusing on the horizontal axis of the Interaction Compass, high-low Connection (see Chapters 1 and 9)	
Initiate conversations	• Give appropriate priority to fostering interpersonal links with colleagues • Take the initiative to talk to someone you don't know or are less familiar with, especially if they seem to have no one to talk with • Pay attention to conventions for greeting people, especially in contexts of cultural diversity
Engage in small talk	• Develop a range of strategies and topics for chatting informally to people you don't know well • Pay attention to people's names, especially ones unfamiliar to you; find out how to pronounce them and try to use them
Seek common ground	• Try to find points of common interest or shared experiences • Talking about shared 'troubles' can help with bonding, but be careful how you handle it • Be cautious about using humour • Find ways of fostering interpersonal relations despite hybrid working
Show care and concern	• Show empathy towards others • Spend time listening to others' when they want/need it • Make allowances for people if you know they are tired and/or stressed
T: Trigger and R: Reactions	• In all aspects of connecting, pay attention to key Triggers (especially Attention and Face) and watch out for any Reactions
Step 2: Engage and Empower Use this stage is to promote cooperation through mutual empowering in relation to work tasks.	
Collaborate with each other	• Work as collaboratively as possible with others • Gather team members who can offer different skills • Support others in appreciating the value of collaboration

Help each other	• Help your colleagues as much as possible • Understand and implement the principle of reciprocity • When giving advice, word it sensitively so you don't sound arrogant
Share information and adjust working styles	• Be aware that information is a form of power; share it in a supportive manner • Be open to different styles of working and ways of doing things and develop ground rules when helpful • Encourage colleagues to share their personal needs and preferences over ways of working
Be courteous	• Do your best to be courteous to colleagues, thanking them, complimenting them, and apologising to them appropriately when the occasion arises

Step 3: Engage and Balance
Ensure you keep various elements in balance, including when engaging in Steps 1 and 2

Balance autonomy-control	• Check how much autonomy you are giving team members • Find out team members' preferences for amount of direction or involvement in decision-making, and make any adjustments needed
Balance directness-indirectness Balance costs and benefits	• Pay attention to the level of directness-indirectness of your language • Adjust the level to suit the People and the Setting. • Be willing to help others but be careful not to be taken advantage of • Fulfil the principle of reciprocity in your dealings with others
Balance individual and collaborative work	• Manage people's time respectfully – not involving them too much or too little • Avoid small group silos as they can be isolating for individuals • Be clear which type of work is best done individually, which in a small group, and which in a large group

The Upward Management Tool: Steps and Prompts

This tool will help you manage relations with your boss. Note that the steps are interconnected; they may occur in any order and almost simultaneously.

Part 4 – Your TRIPS Toolkit

Step 1: Attend and Discern
Use this stage to learn more about your boss's ways of working, how they align with your expectations/preferences, and what aspects (if any) upset or annoy you.

Preferred ways of working	• Discern how your boss likes working: What is particularly important to them and what they get annoyed about • Compare your boss's ways of working with your own and notice how closely aligned or not they are • To gain clarity on these issues, pay close attention to your interactions with your boss. Use the frameworks in Chapter 7 for guidance over what to observe and note • Learn more about working styles from Chapters 7 and 12
Sources of negative reactions	If your boss's behaviour upsets, annoys or challenges you in some way, discern the following: • The features of your boss's behaviour that cause some kind of negative reaction in you – e.g., upset, annoy or challenge you • Note the GAAFFE Triggers they relate to

Step 2: Think and Reflect
Use this stage to think over your own emotional and attitudinal reactions to your boss's behaviour and how seriously it's affecting you.

Your emotional reactions to any challenging behaviour	• Identify the emotions you often experience • Consider how far you disclose your emotions, either verbally or nonverbally • Reflect on your physical health – whether there are any symptoms that could be stress related • Reflect on the impact of your boss's behaviour on your wellbeing

Your attitudes towards your boss	• Consider your attitudes to your boss:
	  o How far do you believe in and trust your boss's professional expertise?
	  o How far do you feel some kind of positive bond with your boss?
	• Reflect on the ways your attitudes to your boss affect the ways in which you react to their dealings/interactions with you

How seriously you are affected	• Reflect on how serious any activations of the GAAFFE Triggers are for you. Consider issues such as:
	  o whether you are unduly controlled
	  o whether you receive unwanted attention or are ignored

Part 4 – Your TRIPS Toolkit

	o whether you are disrespected o whether you are treated unfairly o whether any behaviour (of your boss or what the boss requires of you) is unethical
Step 3: Engage and Tackle Use this stage to address the issues you have identified in Steps 1 and 2. If at all possible, talk with your boss about your concerns and try to work collaboratively on issues	
Seek out support (if needed) for your concerns and emotional reactions	• Identify some people who could give you support over the stresses you are experiencing • Clarify who would be better to avoid talking to (e.g., for confidentiality reasons) • Identify who could give you helpful advice about what action you could take
Try out ways of adjusting	• Find ways to adjust your working style to align better with your boss's preferences • Do this gradually, stretching your comfort zone bit by bit • If possible, work collaboratively with your boss on this • Monitor how successful your adjustments are

If need be, consider alternative solutions	• Balance your current concerns with alternative options; e.g.,
	  o How feasible or desirable it is for you to find another job / resign. Take steps if appropriate
	  o How wise it would be to submit a formal complaint. Take steps if appropriate
	• Explore acceptable workarounds

The Supportive Leadership Tool: Steps and Prompts

This tool will help you become a more supportive leader/boss. Note that the steps are interconnected; they may occur in any order and almost simultaneously.

Step 1: Think and Reflect Use this stage to enhance your self-awareness of features relating to your leadership and management	

Reflect on your people management skills and how others see you	• Reflect on your interactions with your staff. Consider issues such as:
	  o How approachable, caring, and considerate you are, how good at listening
	  o How regularly you give clear explanations, provide

Part 4 – Your TRIPS Toolkit

	supportive feedback, delegate, and give an appropriate amount of guidance o How fairly and respectfully you treat staff, how much you consult with them, and how far you act with integrity • With support from a few trusted colleagues, reflect on how your staff regard your people management skills
Reflect on your leadership values	• Reflect on your leadership values. Consider: o The importance to you of hierarchy and having special privileges o The importance to you of consulting staff and involving them in decision-making o The importance to you of having rules and procedures and of everyone keeping to them o The relative importance to you of staff welfare and organisational targets
Reflect on the bases of your power and that of your staff	Look at Table 8.2 on the bases of power and privilege, and think over: • Which elements give you a lot of power or privilege • Which elements give certain members of your team very little power or privilege • What steps you take to try to minimise any power differentials on people's sense of psychological safety

Step 2: Engage and Connect
Use this stage to build bonds with your team in a range of ways

Connect through informal interaction opportunities	• Create opportunities for your team to meet with you spontaneously • Make sure you don't show favouritism in how often you chat with certain individuals or groups of people • Find ways of retaining connection when people are working remotely
Connect through caring	• Show professional care for everyone in your team • Develop your ability to empathise so you can be sympathetic and adaptable when someone has personal issues that are affecting their work
Connect through openness to feedback	• Encourage people to suggest ideas, e.g., different ways of doing things • Respond constructively when they ask for changes in how you do or manage things • Work on ways of enhancing your own openness to feedback

Step 3: Engage and Balance

Ensure that you mindfully flex and balance two key continua in all your interactions: autonomy-control and directness-indirectness.

Balance how much autonomy or control you manage with	• Flex how much autonomy or control you give your staff
	• Clarify in your mind the factors you need to take into account when doing this
	• Reflect on the ways in which you deal with unacceptable behaviour, considering:
	  o How often you avoid dealing with the issue;
	  o How often you tend to dismiss it, delay dealing with it, deal partially with it, or get someone else to handle it

Balance the directness-indirectness of your communication	• Flex the level of directness of your communication when giving instructions/advice or when making requests • Flex the level of directness of your communication when giving feedback • Clarify in your mind the factors you need to take into account when considering level of directness • Increase the range of your language strategies for varying your level of directness

Chapter 15: The TRIPS Concept Tool Templates

This chapter provides tool templates for reflecting on the TRIPS Concepts.

Triggers: Reflection questions

Use the reflection questions in this template when you want or need to think through the (potential) impact of the GAAFFE Triggers

G: Goals	1. What are your goals? 2. What are other people's goals? 3. How aligned or non-aligned are your goals?
A: Autonomy-control	4. How much autonomy are you allowing or experiencing? 5. How much direction are you giving or experiencing? 6. How suitable is the balance between autonomy and control, for you and others?
A: Attention – non attention	7. How much attention / care / consideration is shown to you and to others? 8. What form does it take or not take? 9. Is it an appropriate amount and type to aid inclusion/sense of belonging without causing discomfort and sense of personal intrusion?
F: Face	10. Are people's face needs (e.g., needs for respect, appreciation) being met? 11. Are people's face sensitivities being threatened?
F: Fairness	12. Is everyone being treated fairly? 13. Is reciprocity occurring?
E: Ethicality	14. Are any ethical issues at stake? 15. If yes, are there any differences in people's stances on the issue?

For background information on the above questions, refer to Chapter 9.

Reactions: Reflection questions

Use the reflection questions in this template when you want or need to think through your or other people's reactions when one or more of the GAAFFE Triggers have been activated.

Part 4 – Your TRIPS Toolkit

Emotional reactions	1. What emotional reactions are you/other people experiencing? 2. How intensely are you/they experiencing them? (Consult Table 3.1 if required)
Displaying emotions	3. How far are you/other people displaying their emotions? 4. What are the display rules/conventions for displaying emotions in this setting? 5. How far are they being upheld? 6. Might there be any cultural differences in the display rules/conventions people uphold?
Regulating emotions	7. How far are you/others regulating or controlling emotions? 8. What strategies are being used or could be used for this?
Perceiving emotions	9. How easy or difficult is it to perceive other people's emotions? 10. How easy or difficult is it for others to perceive your emotions? 11. What signals can provide helpful clues?
Cognitive reactions	12. Was the cause of the issue external or internal to you/the other person? 13. Could it have been controlled? 14. How recurrent is the issue? 15. What person-internal factors might have played a role? 16. What evaluative judgements are being made of you/the other individuals? 17. What is the likely impact on rapport – now and in the future?

For background information on the above questions, refer to Chapter 10.

Interactions: Reflection questions

Use the reflection questions in this template when you want or need to observe, notice, or record what is happening in an interaction.

Ease of mutual understanding	1. Is everyone adjusting their use of language to suit the comprehension level of others? 2. Are you/others checking regularly that everyone is following them?
Message content	3. Is the amount and nature of information that you/others are disclosing suitable/appropriate? 4. How are you/others handling any confidential information?

Communication style	5. Is the level of directness-indirectness that you/others are using suitable, with the meaning clear and manner acceptable? 6. How are you/others handling other communication styles: expressive-restrained, self-enhancing – self-effacing, person-oriented – status-oriented? 7. How well do you/others accept and respond to the different styles?
Communication dynamics	8. How are speaking turns distributed among the people present? 9. How acceptable is this distribution? Is everyone who wishes to participate able to do so? 10. Does any code-switching take place? How do people feel about it?
Microinsults	11. Do any microinsults occur? If so, what form do they take and by whom? 12. How are people responding to the microinsults?

For background information on the above questions, refer to Chapter 11.

People: Reflection questions

Use the reflection questions in this template when you want or need to consider the potential impact of People factors.

Number of people	1. How many people are present? 2. Is the number suitable for the message you/others want to convey?
Individual identity characteristics and personal circumstances	3. What languages do the people present speak and how proficient are they in them? How might language proficiency affect rapport and need to be taken into account to promote participation and inclusion? 4. What are the working style characteristics and personal strengths of the people present and how might they affect rapport and need to be taken into account? 5. What personal circumstances of the people present are you aware of, and how might they need to be taken into account?
Group identity characteristics	6. What are the demographic features of the people present (e.g., age, ethnicity, gender, nationality)? How might they need to be taken into account when managing rapport?

Part 4 – Your TRIPS Toolkit

Association links	7. What professional (e.g., sector) or organisational (e.g., department) groups do the people present belong to? How might their affiliations need to be taken into account when managing rapport? 8. What are the role responsibilities of the people present? Is everyone clear about them? 9. What are the hierarchical relations among the people present? Are there any sensitivities as to how they can best be handled? 10. How well do the people present know each other? How close or distant are they, and how well integrated is each person from that perspective?
Attitude links	11. What is the relationship history among the people present? Is there anything significant that needs to be taken into account? 12. What ingroup/outgroup attitudes exist among the people present? How might they affect relationship management? 13. What potential biases or prejudiced attitudes might the people present have towards each other? How might such biases/prejudice be manifested in what people say or do?

For background information on the above questions, refer to Chapter 12.

Settings: Reflection questions

Physical environment	1. What are the characteristics of the physical environment (e.g., noise, the seating arrangements, the quality of an online connection)? 2. How may the characteristics affect the interaction and people's experience of it?
Psychological atmosphere	3. What adjectives (e.g., stressful, relaxed) would you use to describe the psychological atmosphere? 4. How much psychological safety are you/others experiencing in terms of feeling (a) included, (b) safe to learn, (c) safe to contribute, and (d) safe to challenge the status quo?
Norms	5. What unspoken 'rules' (i.e., common ways of doing things) underlie the way an interaction is handled?

Part 4 – Your TRIPS Toolkit

	6. Is everyone keeping to these unspoken rules? a. If not, what impact is any breach having? b. If not, what might be the reason(s) for breaching the rules?
Regulations	7. Are there any regulations that employees must adhere to? 8. Is everyone keeping to those regulations? a. If not, how might leaders react to a breach? b. If not, what might be the reason(s) for breaching the rules?
Values	9. What are your organisation's espoused (i.e., stated) values? 10. How far are they put into practice? 11. How far do the organisation's values (and the behaviours they encourage) promote or undermine psychological safety? 12. Are there tensions between 'espoused' and 'deep' organisational values (as well as broader societal values)? 13. What is the impact of such tensions on the way employees feel (e.g., cynicism, lack of trust)?

For background information on the above questions, refer to Chapter 13.

Chapter 16: The RelATE family of strategies and concluding comments

The third set of tools that we've introduce you to in the book are the RelATE family of strategies for managing rapport. The table below summarises them.

We recommend using them in conjunction with the TRIPS Challenge Tools (Chapter 14) and the TRIPS Conceptual Tools (Chapter 15).

RelATE Superstrategies	Strategies	Gloss
Attend (pay attention)	Observe	Watch the interaction carefully and people's reactions
	Notice	Notice anything that is unusual or seems to be affecting one or more of the participants
	Discern	Discern the potential impact on rapport of their own and others' behaviour
	Note	Make a mental or written note of what you noticed
	Record	Write down an objective account of what happened or that you noticed
Think	Prepare	Plan for an upcoming event or interaction - thinking through what will be needed
	Reflect	Reflect on anything unusual, annoying, or upsetting by considering the GAAFFE Triggers
	Analyse	Analyse what happened by drawing on all the elements of the TRIPS framework
	(Re)assess	Assess or reassess the situation in the light of your reflections and analyses
	Accept	Accept that your insights may be limited and partial and that any outcomes may not be ideal
Engage	Connect	Build meaningful connections with people
	Empower	Aim to build up and empower others, not devalue them
	Tackle	Find suitable ways of tackling challenging issues - don't ignore or avoid them
	Balance	Flex and balance your handling of the two axes of the Interaction Compass: degree of control versus autonomy and levels of collaborative vs independent working. Similarly, flex and balance styles of communicating and how you prioritise

Part 4 – Your TRIPS Toolkit

We started this book with a problematic working relationship – that between Caleb and his manager. They did not resolve their differences and Caleb soon left his job.

Our hope is that by making the most of the concepts, insights and tools in this book, you will be able to reduce the amount of dissatisfaction, stress and loneliness that occurs in the workplace – yours and that of others.

If you would like to follow up on any of the insights from this book, learn more about the concepts and strategies, and/or receive help in applying them to your work situation, Helen and Domna would be very pleased to support you via their GlobalPeople Consulting (GPC) services. GPC offers an extensive range of tools, services, and resources related to working relationships, rapport, communication, and cultural diversity at work. Amongst them are:

- Diagnostic profilers for purchase, including the RELMAP (Relationship Management Profiler), mentioned in the book;
- Consultancy services, masterclasses and other professional development programmes, including follow-up support to the profiler reports;
- Research services on all aspects of living, working, communicating, and managing relationships in diverse contexts;
- Professional development e-learning content and courses for licensing.

Our website has a large selection of resources and reports which can be downloaded free of charge. **https://globalpeopleconsulting.com/**

Activity and Case Study Answers

These are some suggested answers for the activities and reflection tasks in this book. They are not necessarily comprehensive of all possibilities because people's reactions and interpretations will always be at least partially subjective! Ideally, discuss your thoughts with a colleague. Obviously, we have not commented on questions that relate to your own workplace experience.

Chapter 2
Activity 2.1: Reflecting on rapport triggers
1. Promotion concerns. Two key triggers were responsible for Christoph's reaction. Goals – he very much wanted to be promoted and his boss's stance was thwarting him achieving this goal. Fairness – he knew others (in other departments) had been promoted without having worked for a set period of time. He therefore felt unfairly treated.
2. Recruitment difficulties. Three key triggers were responsible for Marie's reaction. Ethicality – she believed that the lobbying by a staff member to influence the decision process was unethical. Fairness – she believed that being excluded from the interview process was unfair, since she had been found to be without any fault and the appointee would be a member of the team she was leading. Face – she felt the senior manager was not showing her sufficient respect and support.

Case Study 2.2: Giving critical feedback
1. Write more accurately, checking to ensure there are no mistakes.
2. The content of the message was critical of her staff – that they had not been careful enough in their writing. Her hesitation indicates reluctance to cause offence. It is also a form of indirectness that reduces the impact of her message.
3. Admitting her own fault fulfils the same function – to reduce the level of criticism. It also conveys a sense of team focus. Note also that she didn't pick out any particular individuals who could have been particularly to blame.

Case Study 2.3: The local impact of societal and world settings
2. Barbara worked with her team to break the work down into small tasks, with each person knowing what they needed to complete that day in order to feel a sense of achievement. They came back together at the end of the day to review and congratulate themselves. In other words, they shortened their horizon to prevent feeling overwhelmed.

Chapter 3
Case Study 3.1: A disagreement at work
2. Chapter 3 explains what Josh can do!
3. The feelings could fester, with both Josh and Phil failing to work together well, and maybe with Phil being disadvantaged if Josh wrote negative reports about him.

Activity 3.1: Practising Step 1 of the 3R Review Tool
1. Two emotion families were involved:
    - Anger family: annoyed and frustrated; probably moderate (we'd need to ask Josh).
    - Fear family: slight. (Concerned that the client might be dissatisfied)

Activity and Case Study Answers

2. At least the following would be important:
   - P: The individuals' roles and responsibilities, their amount of experience in the role, their relative ages.
   - S: The importance of the client to the company. The organisational culture – how far challenging a superior is encouraged.

Chapter 4
Activity 4.1: Conflict situations
1. Check the contract.
   Contact the technical staff responsible for mending the aircraft and note down details of the exact situation (when the aircraft arrived, when worked started, etc.)
2. Gather all the figures and data.
   Talk with members of the production team, to be clear about any problems.
3. Talk with the chair of the board to gain his perspective.
   Talk with each of the board members privately to find out their positions and what is of most critical importance to each one.

Case Study 4.2: The risk of raising a contentious issue
1. He thought it would be culturally inappropriate because it would be too face-threatening for the Chinese member of staff.
2. She felt uncomfortable leaving the issue unresolved. She felt a strong urge to talk it through.
3. One option would be to talk with an intermediary about the issue, who could then try to resolve matters by talking with both Eleanor and the Chinese member of staff.

Case Study 4.4: Owning racism
1. Her personal story, which concerned the impact of language, referred to an aspect of her identity that everyone could identify with. This enabled others to perceive racism and discrimination in a much more personalised way.

Case Study 4.5: Managing emotions in a contractual dispute
1. It is the equivalent to Step 1 of the Reaction Management Tool explained in Chapter 3. It helps separate out what actually happened from reactions to what happened.
2. It is important to try to really understand the other party's position/concerns and for them to be aware that you are genuinely trying to do this.

Chapter 5
Case Study 5.1: The challenge of silence in meetings
1. She wanted the local staff to share their opinions so that she could benefit from their ideas and suggestions.
2. They found it too face-threatening to do this in a public meeting, in case others disagreed with them. They also felt it would be disrespectful to those in a senior position – people that they would normally just take orders from and obey.

Activity and Case Study Answers

Chapter 6
Case Study 6.1: Unfulfilled responsibilities
1. There could be a range of reasons; e.g., pressure of other work; lost interest in the project; he invited Sarah primarily in the hope/anticipation that he could leave her to do the majority of the work.
2. She felt under pressure to complete the work for the sake of her company's reputation, as well as her own with her line manager.
3. She probably felt happy, maybe even exhilarated during the early fruitful discussions. However, later, when Ervin was doing so little work, she became frustrated about the situation – and probably with him too. As the deadline approached, she is likely to have felt anxious and her emotions may have intensified. Then, when Ervin claimed credit for the report, she would probably have felt angry and maybe resentful towards him.
4. It was unwise insofar as it could encourage Ervin to behave badly like this in the future. On the other hand, Sarah wanted to protect her own reputation for delivering good quality work on time. She could have tried to be firmer with Ervin early on; whether that would have worked is uncertain.
5. Be cautious! If it's important to work with him again, be very clear about the ground rules for collaborating.

Case Study 6.2: A public criticism
1. She didn't understand why a new member of staff would be behaving as though she was her line manager.
2. Olivia's role as project manager could have been made clear earlier.
3. Olivia was upset and embarrassed by Rima's public criticism.

Case Study 6.3: A indirect insult?
1. He almost certainly wasn't being deliberately insulting towards Isaac. Isaac may – or may not – have been offended by it. As we explained in the chapter, microinsults are very subtle forms of communication and different people may react differently.
2. We need to know how comfortable or uncomfortable Isaac really was in using knife and fork. If he was very familiar, he would probably have felt that Leo's comment was patronising. If he was unfamiliar, he would probably have appreciated Leo noticing the issue.

Activity 6.1: Interconnections between people challenges and GAAFFE Triggers
Case Study 6.1: Sarah: Fairness (re division of workload); Autonomy (re needing to ensure completion of the report); Face and Goals (re needing to ensure completion of the report)
Case Study 6.2: Olivia: Face (re the criticism); Attention (re trying to improve relations with Rima)
Rima: Autonomy (re being told what to do by Janet)
Case Study 6.3: Face (re potential criticism)

Case Study 6.4: An agenda ignored
1. He wanted to get to know Helmut first.
2. His boss was very task focused.

Activity and Case Study Answers

3. The client was attaching importance to Attention and Face, while the German company was focusing on achieving the goal of signing a contract as soon as possible.

Case Study 6.5: Ignored at work
1. People often say they feel nervous talking to someone from a different ethnic background, as they are not sure what to say and are afraid of offending. This could be one possible explanation.

Case Study 6.6: Adjusting to an unfamiliar office culture
1. Their practices were very different – she wasn't used to making tea. So she initially felt unable to accept their offer to get her a drink, and later after she had plucked up enough courage to accept, she didn't feel able to reciprocate by offering to make them tea.
2. She plucked up the courage to offer to make them tea. She also started talking about her love of coffee with Vicky.
3. Vicky wrote down a list of places she recommended that Anna May could try going to.

Case Study 6.7: I have ADHD
1. They might feel imposed upon. The GAAFFE Trigger of Autonomy might be activated.
2. She might feel embarrassed to acknowledge her ADHD publicly, fearing that people might look down on her or respond critically. This would activate the GAAFFE Trigger of Face.
3. She wanted to be in the best position possible to respond to any requests she received. She was thereby addressing the GAAFFE Trigger of Goals, both for herself and for her colleagues/clients.

Case Study 6.8: Interpreting a request
1. She didn't want to give the impression she was imposing too much on Anke. She was just being polite and trying to reduce the inconvenience of the request (i.e., she didn't want to activate Anke's GAAFFE Trigger of Autonomy).
2. Shirley had used too many hedges ('no hurry', 'perhaps …), making the date for completing the work too indirect for Anke to interpret.
3. Shirley was shocked that Anke thought she was unclear – she had always regarded herself as speaking clearly. Anke was annoyed with Shirley that she hadn't made the timing clear and now she needed to hurry to complete the work.

Chapter 7
Case Study 7.1: A thwarted personal goal
1. He wanted Jasmine to recruit someone to cover his teaching for the next term while he was on sabbatical leave.
2. There could be various reasons; e.g., wanting to make a good impression in her new strategic planning role; not wanted to be bothered by 'mundane' administrative matters; forgetting about the matter.
3. He could try speaking with someone else in the department who would have the authority to remind Jasmine to address the issue.

Activity and Case Study Answers

Case Study 7.2: Inadequate direction
1. Angela is rarely in the office; when she comes in, it's only briefly; she always has lots of complaints; she gives no clear directions; she's blunt and rude in her communication; she contradicts the decision of her co-director.
2. Face – from the criticism; Fairness – because she's not in the office enough; Fairness – because she doesn't explain clearly what she wants and contradicts her co-director. Maybe also Goals – because Angela's behaviour is hindering her in achieving her project (and maybe career) goals of growing in expertise.
3. Try asking her manager to set priorities and to explain more clearly how she wants the work done.

Case Study 7.3: A bullying manager
1. Heavy workload with tight turnaround times (even requiring weekend work); criticism without clear explanation of how to improve; refusal to discuss workload; shouts at Jingli; conducted a performance management meeting without informing her that this was the case; required standard to be assessed on not identified; status of meetings (i.e., whether they are a performance management meeting or not) not made clear; excluded from meetings that are directly relevant to her work and does not provide any report or account of what was agreed.
2. Intimidation and bullying. Maybe abuse and emotional volatility.
3. Key ones are: Ethicality (re the shouting and bullying, and the way the performance management meeting was conducted); Autonomy (re very tight turnaround times; also lack of direction from her boss re work priorities); Fairness (re failure to explain the standard required). Face and Goals could also be affected.
4. If at all possible, try to get her manager to prioritise the tasks she gives.

Case Study 7.4: Finding a workaround
1. In order to do his job, Raymond needed access to some data that ought to be provided by consultants in different sections of the hospital. However, they did not take time to produce it, and Raymond's boss refused to talk with them about the issue.
2. Try to build good connections with the various consultants.

Chapter 8
Case Study 8.1: A caring boss
1. Spent time getting to know her team; checked how happy and fulfilled they felt; gave support for personal professional development; provided opportunities to work on interesting projects; gave credit for success to the team; celebrated success together; relaxed and had fun together as a team.
2. Able to work on interesting projects; learned a lot from her; could trust her; knew her boss would always support her.
3. She created a lot of trust and goodwill towards her, which in turn meant that her team were prepared to give her a lot of leeway when it came to some of her more challenging behaviours.

Activity and Case Study Answers

Case Study 8.2: Reacting to critical feedback
1. A sense of dread – 'what's coming now?'
2. It was too superficial. She just acknowledged her problem (indicating that it wasn't new information) and said she would work on it – but in unspecific ways. It seemed to close down the conversation.
3. She gave them the opportunity to explain how her poor time management was impacting on them.
4. She needed time to reflect, but by promising to revisit the issue the next day, she showed that she was serious about working through it.

Case Study 8.3: Leading in unfamiliar cultural contexts
1. He was used to giving people a lot of autonomy, but his team wanted much more direction from him. Doing this went against his sense of identity as a leader.
2. His team were used to a leader being much more directive. i.e., Their beliefs about the role responsibilities of a leader were different from his, affecting the balance they wanted on the autonomy–control continuum.
3. We'd recommend that he expand his sense of what it means to be a 'good leader' and stretch a little towards his team's preferred ways of working, while being mindful of his own discomfort while doing so. If possible, he should also try to talk it through with his team, particularly those close to him whom he can trust and from whom he can get good feedback. This should give him ideas for expanding his range of strategies for balancing autonomy–control without feeling or coming across as inauthentic.

Case Study 8.4: Working remotely – connection and control
1. He was put under pressure from his own boss and felt he had no other option.
2. She expected to be able to discuss and negotiate the targets, preferably face to face. She had previously been given a lot of autonomy and couldn't accept now being controlled.

Chapter 9
Case Study 9.1: Expectations of an initial business meeting
1. Jim wanted Mr Iguchi to taste his cheese sample and make an initial decision as to whether the company wished to proceed with discussions. Mr Iguchi wanted to learn more about Jim's company, to visit his premises, and send full information back to head office. He was not in a position to make an initial decision.
2. Jim didn't provide the information that Mr Iguchi was looking for and this led Mr Iguchi to form an initial negative impression of Jim. Jim couldn't work out whether Mr Iguchi was interested or not. Both were frustrated and dissatisfied with each other.
3. Mr Iguchi could have made it clearer what his role responsibilities and processes were – that he didn't have the authority to make a decision and that he needed to send full information back to head office for them to decide. Jim should have checked what was required beforehand and prepared information on his company and product to pass to Mr Iguchi.

Activity and Case Study Answers

Case Study 9.3: Disagreement and face sensitivity
1. She felt that the non-white participants were always portrayed as subordinate to the white participants. She identified with the non-white participants and treating her group as subordinate threatened her group face.
2. She felt that her viewpoint had not been taken seriously and had simply been dismissed. This threatened her personal face.
3. Our identity and sense of worth is associated with the groups we belong to, as well as our individual qualities. So, when Maria felt her group was being disrespected, she reacted as though she had personally been disrespected.

Chapter 10
Case Study 10.1: A failed recruitment interview
1. The interviewer's behaviour activated the Attention Trigger for Delia because she was showing no interest in Delia's views. This in turn might also have been face-threatening for Delia (i.e., Face Trigger). When Delia challenged the interviewer by questioning the value of the activity, this activated the Face Trigger for the interviewer.
2. They felt cold towards each other and seemed to increasingly dislike each other. The interviewer became annoyed and then visibly angry.
3. We are not told, but Delia probably based it on the interviewer's facial expressions, tone, pitch and loudness of voice, maybe gestures.
4. Delia regarded the interviewer as over-confident and arrogant; she also seems to look down on her level of professional expertise.
5. The interviewer should show more interest in the candidate's views and thoughts, while the candidate would be wise to be less explicit in expressing disagreement and criticism. The candidate could also have shown more interest in exploring and understanding the interviewer's perspective, rather than dismissing it straightway. Both interviewer and candidate appeared to approach the interview with rigid expectations, made assumptions about each other from the start, and allowed these assumptions to colour their interaction. They could both have shown much more open mindedness, curiosity, and flexibility in their approach. Delia in particular could have done with more preparation to find out more about the person she was being interviewed by and their professional interests and views.

Chapter 11
Case study 11.1: Informing someone's line manager
1. This was primarily a face threat for Dawei, as Gerald had told his line manager about some of Dawei's performance weaknesses. In doing so, Gerald was portraying Dawei to his line manager as incompetent in certain respects and this would have been embarrassing to Dawei on the one hand, and on the other would have undermined his sense of self-esteem in relation to his line manager. There could also be elements of ethicality. Normally what is shared confidentially should not be shared with others without their permission. This could be seen as a kind of ethical principle which Gerald had breached.

Activity and Case Study Answers

Case study 11.2: A reminder to make tea
1. Initially she was very indirect, but in a light-hearted way.
2. Given that they knew each other well and that they had an agreement to take turns making tea, it's a bit surprising. Being much more direct in these circumstances would normally be fine. It could be that Tom hated taking his turn to make tea and so she broached the issue in a light-hearted way.

Case study 11.3: Showing passion at work
1. The boss seemed to assume that a restrained style was the 'correct' style in order to be professional and that if Vasiliki reflected on her manner, she would realise her 'problem'.
2. It would probably activate her F-Fairness trigger (that her boss was treating her unfairly by expecting her to change) and perhaps her F-Face trigger (that he regarded her as incompetent).

Case study 11.4: Mass emails and seniority
1. The first sentence functioned as a kind of hedge or mitigator, used for politeness reasons – to soften the criticism that followed.

Case study 11.5: Code-switching during international business visits
1. If it was in a social context, it was probably for comfort and convenience. If it was in a meeting, it could have been for any of the reasons listed in the chapter.
2. It emphasised the divisions between them, excluding them both socially and professionally.
3. It seems to have been deliberate – so that Tim wouldn't understand their negative evaluations of what he was saying.
4. Linguistic boundaries are not always airtight. People can often infer meaning from the context, drawing on points that have already been mentioned. Moreover, the author states "the Hebrew language is thoroughly riddled with English names and terms, especially when technical matters are discussed."

Case study 11.6: Who is the manager?
1. The basis of the micro-offence, as reported by the British manager, was the local manager's female gender. However, it is possible that her comparatively youthful age might also have played a role.
2. This was how they dealt with it. They agreed that only the local head would go to first meetings, so the local manager's leadership role was clear. The regional British manager would only go to second meetings, after clients had been told clearly why he was attending the second meeting.

References

Abbajay, M. (2018). *Managing up: How to move up, win at work, and succeed with any type of boss*. Wiley.

Ailon, G. (2007). *Global ambitions and local identities: An Israeli-American high-tech merger*. Berghahn Books.

Alison, E., & Alison, L. (2020). *Rapport. The four ways to read people*. Vermilion.

Allwood, J. (2007). Activity based studies of linguistic interaction. hprints-00460511 Available at: https://halshs.archives-ouvertes.fr/hprints-00460511/document [accessed 26 September 2023].

Barrett, L. F. (2017). *How emotions are made. The secret life of the brain*. Pan Macmillan.

Barrett, L. F., Gross, J. J., Conner Christensen, T., & Benvenuto, M. (2001). Knowing what you're feeling and knowing what to do about it: Mapping the relation between emotion differentiation and emotion regulation. *Cognition and Emotion*, 15(6), 713–724.

BBC Radio 4. (2023). World at One, 23 August.

Belbin, R. M., & Brown, V. (2023). *Team roles at work*. 3rd edition. Routledge.

Blanch-Hartigan, D., Andrzejewski, S. A., & Hill, K. M. (2012). The effectiveness of training to improve person perception accuracy: A meta-analysis. *Basic and Applied Social Psychology*, 34, 483–498.

Blanch-Hartigan, D., Andrzejewski, S. A., & Hill, K. M. (2016). Training people to be interpersonally accurate. In J. A. Hall, M. Schmid Mast, & T. V. West (Eds.), *The social psychology of perceiving others accurately* (pp. 253–269). Cambridge University Press.

Bower, M. (1966). *The will to manage: Corporate success through programmed management*. McGraw-Hill.

Brown, B. (2018). *Dare to lead: Brave work. Tough conversations. Whole hearts*. Random House.

Brown, P., & Levinson, S. C. (1987). *Politeness: Some universals in language usage*. Cambridge University Press.

Byrne, M., Twitchin, J., & Viswalingan, P. (1996). What makes you say that: Cultural diversity at work. VHS recording., SBS-TV.

Canney Davison, S. (1996). Leading and facilitating international teams. In M. Berger (Ed.), *Cross-cultural team building. Guidelines for more effective communication and negotiation* (pp. 158-179). McGraw Hill.

Cardon, P., Okoro, E. A., Priest, R., & Patton, G. (2022). Communication apprehension in the workplace: Focusing on inclusion. *Business and Professional Communication Quarterly*, 86(1), 52–75. For a summary, see https://globalpeopleconsulting.com/speaking-anxiety-at-work-diversity-and-situational-influences

Charan, R., Drotter, S., & Noel, J. (2011). *The leadership pipeline. How to build the leadership powered company* (2nd ed.). Jossey-Bass.

Cialdini, R. B. (2012). The focus theory of normative conduct. In P. A. M. Van Lange, A. W. Kruglanski, & E. T. Higgins (Eds.), *Handbook of theories of social psychology*. Vol.2 (pp. 295–312). Sage.

Cialdini, R. B. (2021). *Influence. The psychology of persuasion*. HarperCollins.

References

Clark, T. R. (2020). *The 4 stages of psychological safety. Defining the path to inclusion and innovation*. Berrett-Koehler Publishers.

Culpeper, J., & Tantucci, V. (2021). The principle of (im)politeness reciprocity. *Journal of Pragmatics*, 175, 146–164.

De Bres, J., & Holmes, J. (2023). Ethnicity and humour in the workplace. In J. P. Gee & M. Handford (Eds.), *The Routledge handbook of discourse analysis*, 2nd edition (pp. 582–594). Routledge.

Debray, C., & Spencer-Oatey, H. (2019). 'On the same page?' Marginalisation and positioning practices in intercultural teams. *Journal of Pragmatics*, 144, 15–28.

Debray, C., & Spencer-Oatey, H. (2022). Co-constructing good relations through troubles talk in diverse teams. *Journal of Pragmatics*, 192, 85–97.

DiStefano, J., & Maznevski, M. (2000). Creating value with diverse teams in global management. *Organizational Dynamics*, 29(1), 45-63.

Dunne, P. (2021). Boards. *A practical perspective*. 2nd ed. Governance Publishing.

Edmondson, A. (2019). *The fearless organization. Creating psychological safety in the workplace for learning, innovation and growth*. Wiley.

Fanshawe, S. (2022). *The power of difference*. Kogan Page.

Fawole, A. A., & Rammala, J. R. (2021). Rapport management in the opening sequence of African and Asian doctors in South Africa. *International Journal of Applied Linguistics*, 31(3), 406-420.

Fletcher, J. K. (1999). *Disappearing acts: Gender, power, and relational practice at work*. MIT Press.

Franklin, P. (2006). *Communicating and cooperating with German business people: A guide for the British*. CD-ROM, Konstanz, KIeM.

French, J. R. P., & Raven, B. (1959). The bases of social power. In D. Cartwright (Ed.), *Studies in social power* (pp. 150-167). University of Michigan.

Frewin, H. (2021). *Better than confidence. The thinking tools you need to get the results you want*. Butterfly House Publishing.

Fukushima, S. (2015). In search of another understanding of politeness: From the perspective of attentiveness. *Journal of Politeness Research*, 11(2), 261–287.

Fuller, P., Murphy, M., & Chow, A. (2020). *The leader's guide to unconscious bias*. Simon & Schuster.

Gross, J. J. (1998). The emerging field of emotion regulation: An integrative review. *Review of General Psychology*, 2(3), 271–299.

Gross, J. J. (2015). Emotion regulation: current status and future prospects. *Psychological Inquiry*, 26, 1–26.

Gurtman, M. B. (2020). Interpersonal circumplex. In V. Zeigler-Hill & T. K. Shackelford (Eds.), *Encyclopedia of personality and individual differences* (pp. 2364–2373). Springer.

Hall, E. T. (1966). *The hidden dimension*. Anchor Press/Doubleday.

Hay, A. (2014). 'I don't know what I am doing!': Surfacing struggles of managerial identity work. *Management Learning*, 45(5), 509–524.

References

Hetrick, S. (2023). *Toxic organizational cultures and leadership. How to build and sustain a healthy workplace*. Routledge.

Hinds, P., & Elliott, B. (2021). WFH doesn't have to dilute your corporate culture. *Harvard Business Review*, 1 February, available at: https://hbr.org/2021/2002/wfh-doesnt-have-to-dilute-your-corporate-culture (accessed December 2023).

Hinton, P. (2023). Rethinking stereotypes and norms in intercultural relations. In T. McConachy & P. Hinton (Eds.), *Negotiating intercultural relations. Insights from linguistics, psychology, and intercultural education* (pp. 95–112). Bloomsbury.

Hogan, C. (2007). *Facilitating multicultural groups. A practical guide*. Kogan Page.

Holmes, J. (2018). Negotiating the cultural order in New Zealand workplaces. *Language in Society*, 47(1), 33–56.

Holmes, J. (2023). Rapport management and microaggression in workplace interaction. In T. McConachy & P. Hinton (Eds.), *Negotiating intercultural relations. Insights from linguistics, psychology, and intercultural education* (pp. 35–53). Bloomsbury.

Jopling, K., McClelland, H., & Proffitt, E. (2023). Loneliness at work: Report for the all-party parliamentary group on tackling loneliness and connected communities. Research conducted by the British Red Cross. https://www.redcross.org.uk/about-us/what-we-do/we-speak-up-for-change/loneliness-at-work Accessed 11 December 2023].

Kahane, A. (2004). *Solving tough problems: An open way of talking, listening and creating new realities* Berrett-Koehler.

Kahn, W. A. (1990). Psychological conditions of personal engagement and disengagement at work. *The Academy of Management Journal*, 33(4), 692–724.

Kandola, B. (2018). *Racism at work. The danger of indifference*. Pearn Kandola Publishing.

Kasumu, S. (2023). *The power of the outsider. A journey of discovery*. Hodder & Stoughton.

Kilmann, R. H. (2023). *Mastering the Thomas-Kilmann conflict mode instrument*. Kilmann Diagnostics.

LaRochelle, J. M., & Karpinski, A. C. (2016). Racial differences in communication apprehension and interprofessional socialization in fourth-year Doctor of Pharmacy students. *American Journal of Pharmaceutical Education*, 80(1), 1-9 (Article 8).

Littlefield, C. (2020). *75+ team building activities for remote teams*. Independently published.

Locher, M. A., & Watts, R. J. (2008). Relational work and impoliteness: Negotiations norms of linguistic behaviour. In D. Bousfield & M. A. Locher (Eds.), *Impoliteness in language: Studies on its interplay with power in theory and practice* (pp. 77–99). Mouton de Gruyter.

Markman, A. (2017). You can't manage emotions without knowing what they really are. In *HBR guide to emotional intelligence* (pp. 31–34). Harvard Business Review Press.

Marriott, H. E. (1990). Intercultural business negotiations: The problem of norm discrepancy. *ARAL Series S*, 7, 33-65.

Matsumoto, D. (2009). Culture and emotional expression. In R. S. Wyer, C.-y. Chiu, & Y.-y. Hong (Eds.), *Understanding culture: Theory, research, and application* (pp. 271–287). Psychology Press.

References

Meyer, E. (2014). *The culture map: Breaking through the invisible boundaries of global business.* Public Affairs.

Molinario, F. (2018). In leadership, relationships matter most. Forbes Newsletter, 24 October 2018.

Molinsky, A. (2013). *Global dexterity.* Harvard Business Review Press.

Molinsky, A. (2016). The feedback sandwich. https://www.andymolinsky.com/reinventing-feedback-sandwich/ Accessed 17 November 2023.

Mutooni, K., Ng'weno, B., & Jordans, E. (2020). Changing leadership perceptions: Leaders in the private sector in Kenya. In E. Jordans, B. Ng'weno, & H. Spencer-Oatey (Eds.), *Developing global leaders. Insights from African case studies* (pp. 211–257). Palgrave Macmillan.

Obama, M. (2022). *The light we carry: Overcoming in uncertain times.* Penguin.

Padilla, A., Hogan, R., & Kaiser, R. B. (2007). The toxic triangle: Destructive leaders, susceptible followers, and conducive environments. *The Leadership Quarterly*, 18, 176–194.

Parkinson, B. (2019). *Heart to heart. How your emotions affect other people.* Cambridge University Press.

Rubin, M. A., Hall, J. A., Curtin, E. M., Blanch-Hartigan, D., & Ship, A. N. (2014). Discussion increases efficacy when training accurate perception of patients' affect. *Journal of Applied Social Psychology*, 45, 355–362.

Scharmer, C. O. (2007). *Theory U: Leading from the future as it emerges.* Berrett-Koehler Publishers.

Schein, E. H., & with Schein, P. (2017). *Organizational culture and leadership* (5th ed.). Wiley.

Shaver, P., Schwartz, J., Kirson, D., & O'Connor, C. (1987). Emotion knowledge: further exploration of a prototype approach. *Journal of Personality and Social Psychology*, 52(6), 1061-1086.

Simon, B. (2004). *Identity in modern society. A social psychological perspective.* Blackwell.

Spencer-Oatey, H. (Ed.). (2007). *e-Learning initiatives in China: Pedagogy, policy and culture.* Hong Kong University Press.

Spencer-Oatey, H. (2008). Face, (im)politeness and rapport. In H. Spencer-Oatey (Ed.), *Culturally speaking. Culture, communication and politeness theory* (pp. 11–47). Continuum.

Spencer-Oatey, H., & Franklin, P. (2009). *Intercultural interaction. A multidisciplinary approach to intercultural communication.* Palgrave Macmillan.

Spencer-Oatey, H., Franklin, P., & Lazidou, D. (2022). *Global fitness for global people: How to manage and leverage cultural diversity at work.* Castledown.

Spencer-Oatey, H., & Kádár, D. Z. (2021). *Intercultural politeness: Managing relations across cultures.* Cambridge University Press.

Spencer-Oatey, H., & Tang, M. (2007). Managing collaborative processes in international projects: Programme management perspectives. In H. Spencer-Oatey (Ed.), *e-Learning initiatives in China. Pedagogy, policy and culture* (pp. 159–173). Hong Kong University Press.

Spencer-Oatey, H., & Wang, J. (2020). Establishing professional intercultural relations: Chinese perceptions of behavioural success in a Sino-American exchange visit. *Journal of Intercultural Communication Research*, 49(6), 499–519.

References

Spencer-Oatey, H., & Xing, J. (2008). Issues of face in a Chinese business visit to Britain. In H. Spencer-Oatey (Ed.), *Culturally speaking: Culture, communication and politeness theory* (pp. 258–273). Continuum.

Sue, D. W., Capodilupo, C. M., Torino, G. C., Bucceri, J. M., Holder, A. M. B., Nadal, K. L., & Esquilin, M. (2007). Racial microaggressions in everyday life: Implications for clinical practice. *American Psychologist*, 62(4), 271–286.

Taser-Erdogan, D. (2022). Careers advancement of women: Applying a multi-level relational perspective in the context of Turkish banking organisations. *Human Relations*, 75(6), 1053–1083.

Thomas, K. W. (1976). Conflict and conflict management. In M. Dunnette (Ed.), *The handbook of industrial and organizational psychology* (pp. 889-935). Rand McNally.

Thomas, K. W. (2002). *Thomas-Kilmann conflict mode instrument*. Kilmann Diagnostics.

Tian, Z. (2023). Relating and rapport management in Chinese-owned companies operating in Kenya. University of Warwick, unpublished PhD data.

Tickle-Degnen, L., & Rosenthal, R. (1990). The nature of rapport and its nonverbal correlates. *Psychological Inquiry*, 1(4), 285–293.

Ting-Toomey, S. (2005). The matrix of face: An updated face-negotiation theory. In W. B. Gudykunst (Ed.), *Theorizing about intercultural communication* (pp. 71–92). Sage.

Ting-Toomey, S., & Chung, L. C. (2005). *Understanding intercultural communication*. Roxbury Publishing Company.

Tomlinson, E. C., & Mayer, R. C. (2009). The role of causal attribution dimensions in trust repair. *Academy of Management Review*, 34(1), 85–104.

Vigier, M., & Spencer-Oatey, H. (2018). The interplay of rules, asymmetries in language fluency, and team dynamics in culturally diverse teams: Case study insights. *Cross Cultural & Strategic Management*, 25(1), 157–182.

Warren, J. (2023). The Ritz London applicant told 'Afro-style' hair was banned. BBC news.

Webster, V., Brough, P., & Daly, K. (2016). Fight, flight or freeze: Common responses for follower coping with toxic leadership. *Stress and Health*, 32, 346–354.

Weeks, J. (2004). Unpopular culture. The ritual of complaint in a British bank. University of Chicago Press.

Williams, N. (2023). It's not about you. A leader's highest calling is to develop other leaders. *Premier Christianity Magazine*, November, 63.

Woolley, S. (2023). McDonalds sexual harassment agreement with the EHRC. https://www.bfawu.org/mcdonalds-sexual-harassment-agreement-with-the-ehrc/ Accessed 28 November 2023.

Index

Abbajay, M. 117
abuse 131, 156, 178, 187, 269
accent 83, 215, 225, 250
acceptable/acceptability 27, 52, 57–59, 100, 135, 159, 178, 184, 185, 255, 260
accept/acceptance (see also: Think and accept RelATE strategy)
acceptance of difference 58, 64, 217, 217, 236
accepted norms/procedures 178, 185, 192
acceptance of offers 105, 199, 268
acceptance of people/ourselves 41, 63, 65, 75, 113, 189, 193, 243
acceptance of behaviour/situations 72, 73, 97, 100, 103, 133, 135, 154, 165, 207, 223, 239, 260, 263, 270
accommodating 56, 57, 111, 205
acronym 83
  GAAFFE acronym 19, 164
  TRIPS acronym 11, 17, 80
adapt (see also: adjust) 113, 124, 132, 256
ADHD 111, 268
adjacency pair 199
adjust 64, 73, 188, 250
adjust behaviour/language/communication 38, 63, 94, 110–113, 115, 121, 152, 154, 160, 202, 211, 253, 255, 259
adjust to cultural differences/changing situations 105, 133, 138, 153, 207, 268
affiliation 7, 28, 168, 170, 173, 219, 251, 261
age 77, 78, 95, 145, 175, 219, 248, 260, 272
agency (see also: control) 168
aggression 84, 98, 113, 131, 186, 190, 239
Ailon, G. 206
alignment 117, 125–130, 132–136, 183, 216, 238, 254, 255, 258
attitudinal alignment 127, 128, 136
  non-alignment 126, 258
  seek alignment 132, 135
  working alignment situations 129, 130
Alison, E. & Alison, L. 167, 186
Allwood, J. 230
ambitious 21, 130, 223
analyse (see: Think and analyse RelATE strategy)

anger 17, 23, 40, 41, 44, 45, 57, 64, 65, 67, 68, 101, 102, 121, 127, 128, 155, 181–185, 187, 189, 198, 265, 267, 271
annoyed 13, 18, 19, 21–23, 25, 31, 36–38, 41, 43, 45, 49–51, 53, 68, 72, 79, 88, 112, 119, 157, 158, 165, 183–185, 195, 197, 199, 204, 212, 221, 247, 249, 254, 263, 265, 268, 271
apologise 29, 112, 253
assertiveness 56, 74
atmosphere (see also: psychological atmosphere) 32, 67, 68, 86, 91, 170, 179, 228, 243, 250
Attend
  Attend – RelATE superstrategy 36, 37, 42, 263
  Attend and discern 77, 82–88, 95, 118, 125–127, 132, 136, 250, 251, 254, 263
  Attend and record 39, 42, 44–48, 51, 53, 134, 247
  pay attention 13, 24, 32, 37, 41, 42, 44, 52, 57, 70, 79, 83, 85, 87, 91, 93–95, 102, 107, 110, 114, 122, 125–127, 184, 191, 196, 204, 209, 212, 216, 246, 247, 250, 252–254, 263
Attention–inattention (GAAFFE Trigger) 9, 10, 14, 20, 21, 34, 37, 48–50, 57, 62, 68, 74, 81, 86, 105, 127, 138, 139, 149, 150, 165, 168, 170–172, 177, 206, 213, 214, 219, 221, 223, 243, 248, 249, 251, 252, 254, 258, 267, 268, 271
attentional deployment 187, 188
attentiveness 170
attitudes (see also: stereotypes) 15, 16, 63, 118, 154, 170, 185, 226, 235, 237, 240
attitudes to time 33, 126, 170, 236, 237
attitudes towards hierarchy–equality 33, 170
attitudes towards others/each other 27, 29, 33, 34, 47, 64, 81,86, 87, 154, 170, 214, 219, 220, 235 ,242, 251, 254, 261
Autonomy–control (GAAFFE Trigger) 9, 10, 14, 20, 34, 37, 48, 57, 62, 68, 74, 86, 87, 110, 113, 116, 118, 120, 121, 127, 138–140, 152–157, 161, 164, 165, 167–171, 177, 179, 180, 200, 202, 221, 241, 243, 249, 251, 253, 257, 258, 263, 267–270
avoidance 17, 19, 26, 28, 39, 44, 64, 66, 68, 70,

Index

72, 74, 91, 94, 98, 106, 111, 133, 153, 156, 157, 167, 183, 186, 187, 189, 206, 212, 214, 225, 232, 235, 236, 247, 250, 253, 255, 257, 263
avoidance conflict management strategy 56–58
axes (see also: interaction compass) 7, 8, 9, 37, 56, 57, 74, 152, 168, 263

balance (see also: Engage and balance RelATE strategy) 20, 102, 109, 110, 113–116, 120, 121, 150, 152, 157, 159, 176, 251, 253, 255, 257, 258, 263, 270
Barrett, L.F. 182
BBC 221
Belbin, R.M. & Brown, V. 217
belonging 28, 75, 81, 96, 98, 104, 173, 174, 188, 214, 219, 224, 238, 243, 258, 261, 271
benevolence 192, 194
bias 22, 29, 223–225, 239, 261
 unconscious bias 224, 226
Blanch-Hartigan, D. 190, 191
body (physical) 40, 189, 190
body language (see: language)
Bower, M. 229
Brown, B. 141, 151, 167, 168, 172, 217
Brown, P. & Levinson, S.C. 167, 168, 172
bullying 122, 124, 131, 136, 156, 269
Byrne, M. 75, 80

Canney Davison, S. 102
Cardon, P. 77
care 37, 41, 67, 82, 107, 142, 143, 149, 150, 161, 222, 252, 255, 256, 258, 269
chair (an event) 21, 61, 73, 85, 88, 89, 91, 251, 266
chairperson 70, 81, 85, 88, 89, 95, 231
change
 change behaviour/opinion/reaction 16, 23, 39, 63, 64, 95, 133, 154, 159, 185, 187, 220, 225, 249, 256, 272
 change language 71, 113, 181, 199, 202, 208
 change relationship 39, 87
 change thinking (cognitive change) 187, 188, 191
 impact of change 5, 133, 187, 207, 237
 physiological change 40, 181
 workplace/societal/world change 4, 32, 33, 95, 102, 137, 138, 178, 233
Cialdini, R. 177, 233
Clark, T. 68, 241, 242, 244
climate (see: atmosphere; psychological atmosphere)
closeness (see: distance–closeness)
code-switching 206–208, 211, 260, 272
cognitive 31, 37, 224
 cognitive change 187, 188, 191
 cognitive reaction 14, 23, 24, 34, 181, 191, 195, 259
 cognitive sensemaking 39, 191, 192, 194
collaborate/collaboration 2, 5, 7, 56, 57, 82, 96, 97, 102, 108, 109, 112, 115–117, 129, 147, 149, 158, 170, 185, 204, 206, 229, 230, 237, 252, 253, 255, 263, 267
colluder 130
comfort zone 102, 133, 138, 255
common ground 58, 66, 74, 79, 105, 106, 215, 252
communication 14, 18, 21, 28, 29, 39, 48, 66, 79, 113, 126, 134, 138, 140, 158, 167, 172, 194, 196–211, 225, 227, 233, 235, 260, 264, 267, 269
 communication clarity (see also: understanding) 83, 84, 94, 250
 communication dynamics 14, 24, 26, 34, 80, 196, 205–208
 communication process 83, 196, 211
 communication style (see also: directness–indirectness) 14, 24, 26, 32, 37, 60, 76, 80, 124, 126, 184, 196, 199–205, 211, 228, 260, 263
 synchronous–asynchronous communication 26, 197, 227
communicative event 30, 31, 47, 58, 59, 166, 197, 205, 208, 229–233, 247
compass (see: interaction compass)
competence 49, 79, 87, 133, 139, 167, 172, 173, 194, 224
complain/complaint 2, 3, 22, 43, 45, 48, 61, 65, 98, 106, 108, 116, 121, 123, 134, 148, 157,

Index

159, 172, 175, 194, 255, 269
compliments 112, 172, 253
confidence 71, 89, 130, 133, 139, 153, 177, 186, 187, 195, 203, 243
conflict 5, 13, 36, 54–74, 102, 130, 131, 141, 160, 165, 172, 180, 185, 186, 238, 249, 266
conflict management strategies 56, 57
confrontation 95, 178, 186
connect (see: Engage and connect RelATE strategy)
connection (see also: attention; interaction compass) 6–8, 57, 60, 66, 71, 74, 139, 140, 147, 151, 152, 154, 155, 168, 170, 171, 186, 188, 252, 256, 261, 270
connection axis/dimension 74, 168, 171
context 4, 12, 13, 17, 19, 28–33, 37, 40, 46, 47, 58, 59, 62, 67, 68, 70, 76–78, 88, 90, 94, 102–104, 107, 108, 146, 148, 154, 194, 196, 198, 199, 201–203, 205, 223, 227–244, 246, 252, 264, 270, 272
contracts 21, 47, 55, 57, 61, 72, 101, 132, 143, 266, 268
control (see also: autonomy–control; interaction compass) 3, 68, 70, 76, 124, 131, 136, 140, 144, 187, 192, 199, 241
control axis/dimension 74, 168–170
control emotions 38, 64, 72, 181, 182, 203, 259
controllability 192, 193
controlled 7, 8, 48, 81, 89, 167, 200, 254, 259, 270
controlling 7, 8, 115, 157, 158, 189, 237, 251
cooperation 37, 56, 57, 74, 96, 101, 102, 108–110, 116, 117, 252
cooperative atmosphere 67, 68, 250
Cooperative Colleague Tool 13, 36, 96, 100–116, 246, 252, 253
cooperative relationship 108, 112, 252
cost–benefit 114, 116
covid-19 pandemic 2, 32, 103, 140, 172, 228, 233, 240
creativity 5, 58, 76, 81, 119, 120, 149, 186, 241
criticise/criticism 19, 26, 28, 29, 65, 68, 88, 98, 116, 121, 122, 151, 157, 159, 173, 178, 212, 213, 225, 234, 241, 242, 265, 267, 269, 271, 272

culture
cultural background 27, 52, 87, 221
cultural climate 14, 227
cultural differences/changes 21, 71, 93, 94, 102, 170, 184, 194, 230, 259
cultural diversity/culturally diverse contexts 31, 60, 180, 211, 235, 244, 252, 264
cultural expectations 31, 153, 154, 158
cultural factors 23, 105, 124, 159, 169, 170, 171
cultural groups 19, 199
cultural knowledge/construction 224, 226
cultural norms/style 58, 59, 158, 160, 197, 205, 213
cultural patterning 228, 230, 232, 239, 244
cultural settings 101, 110, 167, 270
cultural values and principles 32, 33, 228
culture
national culture 31, 32, 52, 58, 59, 76, 154, 228, 230
organisational culture 12, 14, 31, 32, 47, 52, 58, 59, 154, 158, 169, 240, 241, 251, 262, 266
societal culture 32, 52, 158, 169, 230, 232, 238
toxic culture 32, 123, 124, 131, 147, 243
workplace/office culture 3, 4, 105, 124, 137, 242, 268

Debray, C. & Spencer-Oatey, H. 82, 106
decode 196, 210
deference 52, 79, 204, 223
delegate 138, 142, 153, 154, 198, 218, 231, 256
direct 2, 243
(give) direction (see also: control) 9, 121, 127, 136, 152–154, 165, 168, 169, 253, 258, 269, 270
directive 7, 22, 157, 165, 270
directness–indirectness 28, 84, 86, 110, 113–116, 126, 140, 152, 157, 158, 160, 161, 168, 199–202, 250, 253, 257, 260, 272
indirectness 52, 83, 84, 98, 99, 113, 116, 126, 140, 157–160, 186, 200–202, 228, 250, 253, 257, 265, 267, 268, 272
disagreement (see also: conflict) 3, 13, 36, 38, 53–75, 102, 124, 129, 165, 174, 179, 183,

Index

186, 189, 206, 224, 241, 243, 249, 250, 265, 266, 271
discern (see: Attend and discern RelATE strategy)
disclosure-non-disclosure 105, 128, 197, 199, 254, 259
discomfort 88, 92, 238, 258, 270
Discord Management Tool 13, 36, 54, 55, 57, 58, 60, 74, 246, 249
discrimination 3, 28, 81, 82, 86, 103, 104, 146, 156, 188, 215, 219, 225, 266
disrespected 20, 41, 48, 82, 117, 124, 128, 133, 174, 200, 208, 255, 266, 271
distance-closeness 6-8, 12, 22, 29, 65, 71, 139, 148, 158, 168, 170, 171, 201, 206, 213, 223, 236, 247, 251, 261
DiStefano, J. & Maznevski, M. 58
distrust 32, 224, 243
diversity 5, 31, 51, 52, 70, 75, 76, 90, 102, 107, 148, 180, 196, 202, 211, 230, 235, 244, 252, 264
diversity, equity and inclusion (DEI) 76
divisions 3, 21, 96, 107, 120, 224, 267, 272
domination 56, 57, 74, 168, 205, 213, 248
Dunne, P. 54, 63, 70, 141

Edmondson, A. 241
egalitarianism 143, 154, 155
embarrassed 17, 18, 21, 28, 41, 43, 45, 48, 51, 172, 173, 212, 241, 242, 267, 268, 271
emotion 3, 12, 14, 31, 38-53, 58, 67, 70-72, 97, 131, 132, 181-191, 195, 203, 224, 239, 247-250, 254, 265-267, 269
  defining emotion 40
  disagreement and emotion 56-58, 68-74
emotional disclosure/display 52, 70, 128, 185
emotional intelligence 128, 182
emotional management/regulation 23, 38, 39, 42, 53, 54, 64, 72, 73, 123, 183, 185-187
emotional response/reaction 22-24, 34, 39, 43-45, 49, 51, 53, 57, 64, 66, 132, 181, 183-185, 187, 191, 192, 254, 255, 259
emotional support/wellbeing 3, 132,
  identifying emotions 13, 40, 41, 46
  perceiving emotion in others 190, 259
empathy 9, 28, 73, 107, 128, 149, 217, 225, 252, 256

empower (see: Engage and empower RelATE strategy)
Engage - RelATE superstrategy 36, 37, 42, 263
Engage and balance 37, 96, 100, 109, 110, 113-116, 137, 140, 152, 161, 170, 175, 253, 257
Engage and connect 37, 54, 56, 57, 60, 66, 72-74, 96, 100-108, 116, 137, 140, 147-152, 161, 175, 250, 252, 256, 263
Engage and empower 37, 96, 100, 108-113, 116, 175, 252, 263
Engage and tackle 77, 82, 88, 95, 118, 125, 132-136, 251, 255
environment 32, 109, 149, 183, 232, 233, 236, 237, 242, 243, 261
equal/unequal
equal/unequal relations (see also: hierarchy; power distance) 7, 29, 33, 47, 87, 124, 136, 158, 201, 247
equal/unequal opportunities 76, 234
equal/unequal treatment/behaviour 148, 242
equity (see also: fairness) 76, 175, 176, 219
Ethicality (GAAFFE trigger) 9, 10, 14, 20, 34, 48, 63, 86, 118, 122, 123, 127, 138, 139, 152, 165, 177-180, 248, 249, 251, 258, 265, 269, 271
  ethical sense 157, 194, 222, 237
  unethical 20, 48, 130, 136, 255, 265
ethnicity 14, 65, 77-79, 81, 95, 100, 104, 145, 148, 173, 209, 219, 224, 225, 248, 260, 268
evaluate 24, 29, 58, 64, 166, 191, 247, 249
evaluative comment/tone 44, 68, 70, 157, 212
evaluative judgement 12, 22, 23, 39, 43-45, 181, 184, 192, 194, 195, 213, 247, 259
evaluative reaction 34
  negative evaluation of others 19, 21, 23, 64, 212, 231, 272
exclusion 7, 13, 28, 36, 41, 70, 75, 77, 81-83, 85, 87, 88, 91, 95, 96, 102-104, 115, 123, 171, 173, 205-208, 212, 219, 223, 241, 251, 265, 269, 272
expectations 19, 21, 26, 27, 29-31, 33, 51, 52, 60, 63, 71, 91, 113, 155, 158, 166, 169, 171, 175, 185, 186, 196, 197, 199, 203, 204, 209, 220, 221, 227, 229, 231-233, 235, 237, 240, 244, 249, 254, 270-272

Index

adjust expectations 64, 72
cultural expectations 153, 154, 158
mismatched expectations 3, 125, 229
set expectations 95, 140
unmet expectations 19, 31, 91, 197, 221
expertise 28, 73, 76, 79, 81, 83, 128–130, 145, 146, 188, 215, 221, 254, 269, 271
expressive-restrained communication style 199, 203, 260

Face (GAAFFE trigger) 9, 10, 14, 20, 21, 26, 34, 48, 50, 63, 74, 83, 86, 87, 105, 110, 127, 133, 138, 139, 158, 160, 165, 172–175, 177, 180, 200, 202, 218, 248, 249, 251, 252, 258, 267–269, 271
  face enhancing 28, 212
  face support 28, 29, 265
  face threat 26, 28, 49, 59 83, 87, 94, 95, 151, 128, 133, 174, 189, 201, 212, 241, 266, 271
  facework 175
  gain face 172, 173, 175
  give face 172, 173
  lose face 63, 79, 172, 173, 175
Fairness (GAAFFE trigger) 9, 10, 14, 20, 21, 34, 48, 63, 86, 87, 110, 114, 127, 133, 138, 139, 142, 153, 165, 174–177, 203, 214, 219, 221, 223, 235, 248, 249, 251, 258, 269
  (un)fair behaviour 38, 63, 155, 175
  (un)fair judgement 23, 46, 51–53, 191, 194, 203, 247, 249
  (un)fairness and reciprocity 114, 177
  (un)fair representation 174
  (un)fair situation 87
  (un)fair treatment 18, 20, 21, 48, 63, 70, 75, 82, 86, 91, 122, 139, 142, 153, 165, 175, 214, 222, 223, 234, 241, 255, 256, 258, 265, 267, 272
familiarity 7, 14, 29, 30, 59, 79, 86, 92, 93, 95, 97, 105, 196, 197, 206, 220, 223, 229, 252, 267
Fanshawe, S. 104, 226
Fawole, A.A. & Rammala, J.R. 103
fear 32, 40, 41, 57, 58, 68, 72, 181, 182, 185, 187, 189, 224, 265

facing up to fears 65, 66, 152, 157, 189
fear and compliance 124, 130, 146
fear and disagreement 64, 124, 241
fear of annoying/upsetting others 68, 79
fear of consequences 58, 64, 179, 223, 225, 240, 241, 243, 268
fear of losing face/embarrassment 79, 268
fear of speaking (up) 77, 78
feedback
  give feedback 25, 26, 114, 129, 138–140, 142, 157–160, 173, 198, 199, 201, 203, 212, 229, 240, 242, 256, 257, 265
  receive/react to feedback 53, 90, 150–153, 161, 191, 202, 204, 206, 230, 234, 256, 270
Fletcher, J.K. 110
Franklin, P. 9, 60, 180, 211, 244
freedom (see: autonomy)
French, J.R.P. & Raven, B. 221
Frewin, H. 187, 188, 195
frightened 41, 222
frustrated 31, 41, 43–45, 49, 51, 72, 75, 76, 96, 97, 113, 119, 151, 166, 197, 202, 216, 241, 265, 267, 270
Fukushima, S. 170
Fuller, P. 104

GAAFFE Triggers (see: triggers)
global 2, 38, 107, 149, 174, 180, 211, 215, 244
Goals (GAAFFE trigger) 9, 10, 14, 20, 21, 26, 31, 34, 48, 49, 62, 81, 86, 87, 117–120, 127, 138, 139, 157, 158, 165–167, 179, 200, 202, 214, 222, 230, 237, 240, 241, 248–251, 258, 265, 267
  desired/desirable goals 23, 39, 64, 88, 103, 117, 118, 153
  flexibility/realism over goals 63, 72, 73, 120, 133, 154, 250
  support/understand others' goals 49, 51, 62, 71, 100, 108, 116, 153, 179
  thwarted/unfulfilled goals 48, 49, 62, 119, 136, 158, 179, 268, 269
grateful (see: thank)
greet 102–104, 131, 199, 252
Gross, J.J. 181, 186, 187, 189

Index

group (see also: identity) 14, 28, 47, 73, 75, 77, 81–84, 89–92, 95, 98, 107, 111, 115, 145, 148, 173, 174, 187, 199, 219, 225, 230, 236, 241–243, 250, 253, 271
ingroup/outgroup 28, 79, 84, 98, 99, 139, 219, 224, 261
Gurtman, M.B. 168

Hall, E.T. 171
harassment 156, 157, 172
harmony 9, 55, 79, 236, 241
Hay, A. 139, 226
health 3, 5, 6, 49, 50, 182, 190, 234, 254
hedging 26, 49, 73, 159, 188, 201, 202, 268, 272
hesitation 26, 84, 85, 89, 103, 186, 201, 265
Hetrick, S. 124
hierarchy (see also: power distance) 14, 29, 33, 129, 143, 154, 170, 204, 223, 236, 237, 256
Hinds, P. & Elliott, B. 107
Hinton, P. 211, 224, 226
Hogan, C. 67, 70
Holmes, J. 25, 28, 99, 201, 205, 206, 209, 211, 212
humiliated 41, 172, 173
humour 106, 107, 252
hybrid working 5, 33, 107, 108, 140, 154, 161, 192, 252

identity 12, 17, 71, 78, 81, 95, 105, 128, 139, 141, 145, 148, 154, 161, 172, 173, 189, 214– 220, 226, 251, 260, 270
diverse identity backgrounds 5, 52
group identity 27, 28, 34, 52, 86, 87, 145, 148, 173, 214, 215, 219, 224, 251, 260, 271
individual identity 27, 28, 34, 87, 214, 215, 251, 260, 266
social identity theory 224
ideology 28, 55, 63, 224
impolite (see: rude)
imposition 105, 139, 155–157, 167, 200, 221, 235, 268
inappropriateness 48, 117, 131, 132, 135, 156, 167, 205, 213, 266
inclusion 3, 41, 146, 171, 174, 241–244, 258

inclusion–exclusion 7, 205, 251
inclusion in meetings/discussions 75–95, 212, 260
inclusion and psychological safety 241–244
independence/independent working 121, 140, 263
indirectness (see: directness)
innovation 5, 70, 76, 243, 244
insult 98, 99, 116, 173, 177, 204, 210, 267
integration 56, 57, 103, 261
integrity 138, 142, 179, 192, 194, 256
intention 149, 152, 166, 197, 208–210
Interaction (TRIPS element) 11, 12, 24–27, 196–211
interaction mode/manner 67–70, 126, 250
interaction compass 7–9, 37, 56, 57, 74, 101, 147, 152, 156, 168–171, 252, 263
intercultural 51, 52, 166, 180, 211, 226, 228, 244
intercultural negotiations 166
interpersonal 9, 57, 81, 100–102, 107, 108, 116, 129, 130, 147, 151, 168, 170, 183, 252
interpersonal circle 7
interrupt 70, 79, 80, 85, 87, 93, 174, 205, 231
intimidation 68, 131, 156, 160, 222, 269
isolation 41, 73, 96, 103, 178, 253

Jopling, K. 5
joy 40, 41, 182
judgements (see also: evaluate) 12, 22, 23, 30, 34, 38–40, 43–46, 51–53, 70, 74, 104, 112, 130, 152, 170, 171, 175, 181, 184, 187, 188, 192–195, 203, 213, 215, 247, 248, 259
justice 110, 175

Kahane, A. 67
Kahn, W.A. 240, 241
Kandola, B. 208
Kasumu, S. 31
Kilmann, R.H. 56, 57

language
body language 52, 80, 92, 197
foreign language/native language 28, 71, 201. 260

Index

language adjustment 94, 111, 259
language code/other languages 172, 196, 272
language and culture 102
language fluency/proficiency 28, 83–86, 89, 93, 94, 113, 145, 146, 206, 215, 251, 260
language use and interpretation 99, 131, 177, 196, 197, 204, 206–208, 216, 220, 223, 253, 257, 266
working language 79, 83, 93, 94, 145, 146, 197, 202
leadership (see also: values) 32, 76, 81, 117, 237, 241, 255, 256, 272
   Supportive Leadership Tool 13, 36, 140–161, 246, 255
linguistics 26, 54, 99, 199, 200, 205, 207, 210–212, 226, 228–230, 272
links between people 12, 14, 27, 29, 34, 46, 47, 59, 100, 108, 112, 116, 158, 212, 219, 220–226, 247, 251, 252
   association links 220, 223, 261
   attitude links 223, 261
listen 2, 63, 68, 69, 70, 79, 84, 89, 90, 93, 98, 107, 108, 111, 140, 142, 151, 156, 159, 250, 252, 255
Littlefield, C. 107
Locher, M.A. & Watts, R.J. 210
loneliness 5, 6, 41, 103, 264
love 40, 41, 106, 182, 268

manage up/down 117
Markman, A. 41
Marriott, H.E. 166
Matsumoto, D. 184
mediator 53, 55, 58
Meyer, E. 159
microaggression/micro-incivility/microinsult 14, 95, 98–100, 104, 105, 108, 116, 173, 196, 208–211, 225, 260, 267, 272
micromanagement 3, 7, 131, 138, 153, 167
mindfulness 17, 32, 74, 107, 120, 148, 170, 171, 196, 197, 202, 204, 206–210, 222, 223, 225, 257, 270
minority 14, 76, 139
mismatch 5, 9, 124, 196

mistrust 3
misunderstandings (see also: understanding) 31, 52, 197
mitigation (see: hedging)
modest 26, 203
Molinario, F. 137
Molinsky, A. 159, 160
monitor 95, 140, 153, 197, 242, 243, 251, 255
motivation 2, 5, 84, 88, 130, 138, 139, 147, 218, 221
Mutooni, K. 178

names 26, 71, 97, 104, 105, 204, 209, 252, 272
nationality 81, 87, 145, 209, 224, 260
national culture (see: culture)
neglect 48, 56, 57, 146, 156, 214
negotiation 33, 55, 72, 101, 113, 124, 133, 166, 172, 197, 207, 211, 226, 227, 235, 250, 270
nervous 54, 59, 93, 139, 158, 189, 268
nervous system 189
neurodiversity 28, 113, 145
nonverbal 69, 70, 103, 128, 170, 175, 181, 190, 191, 197, 243, 250, 251, 254
norms 14, 30, 31, 52, 58, 59, 70, 86, 87, 107, 153, 158, 184, 197, 205, 213, 224, 226–230, 232, 233, 235, 238, 240–242, 244, 251, 261
   descriptive norms 233, 235
   injunctive norms 233

Obama, M. 65, 188, 189
obligation 158, 177, 220
offence 22, 57, 99, 104, 107, 113, 114, 158, 167, 173, 175, 180, 198, 202, 204, 209, 210, 213, 265, 267, 268
openness 53, 54, 64, 68–71, 74, 150, 250, 256
orders 167, 180, 266
organisation (see also: values)
organisational culture (see: culture)
organisational learning 5
organisational setting 14, 31, 32, 34, 227, 228, 238, 247
othering 102, 107
outsider 75, 84, 87, 98, 100, 208, 209
overlap (see also: turns) 28, 79, 87, 92

Index

Padilla, A. 130
pandemic 2, 5, 32, 33, 103, 140, 149, 172, 228, 233, 240
Parkinson, B. 181, 183
participation, 75–95, 105, 205, 208, 213, 238, 239, 246,250, 251, 260
Participation Management Tool 13, 36, 82–95, 246, 250, 251
patronising 267
patterns of behaviour (see also: culture patterning; norms) 109, 134, 232, 233
   language use patterns 84, 92, 113, 197, 213
   manager/leader behaviour patterns 126, 128, 147
   strategy patterns 37, 159
   work patterns 5, 33, 199
   pausing 25, 85, 94
People (TRIPS element) 11, 12, 27–29, 212–226
   number of people 14, 27, 28, 34, 212–214, 226, 260
performance 21, 61, 65, 121, 122, 139, 189, 190, 194, 198, 199, 212, 240, 271
performance management 138, 269
performance monitoring/reviews 140, 153, 203, 229
   relationships and performance 5, 58
person-oriented – status-oriented communication style 199, 204, 260
personality 12, 28, 79, 84, 93, 129, 172, 199, 215, 216
politeness 13, 133, 167, 170, 172, 176, 180, 194, 200, 204, 220, 226, 244, 268, 272
power 7, 23, 31, 67, 79, 109, 117, 119, 121, 137, 141, 154, 161, 168, 170, 178, 199, 220, 226, 233, 241, 243, 256
   coercive (negative) power 136, 221
   expert power 41, 79, 151, 221, 223
   legitimate (authority) power 145, 221, 222
   power and information 110, 199, 253
   power and privilege 140, 144–147, 256
   power and psychological safety 124
   power distance 33, 58, 158, 170, 221–223, 236
   referent (respect) power 221

reward (positive) power 136, 138, 145, 221–223
pragmatics 13, 168, 170, 172, 176, 220
prejudice 224, 225, 261
prepare (see: Think and prepare RelATE strategy)
progress
   progress in career 189, 239, 241, 250
   progress in handling disagreement 55, 72, 250
   progress with project/task 97, 193, 230
promotion 21, 24, 76, 119, 120, 138, 184, 221, 223, 234, 239, 240, 265
psychology/psychological 7, 13, 28, 31, 40, 130, 168, 170, 211, 219, 221, 226, 236, 242, 261
psychological atmosphere 14, 30–32, 124, 227, 240, 251, 261
psychological safety 31, 32, 50, 58–60, 68, 69, 80, 91, 124, 129, 130, 136, 137, 144, 146, 147, 179, 221, 222, 240–244, 251, 256, 261, 262
psychologist 7, 28, 41, 68, 168, 175, 177, 181, 183, 186, 187, 214, 224, 233

race 71, 77–79, 104, 174, 188
racism 65, 71, 215, 266
rapport (see also: TRIPS rapport management framework)
   aim and meaning of rapport 9–11
Reaction (TRIPS element) 11, 12, 17, 22–24, 181–195, 258–259
Reaction Management Tool 13, 36, 39, 41–54, 64, 246, 247, 266
Reassess (see: Think and reassess)
reciprocity 114–116, 176, 177, 253, 258
record (see: Attend and record RelATE strategy)
reflect (see: Think and reflect RelATE strategy)
reframing 133, 188, 189
regulations 14, 18, 30, 32, 143, 180, 227, 228, 233–235, 240, 262
RelATE family of strategies 12, 14, 36, 37, 39, 42, 60, 82, 101, 125, 141, 246, 263
RelATE superstrategies 36, 37, 42, 263 (see

Index

also: Attend, Think, Engage)
relationship
  defining relationship 6–8
  relationship and rapport 9–11
  role relationship 6, 7, 13, 20, 124
remote working/interaction 3, 5, 107, 140, 149, 154–156, 161, 256, 270
resentment 28, 41, 81, 95, 109, 114, 121, 133, 212, 267
respect 20, 41, 47, 58, 59, 69, 75, 127, 129, 130, 133, 142, 145, 155, 165, 172, 173, 200, 253, 256, 258, 265
rights 29, 55, 113, 123, 176, 178, 220
risk 14, 19–21, 23, 26, 29, 32, 34, 39, 49, 50, 54, 57, 58, 63, 65, 73, 83, 85, 88, 102, 110, 124, 129, 130, 132, 146, 157, 164, 167, 172, 173, 180, 194, 202, 222, 227, 232, 243, 266
role (see also: relationship)
role responsibilities 14, 27, 29, 47, 49, 52, 154, 158, 201, 220, 221, 223, 231, 232, 235, 247, 251, 261, 270
Rubin, M.A. 191
rude 23, 84, 117, 121, 128, 194, 205, 231, 269
rules 95, 111, 143, 225, 228, 235, 236, 244, 253, 256, 259, 261, 262, 267
  display rules 184, 185, 259
  ground rules 111, 253, 267
  national rules 32, 228
  prescriptive and proscriptive rules 233, 234
rules and regulations 30, 32, 228, 233–235

sadness 40, 41, 44, 45, 96, 182
safety (see: psychological safety)
Scharmer, C.O. 67
Schein, E.H. 242
self 138, 147, 240
  self-assured/self-confident 79, 85, 128, 133, 174, 239
  self-awareness 23, 53, 137, 139, 141, 161, 203, 255
  self-blame 133
  self-care (vs. care for others) 143, 144
  self-direction (see: autonomy)
  self-disclosure 105, 197
  self-doubt 79, 139
  self-enhancing – self-effacement communication style 26, 199, 203, 260
  self-esteem/self-worth 128, 172–174, 271
  self-identity/self-image 139, 175, 240
  self-reflection 16, 64, 157
sensemaking 39, 93, 191–194
sensitivity 7, 9, 11, 12, 19, 21, 34, 49, 54, 62, 71, 73, 76, 86, 90, 95, 104, 115, 142, 146, 150, 164, 174, 175, 183, 214, 225, 253, 258, 261, 271
Setting (TRIPS element) 11, 12, 14, 17, 19, 24, 29–34, 46, 47, 51, 52, 59, 62, 66, 86, 99, 152, 154, 158, 166, 169, 184, 190, 196, 197, 199, 201, 213, 227–244, 246–249, 251, 253, 261
  communication/interaction setting 12, 14, 29, 30–32, 167, 197, 227, 228, 236
  cultural setting 101, 110, 167, 270
  organisational setting 12, 14, 30, 32, 34, 223, 227, 228, 238, 247
  societal/regional/world setting 30, 32–34, 146, 223, 227, 228, 238, 247, 265
shame 41, 141, 172, 173, 225
Shaver, P. 182
shocked 38, 123, 229, 268
sidelined 75, 223, 239
silence 48, 68, 70, 75, 76, 81, 87, 91–93, 106, 129, 205, 266
Simon, B. 224
slang 83, 84, 87, 94, 250
small talk 52, 104, 252
socialise 59, 148, 223
socialised (culturally) 199, 229, 243
speak up/out 77, 79, 81, 90, 130, 222, 242
speed
  speed of speech 80, 83–85, 92–94, 111, 205, 208, 250
  speed of working 61, 126, 216
Spencer-Oatey, H. 9, 15, 30, 75, 82, 106, 111, 114, 153, 158, 166, 172, 173, 176, 180, 198, 211, 226, 229, 231, 244
status 103, 139, 172, 173, 204, 209, 221, 236, 240, 269
stereotypes 52, 81, 87, 219, 223, 224, 226
stories/storytelling 3, 71, 104, 188, 189, 266

Index

strategies (see: RelATE family of strategies)
strengths 21, 151, 198, 203, 217–219, 260
 management strengths 141–143, 147, 161
 strengths approach 217–219
 work-related strengths 215, 217–219
stress 3, 32, 33, 64, 72, 86, 89, 96, 115, 121, 123, 128, 132, 149, 150, 155, 188, 216, 234, 240, 243, 252, 254, 255, 261, 264
style
 style of communication (see: communication)
 style of working (see: working style)
Sue, D.W. 102, 208, 210
support/supporting 2, 16, 37, 41, 44, 46, 65, 73, 82, 96, 100, 107, 149, 174, 229, 233, 241, 252
 be/feel supported 21, 23, 41, 232, 240, 243, 256
 be supportive/provide support 15 50, 70, 96, 100, 112, 114, 116, 129, 130, 139, 149, 150, 153, 161, 174, 179, 192, 206, 217, 218, 234, 242, 243, 252, 253, 255, 256, 264, 269
 lack of support 156, 265
 mutual support 96, 103, 108, 109, 149
 seek support 132, 134–136, 255
Supportive Leadership Tool (see: leadership)
surprise 40, 59, 78, 123, 159, 160, 182, 184, 198, 272

tackle (see: Engage and tackle RelATE strategy)
talk over (see: overlap)
task–relationship balance 33, 101, 102, 107, 112, 129, 165, 167, 236, 237
team(s) 2, 3, 6, 21, 29, 33, 61, 75, 80–84, 91, 93, 95, 96, 102, 107–109, 113, 115, 121, 140, 146–152, 155, 174, 188, 192, 194, 200, 204, 206, 208, 209, 211, 213, 217, 228–230, 235, 240, 256, 265, 269, 270
 diverse and remote teams 5, 58, 107
 team leader/manager 25, 29, 61
 team meeting/discussion 25, 28, 83, 174, 208, 213
 team member(s) 9, 21, 25, 26, 28, 65, 84, 87, 88, 98, 107, 111, 146, 158, 218, 223, 229, 230, 242, 252, 253, 256, 265
 team spirit/support 96, 107, 109, 256
teamwork 75, 80, 88
tensions 5, 53, 59, 69, 98, 100, 115, 116, 140, 161, 262
thank 18, 104, 151, 168, 198, 253
Think – RelATE superstrategy 36, 37, 42, 263
 Think and accept 37, 54, 60, 73, 74, 250
 Think and analyse 77, 82, 86–88, 95, 251
 Think and prepare 60, 68, 72, 74, 102, 249
 Think and reassess 40, 42, 51, 53, 249
 Think and reflect 39, 42, 48, 51, 53, 118, 125, 127, 132, 134, 136, 137, 140, 141, 150, 161, 247, 254, 255
Thomas, K. 56, 57
Tian, Z. 175, 179
Tickle-Degnen, L. & Rosenthal, R. 190
time management 97, 236, 270
time orientation 236
Ting-Toomey, S. 172
Ting-Toomey, S. & Dorjee, T. 211
Tomlinson, E. & Mayer, R.C. 191
tools/toolkit (see: TRIPS tools/toolkit)
trigger (GAAFFE triggers; see also: Goals; Attention; Autonomy; Face; Fairness; Ethicality) 7, 9–12, 14, 17, 19–27, 29–32, 34, 38, 41, 48–51, 53, 57, 61–64, 66, 74, 81, 83, 86, 100, 102, 105, 110, 112–114, 118, 120–123, 127, 133, 138, 139, 149–153, 157, 158, 164–180, 183, 184, 189, 191, 195–200, 203, 208, 212–214, 219, 221–223, 229–231, 235, 246, 248, 249, 251, 252, 254, 258, 263, 265, 267, 268, 271, 272
TRIPS rapport management framework 4, 10–13, 15, 17–34, 37, 38, 52, 53, 58, 162, 164, 172, 180, 181, 190, 196, 212, 227
TRIPS tools/toolkit (see also: Cooperative Colleague Tool; Discord Management Tool; Participation Management Tool; Reaction Management Tool; Supportive Leadership Tool; Upward Management Tool)
TRIPS challenge tool templates 14, 247–257
TRIPS concept tool templates 14, 46, 258–262
trouble 54, 106, 119, 170

Index

troublemaker 130, 241
troubles talk 106, 252
trust 71, 128, 137, 194, 224
  build/create trust 3, 71, 74, 102, 151
  level of trust 57, 67, 110, 207, 213, 262
  mutual trust 9, 23, 59
  need for/importance of trust 2, 241
  trust others/trusted by others 53, 132, 142, 149-151, 154, 219, 225, 236, 237, 254, 256, 269, 270
  undermine trust 97, 199
turns/turn-taking 26, 70, 76, 79, 83-87, 89, 92, 93, 95, 200, 201, 205, 208, 213, 214, 231, 251, 260, 272

unacceptable 34, 130, 156, 184, 217, 223, 257
unaccepted 20, 79
uncertainty 5, 18, 32, 72, 103, 148, 149, 151, 187, 202, 207, 210, 236, 237, 240, 267
unconscious bias (see: bias)
understanding (see also: communication) 31, 37, 73, 88, 153, 166, 250, 259
  difficulty in understanding 79, 83, 84, 197, 202
  gain/promote understanding 51, 93, 207, 225
  little/different understandings 2, 194, 230
  mutual understanding 14, 16, 55, 57, 66, 68, 70, 71, 84, 94, 117, 124, 171, 186, 197, 211, 220, 231-233
  understanding emotions 39-41, 181, 195
unequal (see: equal/unequal)
unfair (see: Fairness)
upset 13, 18, 22, 23, 36-38, 43, 49, 50, 53, 54, 64, 68, 112, 123, 127, 134, 155, 158, 165, 173, 174, 179, 186, 189, 195, 197, 198, 204, 234, 241, 247, 249, 254, 263, 267
Upward Management Tool 13, 36, 118, 124, 125, 127, 136, 246, 253

value 15, 58, 66, 107, 109, 114, 116, 150, 188, 218, 252, 271
values (see also: cultural) 14, 28, 30, 138, 140, 141, 147, 153, 157, 167, 170, 177-179, 199, 204, 215, 223, 227, 228, 235-240, 256, 262
  leadership values 143, 144, 161, 256
  organisational values 32, 228, 237, 238, 239, 262
Vigier, M. & Spencer-Oatey, H. 111, 211

warmth-antagonism 9, 190
Warren, J. 215
weaknesses (see also: strengths) 21, 142, 154, 161, 198, 217, 271
Webster, V. 131, 134, 156
Weeks, J. 200
welfare 49, 124, 144, 199, 256
wellbeing 3, 5, 6, 76, 117, 128, 135, 139, 140, 147, 218, 224, 225, 237, 240, 241, 254
Williams, N. 149
Woolley, S. 157
workarounds 109, 119, 134, 135, 255, 269
working style 14, 28, 46, 47, 55, 111, 113, 126, 127, 132, 133, 136, 199, 214-217, 219, 226, 251, 253-255, 260
workload 216, 267, 269

www.ingramcontent.com/pod-product-compliance
Lightning Source LLC
Chambersburg PA
CBHW071956290426
44109CB00018B/2038